JOHN KEATS

JOHN KEATS

Robert Woof
Stephen Hebron

THE WORDSWORTH TRUST
1995

Exhibition sponsored by **KPMG**

Typeset in Garamond by the Wordsworth Trust
Printed by Titus Wilson, Kendal

ISBN 1 870787 15 3

Contents

Sponsor's Preface

It is particularly gratifying in this time of economic hardship that KPMG have been able to help the Wordsworth Trust by sponsoring this wonderful celebration of the bicentenary of John Keats.

KPMG have long held the view that the private sector should help the arts wherever possible, and so enable the public to have the opportunity to see and enjoy great works of art from different sources in one place at the same time.

We would like to take this opportunity to congratulate and thank all those who have made it possible, and in particular the Wordsworth Trust, its Director and staff, for all the hard work they have done.

Peter Brown
Managing Partner, KPMG

ACKNOWLEDGEMENTS

The Trustees of the Wordsworth Trust would like to thank the many people and institutions who have helped to make possible this celebration of the bicentenary of John Keats. This book records the exhibition that opened in Grasmere on 14 July 1995 (until 30 September) and reopened at the British Library on 11 October (until 8 January 1996). The attempt is to give a cultural context for the better understanding of Keats's story and achievements.

The assembling of so many treasures is the gift of so many curators and scholars. We thank first all at the British Library who have worked with us over the last year. Jane Carr, as Director of Public Services, invited the Wordsworth Trust to bring the exhibition to the British Library, and her colleagues, Alan Sterenberg, Janet Backhouse and Shelley Jones, with Sally Brown from the Department of Manuscripts and Elizabeth James from the Department of Books, have facilitated the loans and planning. It has been a delightful and creative collaboration.

Other institutions have given more than customary courtesy. The Victoria & Albert Museum has lent from several departments, pre-eminently from Prints and Drawings, but in addition the Tassie Gems from Sculpture, and the Edmund Kean material from the Theatre Museum. Our especial thanks to Susan Lambert, Janet Skidmore, Chris Titterington, Margaret Benton and Jim Fowler (the last two at the Theatre Museum). The National Portrait Gallery provided a major series of portraits of the Keats circle, and we are especially grateful to Kai Kin Yung and Jonathan Franklin for their help. Visits to Keats House, Hampstead, have allowed us access to many important images and documents, but not least the pleasure of talking to Christina Gee on many research matters.

There are many individuals who have helped with our research: Colonel Skinner at Apothecaries' Hall; Stephen Wildman at Birmingham City Art Gallery; Christopher Brown at the National Gallery; Kim Sloan of the Department of Prints and Drawings at the British Museum; Lynn Romig at the British Museum Publication Department; Ian Jenkins from the Department of Greek and Roman Sculpture; Vivien Knight at the Guildhall Art Gallery, and Ralph Hyde and John Fisher from the Guildhall Library; Richard Wood of the Usher Art Gallery, Lincoln; Charles Nugent of the Whitworth Art Gallery, Manchester; Sarah Richardson at the Laing Art Gallery, Newcastle upon Tyne; John Murdoch, Sarah Hyde and Uta Kornmeier at the Courtauld Institute. In our pursuit of the medical background of Keats, we were helpfully advised by Robert Knight of Guy's Hospital, Chris Lawrence of the Wellcome Institute, and William Schuchbach, the Keeper of Prints at the Wellcome Library. Further, Ghislaine

Lawrence, Curator of Clinical Medicine at the Science Museum, helped us find the appropriate medical instruments and interpret more correctly their use. There are special debts which include kindness and friendship, to Reg Alton; Paul Betz; Geoffrey Bindman; Gerald Burdon; Roy Davids; Malcolm Dyer; Arthur Freeman; Alan Haydon; Michael Jaye; Rachel Moss; the late Dallas Pratt; Chris Sheppard; Susan Sloman; John Spedding; Charles Warren; Duncan Wu.

An exhibition on this scale is a major logistical enterprise. I have to thank my colleagues at Grasmere for their great patience and their many skills. Jeff Cowton, our Curator and Registrar, has, from its inception, given the project his customary stamina and excellence; he wishes to record his special gratitude to a dedicated and professional team, many of whom are volunteers or members of a training programme. Alex Black has been our indefatigable photographer; and Sally Woodhead and Martin Oldham have helped the authors to keep to the timetable amongst many pressures and difficulties. Stephen Hebron has been an heroic force who over two years has kept his eye targeted on the Keats exhibition, giving many extra hours to the research and the drafting of material. Further, he has single-handedly designed the catalogue and typeset it. In all this, he would like to acknowledge the support of Oliver Turnbull, who has managed the printing at Titus Wilson.

No exhibition can survive without financial support. The exhibition would have been impossible but for the generous grants received from Mrs Valerie Eliot, from Mrs Drue Heinz (courtesy of the Drue Heinz Foundation and the Wordsworth Trust America), whose initial commitments alone made this publication possible. We have, further, had support from Northern Arts, who have seen the exhibition as a forerunner to that in 1996 on Keats's friend, the painter Benjamin Robert Haydon. Lord Gowrie has kindly given the exhibition his own effective encouragement. The Esmée Fairbairn Charitable Trust, following visits from Penelope Hughes-Hallett and Margaret Hyde, has given generous and sensitive support throughout a difficult year.

I have one personal debt which no thanks here can represent, and that is to Pamela Woof, who has shared with us her scholarship and her flair for enjoying Keats in all his writing, enabling us all the better to savour every precise nuance.

Robert Woof
Director

JOHN KEATS: AN INTRODUCTION

Every reader of Keats has cause to mourn and to rejoice; every reader comes to know the truth of his realisation that 'in the very temple of Delight / Veiled Melancholy has her sovran shrine'. We rejoice that Keats was born two hundred years ago on 31 October, and that his poetry has been, is and will be read and loved all over the world; and we grieve that he had so little time, less than twenty-six years; 'The lyf so short, the craft so long to lerne', wrote Chaucer four hundred years before Keats arrived to show that in a life shorter by far than most the craft could be learned to such perfection. Later in the Nineteenth Century, thinking over his immediate predecessors, Matthew Arnold thought that Keats had a 'more consummate poetic gift' than either Wordsworth or Byron, the poets of his century that he most admired; but Keats, alas, 'died having produced too little and being as yet too immature to rival them'. Time has not accepted Arnold's hesitancies, and has certainly rejected Keats's own proposed epitaph: 'Here lies one whose name is writ in water'. Keats is a major poet, one among that great Romantic pantheon – Wordsworth, Coleridge, Byron, Shelley and Blake.

Son of the head ostler at the Swan and Hoop, Finsbury, London, Keats was fatherless at nine and orphaned at fourteen. He became 'head' of his family, his two brothers, George and Tom, and his sister, Fanny. It was a role to which he rose, even though he was frustrated in his powerlessness to do more than contradict or incense his surviving guardian, the solicitor, Richard Abbey. His care for his brothers and his young sister was constant. When, in March 1817, he and Tom and George lived under the same roof for the first time in some years, the sense of domestic peace that Keats felt is expressed in his sonnet beginning:

> Small, busy flames play through the fresh-laid coals,
>   And their faint cracklings o'er our silence creep
>   Like whispers of the household gods that keep
> A gentle empire o'er fraternal souls.

It is later to these 'fraternal souls' that many of Keats's most marvellous letters are written. Events in his younger siblings' lives were crucial to him: George's decision to emigrate to America in June 1818, the suffering and death from tuberculosis of Tom later that year, the half-seclusion of Fanny with the hostile Abbeys.

But at the same time that fraternal loyalty was supplemented by his gift for intense friendships, friendships for those who could nurture his deep need to be alive in the imagination, feed his appetite for literature and his ambition to be a writer. Those friends were often mentors. Charles Cowden Clarke, the son of the headmaster of Enfield School, was one of the earliest to supply Keats with books, but beyond that, to share in the reading and the discussion of poetry. 'You first taught me', wrote Keats in his verse-letter of September 1817, 'all the sweets of song', and he goes on to spell out some of the elements of that youthful literary education:

> Spenserian vowels that elope with ease,
> And float along like birds o'er summer seas;
> Miltonian storms, and more, Miltonian tenderness;
> Michael in arms, and more, meek Eve's fair slenderness.
> Who read for me the sonnet swelling loudly
> Up to its climax and then dying proudly?
> Who found for me the grandeur of the ode,
> Growing, like Atlas, stronger from its load?
> Who let me taste that more than cordial dram,
> The sharp, the rapier-pointed epigram?
> Showed me that epic was of all the king,
> Round, vast, and spanning all like Saturn's ring?
>   (ll.56-67)

Walking 'through shady lanes' or 'in a chat . . . at nightfall among your books', Keats came, through Clarke, to an exploration of the major English writers – and these included Chatterton, and, on the evidence of Clarke's commonplace book, Wordsworth. They included, of course, Shakespeare.

Cat. 2 Frederick Lewis,
View at Enfield

Cat. 4 Charles Cowden
Clarke by an unknown artist

Clarke provided for Keats what many of us too have had, and we can understand Keats's excitement; he provided the seminal literary images that last a lifetime:

> The hand of Brutus, that so grandly fell
> Upon a tyrant's head. Ah! had I never seen,
> Or known your kindness, what might I have been?
> What my enjoyments in my youthful years,
> Bereft of all that now my life endears?
>
> (ll.71-5)

The great writers stayed with Keats, and his commitment, and his ambition as a poet were undeviatingly to the weightiest figures in literature. Virgil he had known in Latin at school, Homer famously through Chapman's translation, Petrarch and Boccaccio through Hunt and Reynolds: finally, Dante came to be a presence: Keats took Henry Cary's translation of *The Divine Comedy* with him when he walked through the north of England and into Scotland in the summer of 1818. Clarke had set it all going while Keats was in his early teens, a boy at school; poetry became part of his life, and as such, and inevitably, it became a central subject of his own poetry.

Awareness of the literature of the past did not mean that Keats ignored the writing of his contemporaries. He knew Mary Tighe's *Psyche* (first published in Ireland in 1805), and he got to know well the writing of the first 'famous' poet to whom Charles Cowden Clarke introduced him, Leigh Hunt. With Hunt, too, when Hunt was living at the Vale of Health, Hampstead Heath, the reading and talking about literature continued:

> For I am brimful of the friendliness
>   That in a little cottage I have found;
> Of fair-haired Milton's eloquent distress,
>   And all his love for gentle Lycid drowned;
> Of lovely Laura in her light green dress,
>   And faithful Petrarch gloriously crowned.
>
>   ('Keen, fitful gusts are whispering here and there')

The two men sharpened their writing skills, setting themselves a challenge of providing each a sonnet on a set subject in a given time. To such an exercise we owe Keats's finely-shaped sonnet, 'On the Grasshopper and Cricket': 'The poetry of earth is never dead', with its clear differences of heat and frost, singing and silence, and, in the end, these opposites coming together in ambiguous identification within the mind of the poet:

> On a lone winter evening, when the frost
>   Has wrought a silence, from the stove there shrills
> The Cricket's song, in warmth increasing ever,
> And seems to one in drowsiness half lost,
>   The Grasshopper's among some grassy hills.

The sonnet is prophetic of those great later meditations in both narratives and in the Odes on where reality is – inside, or outside, the mind?

For a time, it must be said, some of Keats's own writing was influenced by Hunt's too easy style, his fanciful imagery, his loose rhyming; and Keats was also drawn to the rather rebellious tone of Hunt and his circle, so evident in *The Examiner*, the anti-government paper, which Hunt edited. The initial harvest of the friendship with Hunt was the publication of some of Keats's sonnets in that weekly paper and, more, his introduction to and immediate friendship with figures such as Benjamin Robert Haydon, a painter as ambitious in his art as Keats was in poetry; or William Hazlitt, whose essays and lectures soon revealed to Keats that here was the most acute critic of the age. Keats was able to hold his own in their society, and beyond that, in every case to provoke a keen interest in his destiny. It was friendship with Hunt that led him to meet Shelley, friendship with Haydon that brought him to meet Wordsworth. Shelley's *Alastor* (1816) may have been an example of a long poem that enticed Keats to write the 4,000-line *Endymion*, but it was not until Keats's third volume of poems, published in 1820, that Shelley recognised that here was a genuine talent, a writer who could become the first of poets. With Wordsworth there was a generation-gap: Wordsworth, fed by Haydon's gossip, feared that Keats was not keeping good company, in that he spent his time with Hunt or Hazlitt or Reynolds; but Wordsworth knew that this young poet, who once read the 'Hymn to Pan' (from *Endymion*) to him, promised a great deal. Wordsworth's reported remark, 'a pretty piece of Paganism', on hearing Keats read, is certainly not overgenerous, but it is not imprecise.

But beyond all these friendships (and he had many acquaintances), the closest to Keats were Benjamin Bailey, an Oxford undergraduate (later a clergyman in Ceylon and an admiring correspondent of Wordsworth), and John Hamilton Reynolds, ardent to be a writer, but who, with some self-dismay, finally settled for less and became a lawyer. It was friends of this calibre, with their serious commitment to become poets, that inspired Keats to write to them his most serious letters. The nature of the poet is a central theme. We see him define it as possessed pre-eminently by Shakespeare – his having a 'negative capability' – the capacity to enter into the life of characters so that the poet is outside the moral simplicities and has as much delight in the villain as in the heroine, in an Iago as in an Imogen. And in one of the great letters that he writes to Reynolds, in April

Benjamin Bailey by an unknown artist *(Keats House, Hampstead)*

1818, he makes the recognition that it is the poet's job to be a part of the development of knowledge, particularly psychological knowledge; Keats believed in progress, and he concludes that it is Wordsworth rather than Milton that he must follow, the Wordsworth of 'Tintern Abbey', who had begun to explore the dark passages of thought. It is Keats's hope that he will reach and go beyond Wordsworth and take further 'the grand march of intellect.' Keats, a poet in his letters as in his verse, expresses his meaning in images.

> I will return to Wordsworth—whether or no he has an extended vision or a circumscribed grandeur—whether he is an eagle in his nest, or on the wing—And to be more explicit and to show you how tall I stand by the giant, I will put down a simile of human life as far as I now perceive it; that is, to the point to which I say we both have arrived at—' Well—I compare human life to a large Mansion of Many Apartments, two of which I can only describe, the doors of the rest being as yet shut upon me—The first we step into we call the infant or thoughtless Chamber, in which we remain as long as we do not think—We remain there a long while, and notwithstanding the doors of the second Chamber remain wide open, showing a bright appearance, we care not to hasten to it; but are at length imperceptibly impelled by the awakening of the thinking principle—within us—we no sooner get into the second Chamber, which I shall call the Chamber of Maiden-Thought, than we become intoxicated with the light and the atmosphere, we see nothing but pleasant wonders, and think of delaying there for ever in delight: However among the effects this breathing is father of is that tremendous one of sharpening one's vision into the heart and nature of Man—of convincing ones nerves that the World is full of Misery and Heartbreak, Pain, Sickness and oppression—whereby This Chamber of Maiden Thought becomes gradually darken'd and at the same time on all sides of it many doors are set open—but all dark—all leading to dark passages—We see not the ballance of good and evil. We are in a Mist—*We* are now in that state—We feel the "burden of the Mystery," To this point was Wordsworth come, as far as I can conceive when he wrote 'Tintern Abbey' and it seems to me that his Genius is explorative of those dark Passages. Now if we live, and go on thinking, we too shall explore them. He is a Genius and superior [to] us, in so far as he can, more than we, make discoveries, and shed a light in them—Here I must think Wordsworth is deeper than Milton—though I think it has depended more upon the general and gregarious advance of intellect, than individual greatness of Mind—
>
> (Keats to Reynolds, 3 May 1818)

The ambition to be a poet, and the friendships that fostered this, these were vital to Keats.

Cat. 102 William
Wordsworth by Haydon
(study for *Christ's Entry
into Jerusalem*), *c* 1817

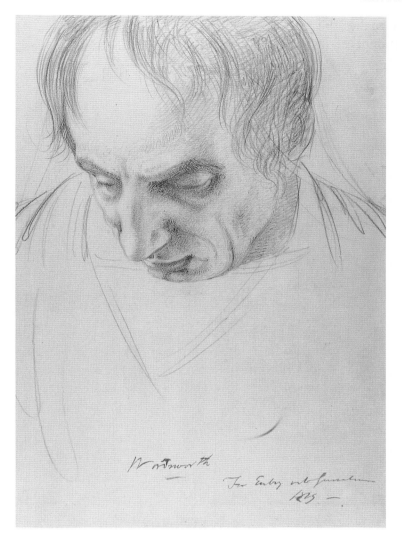

Another aspect of his life is more surprising, indeed, peculiar to him alone among the Romantic poets. At the age of fourteen, he was apprenticed to Thomas Hammond, an apothecary of Enfield. At nineteen, he entered Guy's Hospital, and spent nearly a year in formal training; in the very first months he was picked out by the surgeons of the hospital, headed by Astley Cooper, to be a dresser on the wards. Clearly, Keats was seen as one who might proceed, after his apothecary's examinations (after nine months), to qualify as a surgeon. The hospital gave him a thorough knowledge of death and decay, of the low somatic aspects of human life (insofar as medicine understood them in those days). Keats would be aware of the imprecision of surgeons, the likelihood of death under the knife, and the general prevalence of disease within the hospital. (He was dresser to the surgeon William Lucas Jr, whose recklessness in taking the knife through vital organs horrified colleagues such as Astley Cooper: Lucas's nickname was 'the Butcher'.) Keats would also be aware that the hospital was a place where those who wished to help humanity through medicine could fulfil a

great need. All we know is that when Keats, in an exemplary and expeditious fashion completed his apothecary's examinations in July 1816, he had decided not to continue with his medical studies. Some might speculate that he found the work distasteful. But the more likely reason is his overwhelming belief in himself as a poet. Near the beginning of the second version of 'Hyperion', usually entitled 'The Fall of Hyperion: A Dream', the would-be poet in his dream hears a voice telling him to climb some huge marble steps towards an altar, or he will die. He almost dies, but manages the climb and enters into conversation with the voice that comes from a 'tall shade, veiled in drooping white'. The voice accuses him of being merely a dreamer:

> Art thou not of the dreamer tribe?
> The poet and the dreamer are distinct,
> Diverse, sheer opposite, antipodes.
> The one pours out a balm upon the world,
> The other vexes it.
>
> (ll.198-202)

The true poet, in other words, is a healer. The dreamer accepts the distinction between true poet and 'mock lyrists, large self-worshippers . . . careless hectorers in proud bad verse', and, instead of asking where he himself is placed, he inquires into the identity of the veiled speaker and of the great image above the altar. The response to this, by implication – for he does not in any self-regarding way stop to comment – is that he is a true poet, for the veiled figure thinks him worthy, after due sacrifice, to contemplate and experience great suffering: to explore, in the words of Keats's letter, the dark passages. She is Moneta, priestess of the long-ago defeated Saturn, 'Sole priestess of his desolation', and she gives the poet the experience of suffering in two ways: one is to reveal her face, a face of total anguish yet with eyes benign and wholly impersonal; the other is to tell the story of the Titans' loss and Saturn's eternal despair in defeat. It is his statue that surmounts the altar. Here is the passage describing the face that has known, and will always know, grief, and yet has eyes of wide general compassion, the eyes of a healer. The face reveals what poetry is about. Keats writes here in a calm and measured verse. Perhaps the visionary power and the solemn dignity of 'The Fall of Hyperion' is Keats's fullest tribute to Dante.

> . . . yet I had a terror of her robes,
> And chiefly of the veils, that from her brow
> Hung pale, and curtain'd her in mysteries
> That made my heart too small to hold its blood.
> This saw that Goddess, and with sacred hand
> Parted the veils. Then saw I a wan face,
> Not pin'd by human sorrows, but bright blanch'd
> By an immortal sickness which kills not;
> It works a constant change, which happy death
> Can put no end to; deathwards progressing
> To no death was that visage; it had pass'd
> The lily and the snow; and beyond these
> I must not think now, though I saw that face—
> But for her eyes I should have fled away.
> They held me back, with a benignant light,
> Soft mitigated by divinest lids
> Half closed, and visionless entire they seem'd
> Of all external things—they saw me not,
> But in blank splendour beam'd like the mild moon,
> Who comforts those she sees not, who knows not
> What eyes are upward cast.
>
> (ll.251-71)

If the practical world of medicine, with its high moral purpose of physical healing, was rejected by Keats, it was because he was moving towards an even higher destiny, that of the poet-healer. But his early training gave him the vision which could only come from his education as a scientist. By contrast, his near-contemporaries – Wordsworth, Coleridge, Byron and Shelley – had predominantly a classical training. Blake's background was also different from the norm, but he draws upon a Non-Conformist vitality that stretches back to the independent chapels of the Seventeenth Century. When one considers the numerous teachers who instructed Keats at the United Hospitals – Guy's and St Thomas's – one becomes aware of how extensive was Keats's practical knowledge, not only of anatomy and physiology, but also of basic chemistry and, above all, of botany. That as part of his training Keats had to go on field-trips with William Salisbury meant that he had a precise knowledge of the flowers in their perpetual cycle of change and decay. When Wordsworth writes of flowers – daffodils, the daisy, or the lesser celandine, for instance – his inclination is to moralise over their significance. For Keats they are just themselves, factors in the ever-changing process, constant only in growth and decay. Almost every line of Keats is imbrued with a sense of a physical universe that is a kind of wonder; its secrets were becoming known in a secular revelation to figures as diverse as Humphry Davy, John Hunter or Keats's own teachers, Astley Cooper, Alexander Marcet, John Henry Green, James Curry, or his examiner, William Brande of Apothecaries' Hall.

Beyond Keats's commitment to the art of poetry, and his knowledge of the world through the eye of science (rather than, say, through, religious terminology), there is a third and powerful influence, that from Keats's ever-growing interest in art. By meeting Leigh Hunt and Benjamin Robert Haydon, Keats had access to massive print collections (the means through which most Old Masters were available). True, the British Institution and the Royal Academy were among the galleries that gave regular displays of great pictures, but Keats's knowledge of Raphael, Titian, Claude, Poussin, and even of recent artists such as Sir Joshua Reynolds or Benjamin West, would be largely through the medium of prints. Ian Jack, in his *Keats and the Mirror of Art* (1967), establishes how the visual arts offered to Keats a medium other than words in which the imagination could stray, could build upon, use and reject in the constant quest towards remedies for, and even celebrations of, our living in a world of pain. The paintings that Keats found most suggestive were often on classical themes – rather than on Christian topics, for example (and there are many of these printbooks). But then, Keats knew Ovid's stories well, and quite unexpectedly in Wordsworth's *Excursion* (1814) he came across a passage uncharacteristic of

Cat. 57 Benjamin Robert Haydon by Sir David Wilkie

that matter-of-fact, even novelistic poet, a passage delighting in the way that, as Wordsworth's fancy has it, forces and animations of the natural world were transformed into Gods, Nymphs, Naiads and Oreads by the 'swains of pagan Greece'. In Haydon's copy of *The Excursion* (now at Cornell University) this passage is marked as being admired by Keats:

> Once more to distant ages of the world
> Let us revert, and place before our thoughts
> The face which rural solitude might wear
> To the unenlightened swains of pagan Greece.
> — In that fair clime, the lonely herdsman, stretched
> On the soft grass through half a summer's day,
> With music lulled his indolent repose:
> And, in some fit of weariness, if he,
> When his own breath was silent, chanced to hear
> A distant strain, far sweeter than the sounds
> Which his poor skill could make, his fancy fetched,
> Even from the blazing chariot of the sun,
> A beardless Youth, who touched a golden lute,
> And filled the illumined groves with ravishment.
> The nightly hunter, lifting a bright eye
> Up towards the crescent moon, with grateful heart
> Called on the lovely wanderer who bestowed
> That timely light, to share his joyous sport:
> And hence, a beaming Goddess with her Nymphs,
> Across the lawn and through the darksome grove,
> Not unaccompanied with tuneful notes
> By echo multiplied from rock or cave,
> Swept in the storm of chase; as moon and stars
> Glance rapidly along the clouded heaven,
> When winds are blowing strong. The traveller slaked
> His thirst from rill or gushing fount, and thanked
> The Naiad.—Sunbeams, upon distant hills
> Gliding apace, with shadows in their train,
> Might, with small help from fancy, be transformed
> Into fleet Oreads sporting visibly.
> The Zephyrs fanning, as they passed, their wings,
> Lacked not, for love, fair objects whom they wooed
> With gentle whisper. Withered boughs grotesque,
> Stripped of their leaves and twigs by hoary age,
> From depth of shaggy covert peeping forth
> In the low vale, or on steep mountain-side;
> And, sometimes, intermixed with stirring horns
> Of the live deer, or goat's depending beard,—
> These were the lurking Satyrs, a wild brood
> Of gamesome Deities; or Pan himself,
> The simple shepherd's awe-inspiring God!
>
> (Book IV, ll.847-87)

ORIGINAL POETRY.

TO HAYDON,

WITH A SONNET WRITTEN ON SEEING THE ELGIN MARBLES.

HAYDON! forgive me that I cannot speak
  Definitively on these mighty things;
  Forgive me that I have not Eagle's wings—
That what I want I know not where to seek:
And think that I would not be overmeek
  In rolling out upfollow'd thunderings,
  Even to the steep of Heliconian springs,
Were I of ample strength for such a freak—
Think too, that all those numbers should be thine;
  Whose else? In this who touch thy vesture's hem?
For when men star'd at what was most divine
  With browless idiotism—o'erwise phlegm—
Thou hadst beheld the Hesperean shine
  Of their star in the East, and gone to worship them.

ON SEEING THE ELGIN MARBLES.

My spirit is too weak—Mortality
  Weighs heavily on me like unwilling sleep,
  And each imagined pinnacle and steep
Of godlike hardship, tells me I must die
Like a sick Eagle looking at the sky.
  Yet 'tis a gentle luxury to weep
  That I have not the cloudy winds to keep,
Fresh for the opening of the morning's eye.
Such dim-conceived glories of the brain
  Bring round the heart an undescribable feud;
So do these wonders a most dizzy pain,
  That mingles Grecian grandeur with the rude
Wasting of old time—with a billowy main—
  A sun—a shadow of a magnitude.   J. K

Cat. 42 Publication in *The Examiner* of 9 March 1817 Keats's sonnets to the Elgin Marbles

Such authority would confirm Keats in his love of classical art. And then, there were the Elgin Marbles. Keats was close to the controversy surrounding their coming to London. It was Haydon's advocacy of their importance, and his powerful agitation that ensured that the government bought these wonderful sculptures for the nation. The Elgin Marbles represented for Keats a heroic challenge that he felt that he could hardly attempt to compete with, much less equal in poetry:

> My spirit is too weak—mortality
>   Weighs heavily on me like unwilling sleep,
>   And each imagined pinnacle and steep
> Of godlike hardship, tells me I must die
> Like a sick Eagle looking at the sky.
>
> ('On Seeing the Elgin Marbles', ll.1-5)

The sublimity of power that was still there, and the further sublimity that could only be imagined, oppressed and paralysed him. The fragmentary ruined state of the Marbles was comment enough on the permanence of high art. Such achievement, such aspiration, and such decay, like other 'dim-conceivèd glories of the brain', could only

Bring round the heart an undescribable feud;
So do these wonders a most dizzy pain,
  That mingles Grecian grandeur with the rude
Wasting of old Time—with a billowy main—
  A sun—a shadow of a magnitude.

(Ibid, ll.10-14)

Yet, they represent a theme that was to recur again and again in Keats: how is it possible for the human and the immortal to coexist? Keats felt it a challenge to present the ancient gods of Greece within a matter-of-fact human world; it meant that his poetry would inevitably take a symbolic turn. Contemporary artists had similar leanings. Keats would know of that new and fine body of watercolourists who, from 1804, had set up the increasingly influential Watercolour Society. Painters such as Joshua Cristall and William Havell made it their practice to animate a particular, even a well-known scene, a Lake District landscape, for instance, that was already much painted, by placing in it figures from a classical past. The unlikely costume of these persons in tunics or togas, did much to establish the artists' meaning, that this England was indeed Arcadia.

Keats, of course, was aware of painters among his contemporaries other than those who mingled the classical with everyday reality. His friend Haydon was a historical painter. as was another of their circle, William

Cat. 113 Joshua Cristall, *View of Borrowdale with Classical Figures*

Cat. 61 Lifemask of Keats
by Haydon, 1816

Hilton: both, for a moment, set aside their more ambitious work to do portraits of Keats. Hilton's was based upon a miniature, one of the more matter-of-fact ones, by a younger artist, Joseph Severn, whose care for Keats in his last weeks, and Shelley's public praise of this in the Preface to *Adonais*, was to give Severn a kind of fame, and contribute to the success of his career as an artist. Haydon made a drawing of Keats – it was a study for his large painting, *Christ's Entry into Jerusalem*; he also made a lifemask. In his *Christ's Entry*, he was to place his gaunt, thoughtful head of Wordsworth – by far the best image of the older poet ever made – to the front of his vital head of Keats, the young man's mouth open as if in eager conversation. Haydon was making the contrast between Youth and Experience: the one astonished with wonder, the other naturally reverential in the presence of Christ. Haydon's placing Wordsworth and Keats together is an original and creative juxtaposition, a statement of literary criticism. In seeing his friends, Haydon and Hilton, at work, Keats would be aware of their basing their fictional and historical painting upon studies and observation within their studios. But equally, he obviously could not have failed to notice those landscape artists whom the Twentieth Century regards as the finest of the Romantic period – Peter De Wint, for instance,

John Keats by Haydon (study for *Christ's Entry into Jerusalem*), c. 1816 *(National Portrait Gallery, London)*

Hilton's brother-in-law, or William Turner of Oxford, both artists whose symbolic statement is implicit in their dexterous facility with light and shade which define and sculpt the ever-varying English landscape. Both would and do appeal to patriotic feeling. Keats, too, despite his Grecian subjects, writes about England; here, in a sudden, celebratory passage from the letter-journal to Tom of his tour through the Lakes, 1818, he describes his deep delight in watching children dance at the village inn in Wigton:

> July 1st—We are this morning at Carlisle—After Skiddow, we walked to Ireby the oldest market town in Cumberland—where we were greatly amused by a country dancing school, holden at the [Sun], it was indeed "no new cotillon fresh from France." No they kickit & jumpit with mettle extraordinary, & whiskit, & fleckit, & toe'd it, & go'd it, & twirld it, & wheel'd it, & stamp'd it, & sweated it, tattooing the floor like mad; The differenc[e] between our country dances & these scotch figures, is about the same as leisurely stirring a cup o' Tea & heating up a batter pudding. I was extremely gratified to think, that if I had pleasures they knew nothing of, they had also some into which I could not possibly enter I hope I shall not return without having got the Highland fling, there was as fine a row of boys & girls as ever you saw, some beautiful faces, & one exquisite mouth. I never felt so near the glory of Patriotism, the glory of making by any means a country happier. This is what I like better than scenery. I fear our continued moving from place to place, will prevent our becoming learned in village affairs; we are mere creatures of Rivers, Lakes, & mountains.

Keats's patriotism is not of the hortatory kind that Wordsworth sometimes uses—'Milton! thou shouldst be living at this hour: / England hath need of thee'. Keats here seems more celebratory, touched with a democratic impulse, and imbrued with a passionate sense that England was the proper and worthy place of his endeavour, of his exploration of the great themes: love and death, beauty and truth.

Keats felt in his first draft of the Preface to *Endymion* that he had to point out the poem's faults, and at the same time he admitted his unwillingness to take the time to correct them; he was impatient to move on, to write something else, to be judged only at the highest level:

> I fought under disadvantages. Before I began I had no inward feel of being able to finish; and as I proceeded my steps were all uncertain. So this Poem must rather be consider'd as an endeavour than a thing accomplish'd; a poor prologue to what, if I live, I humbly hope to do. In duty to the Public I should have kept it back for a year or two, knowing it to be so faulty: but I really cannot do so:—by repetition my favorite Passages sound vapid in my ears, and I would rather redeem myself with a new Poem—should this one be found of any interest.

Cat. 128 John Keats by Charles
Wass after William Hilton, 1841

Keats recognised that this long poem was necessary to demonstrate his capacity to compose, organise, create the machinery of a substantial narrative poem; but he knew, almost as his readers of today know, that in *Endymion* this was not quite achieved, even though the poem is flickering with interest throughout, seminal of themes he was to develop further.

It is perhaps for a similar reason, of wanting to test himself beside the greatest of writers, that he felt drawn to the idea of writing a tragic drama. But *Otho the Great* is not an important work; it seems not so significant as, say, *The Borderers* or *Osorio* (*Remorse*) in the early careers of, respectively, Wordsworth and Coleridge. For them, the plays were a lesson in how to find the root of their poetry in spoken speech. Keats's play seems not to have so full an impact on his art; the plot was, after all, Charles Brown's, and the play was written at speed; a text versified than a theme explored. But Keats still pursued drama, and this was closely related to his admiration of Edmund Kean, a figure, like himself, small in physical height, and, from the drawings that survive, rather similar in appearance. Both poet and actor shared a vitality, and a wish to reform the art they practised. Keats is blatant in his wish to follow Kean and, in composing *Otho the Great*, he believed the play's success would depend on Kean's being able to play the lead. That Keats's serious exploration of drama as a form was going to continue is clear from the fragment *King Stephen*, itself more impressive than anything in *Otho the Great*.

But such attempts at works on a larger scale were not Keats's normal composition, which was clearly the shorter poem – the sonnet most frequently, but, equally significant, the verse-letter, which had an intimacy, simulating conversation with a friend. As we have already established, Keats's letters themselves are proto-poems, so full of a teeming energy that expresses itself in images, and thus demanding that the reader confront the fine intellectual power coursing through the author's mind. The prose letters share with the sonnets and the verse epistles an imperative mental and emotional exploration, for the writer himself is the confessing hero. Inevitably, this stance of intimacy, enhanced by a language freshly coined, leads to the great Odes.

The ode, before Keats wrote odes, might have been looked upon as a heroic lyric, the highest form of poetry devoted to a public theme. Keats made that public theme not a concern for events on a national stage, but for the pursuit of the highest (which includes the idea of their being commonplace) philosophical questions. The very enquiring mood that Keats brings to the Odes is part of their fine weighted thought. But more, like ancient odes in drama, they are antiphonal in structure; an idea advanced will induce the poet to think of and embrace a very opposite line of argument. The poet understands, with Socrates, that truth comes out of dialogue. It is a sophisticated movement, natural to the sonnet as Keats used it, where octet and sestet can easily contain reversal. When Keats turns to the ode, he is able to run each technically similar and complex stanza as a separate swing of the dialectical argument, with sometimes the stanza itself containing an antiphonal element. The Odes are in some ways short sonnet-sequences, but with the 'sonnets' bound together more closely than in any sequence we might read, say, from the Elizabethan period. They are personal meditations as well as formal poems.

Before discussing particular Odes, we should keep in mind that Keats sought for a real success in narrative. A group of major, if variable, tales was published in 1820. 'Isabella' seemed to Charles Lamb Keats's most important work when he reviewed the 1820 volume; twentieth-century readers will find Keats's attacks upon Isabella's paranoid and murderous brothers too crudely political; the brothers are less themselves than representations of a merchant and exploitative class:

> For them the Ceylon diver held his breath,
>   And went all naked to the hungry shark;
> For them his ears gush'd blood; for them in death
>   The seal on the cold ice with piteous bark
> Lay full of darts; for them alone did seethe
>   A thousand men in troubles wide and dark:
> Half-ignorant, they turn'd an easy wheel,
> That set sharp racks at work, to pinch and peel.
>
>   (Stanza 15)

Cat. 221 William Holman Hunt, *Isabella and the Pot of Basil*

This material is not from Keats's main source, Boccaccio; and all sense in the original that Lorenzo was pursuing Isabella for selfish ends is suppressed; for Keats, Isabella is not a figure to be rescued from a seducer, but a girl oppressed by a tyrannous family. She has lost love, a love brought so slowly and painfully from the depths of being into articulation and secret expression. Keats vividly depicts the brothers riding with 'their murder'd man', and after the death and the macabre reburying of the head by Isabella in the pot of basil, he concentrates on Isabella's psychological state, her displaced obsession, hardly now for the dead lover, but strangely for the growing plant in the pot. It is only after Keats's death, with the publication of some of John Hamilton Reynolds' attempts at Italian themes in his *Garden of Florence* (1821), which have a modern, rather than a Chaucerian, style, that it becomes clear that Keats and his friend had set out on an ambitious scheme, of which 'Isabella' was but a part. Reynolds explained:

> The stories from Boccaccio (The Garden of Florence, and The Ladye of Provence) were to have been associated with tales from the same source, intended to have been written by a friend;— but illness on his part, and distracting engagements on mine, prevented us from accomplishing our plan at the time; and Death now, to my deep sorrow, has frustrated it forever.
>
> He, who is gone, was one of the very kindest friends I possessed, and yet he was not kinder perhaps to me, than to others. His intense mind and powerful feeling would, I truly believe, have done the world some service, had his life been spared—but he was of too sensitive a nature—and thus he was destroyed! One story he completed, and that is to me now the most pathetic poem in existence!

In his treatment of Lamia, Keats was similarly independent of his source. The note in Burton's *Anatomy of Melancholy* was seed enough:

> Philostratus, in his fourth book *de vita Apollonii* hath a memorable instance in this kinde, which I may not omit, of one Menippus Lycius, a young man 25 years of age, that going betwixt Cenchreas and Corinth, met such a phantasm in the habit of a fair gentlewoman, which taking him by the hand, carried him home to her house, in the suburbs of Corinth, and told him she was a Phoenician by birth, and if he would tarry with her, *he should hear her sing and play, and drink such wine as never any drank, and no man should molest him; but she being fair and lovely, would live and die with him, that was fair and lovely to behold.* The yong man, a philosopher, otherwise staid and discreet, able to moderate his passions, though not this of love, tarried with her a while to his great content, and at last married her, to whose wedding, amongst other guests, came Apollonius; who, by some probable conjectures, found her out to be a serpent, a lamia; and that all her furniture was like Tantalus gold, described by Homer, no substance, but meer illusions. When she

saw herself descried, she wept, and desired Apollonius to be silent, but he would not be moved, and thereupon she, plate, house, and all that was in it, vanished in an instant: *many thousands took notice of this fact, for it was done in the midst of Greece.*

Keats's treatment of the sexuality of Lamia, the snake who turns into a woman, was so impressive that it oppressed some of Keats's contemporaries: its sensuality seemed to them alienating, the emphasis on the physical aspects of metamorphosis seeming at once both matter-of-fact and sensational. Keats adds the prelude that tells of a quest for love where immortal seeks immortal – Hermes seeks a Nymph and gains her:

> Into the green recessèd woods they flew;
> Nor grew they pale, as mortal lovers do.

Their love is not changeable and finite. The implication is that in the actual world lovers are less blessed. It is the main story of 'Lamia' that carries the stresses and ambiguities; Lycius is a mortal youth, Lamia an immortal being; when first we meet her she is a brilliant serpent, soon, with Hermes' help, a beautiful woman with magic powers. These lovers are not equal. But the love between them is felt and true, and our sympathies are with Lamia, who has become, despite her special immortal strengths, vulnerable because she loves. Her transforming strength is allied to that (most human) weakness and in her love she capitulates to Lycius' masterful demand that their love be made public by a wedding ceremony. Lycius was unable to recognise that their passion – and this is a dimension of the erotic – had to be kept private. We, the readers, know that Lamia is not the woman she seems, and that Lycius, from one point of view, is not 'failing' Lamia by having thoughts of the wider world beyond her; it is part of his identity as a young man in society. Nor is he being untrue to another aspect of himself when he gives himself to love, and it is we, not Lycius, who see that the banquet-room, 'mimicking a glade' with palms and plantains and 'creeping imageries of slighter trees' is illusory, is not the 'green-recessèd woods' where equal love is consecrated. Yet Lamia has a reluctant pride in it all, paces about in a 'pale contented sort of discontent'. The uninvited guest, the philosopher and tutor Apollonius, turned into an old austere grim father-figure, a narrow rationalist, by Keats, remorselessly stares Lamia into 'truth', declares her serpent. It is like a death to her; she vanishes. Lycius, 'saved' from illusion, dies at once. It is a moral tale, but we do not accord it a moral response. Our sympathies flicker fitfully. Keats's exploration is psychological not ethical. While writing a fabulous tale he moves into the 'dark Passages' of man's love and desire for woman, his fear of being overwhelmed by love; of youthful reason's need to forget itself in feeling and old reason's rejection of all illusion; of woman's being part enchanter who offers seeming immortal moments, and part serpent who, despite all good feeling, destroys. There are no emotional certainties. Keats in the poem shifts allegiances and explores ambiguities more interestingly than on one celebrated occasion when he, in mischievous mood perhaps, yet significantly, condemned reason and scientific analysis as too often destructive. At the famous dinner at Haydon's studio, on 28 December 1817, with Lamb, Wordsworth and others present, Keats proposed a toast of 'Confusion to the memory of Sir Isaac Newton for spoiling the poetry of the rainbow by reducing it to a prism' (Haydon to Wordsworth, 16 October 1842).

In 'The Eve of St. Agnes', the balance is between light and dark. The tale has a frame of coldness and death: the frozen world at the beginning, and the ancient Beadsman with his terrifying knowledge of the cold of the dead; and at the end, after the sharp sleet of the storm, the death of the old nurse, Angela, and that of the Beadsman too, who 'For aye unsought for slept among his ashes cold.' It is so cold, that the dead themselves are imagined as able to feel the ferocious chill. In contrast, the main story of Porphyro and Madeline is a triumph of youth (which, it is hinted more than once, has a charmèd life and magical powers). The suggestion (by Jack Stillinger) that the plot is a hoodwinking of both the chaperone, Angela, and Madeline herself, seems an ingenious argument; at the same time, it misses the point of this richly patterned and celebratory poem. It is in the depiction of Madeline, at times as a bird, at times as an angel (though hardly within a Christian context), that the reader sees her as a princess to be desired. Porphyro's finest moment is not so much his meeting with Madeline herself, as the preparation of the majestic feast, laid out so ritualistically. This courtship represents a generosity, promises a fertility. Keats's friends urged him not to have Porphyro make love with Madeline, but for Keats the dream that she inhabited had to be made one with the actual

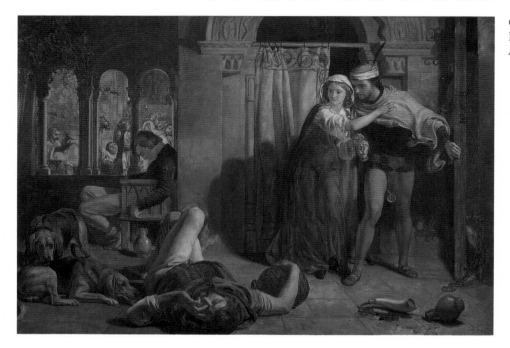

Cat. 219 William Holman Hunt, *The Flight of Madeline and Porphyro*

world. Here, indeed, is an example, almost literal, of how imagination may be compared to Adam's dream: he (or she) awoke and found it truth. At the moment of Madeline's awakening in the real, the fallen, ordinary world, she sees Porphyro as a vulnerable, fearful man, unlike his visionary self in her dream:

> How chang'd thou art! how pallid, chill, and drear!

But as she voices her own fear and her need for him, Porphyro becomes the vision of himself, for the moment immortal, 'Beyond a mortal man impassioned far'; and whatever the storm can do later, whatever changes are in store for the lovers, they share, as he melts into her dream, this brief intensity. The piled fruit, the elaborate shrine-like room, the lute song, are properly in place for Madeline's rite of passage from cold chastity to the warmth of shared real experience and the ability to go out into the storm. Even the storm is as ambiguous as much else in the poem; it both protects the lovers from discovery and presages their mortal struggles.

They leave, not changing the world, but abandoning it. The dragons are not killed (as they would be in Spenser's *Faërie Queene*) but are left sleeping; the lovers have rescued themselves, but the society they escape is left to its own triviality of corruption. Keats's friend Richard Woodhouse thought the conclusion had a cynicism learned from Byron; but it seems otherwise, and that for Keats, the world of nightmare and of death were the proper images balancing those where love so convincingly, if unexpectedly, conquered.

It was the fragmentary 'Hyperion' that most impressed Shelley in Keats's last volume. Only the first version was published in 1820, with the subtitle, 'A Fragment'. The second version, with its prefatory meeting between the poet and Moneta (which we have already discussed), encapsulates in shorter form the themes of the first. In the first 'Hyperion' the implicit theme is Keats's deep-held belief that change is the permanent reality, and the unchanging Titans defy that law. But the moment where the tale breaks off is with the coming of the young god, Apollo, who is in stark contrast with the fallen figures of Saturn, Thea and Enceladus, all marked with a gigantic lassitude; more importantly, Apollo is in contrast to 'blazing Hyperion on his orbit fire': they both have beauty and vitality; both, in their turn, rule the sun but it is Apollo alone who desires knowledge, wants everything – 'sovran voices, agonies, Creations and destroyings'. And this he receives. In the final surviving episode of the fragment Apollo meets the female figure Mnemosyne, goddess of Memory, and she guides the god to knowledge, even though she remains silent:

> Mute thou remainest—mute! yet I can read
> A wondrous lesson in thy silent face:
> Knowledge enormous makes a God of me.
> (Book III, ll.111-3)

The knowledge contains the painful and it brings pain, even physical anguish. Apollo dies into real godhead as he acquires Mnemosyne's knowledge. His suffering pain and his knowledge of it mean that he is god of far more than Hyperion was: he is the god of Poetry. The fragment ends with Apollo's shriek, perhaps foretelling the tragic vision of poetry. But he will have his lyre, will create and make music. Keats died too soon but clearly he knew what was required and where he was going.

The popularity of one narrative, 'La Belle Dame sans Merci', might have surprised Keats. Here again, there are two versions, and the earlier seems the better. It is a short poem, bare in setting, incantatory, like a ballad in its language; little happens beyond the telling of a meeting with a lady, her strange language, her singing, her gift of food, his belief in her love, his abandonment by her, his destructive dream of other men, kings and princes, who are yearning even to death, his awakening to a cold world and his utter inability to live in it any more. It is clear, detailed, and thoroughly mysterious. There is no explanation by the poet, no summary, no moralising. Was it vision, illusion, an insight into paradise, an enchantment that destroys? We have no answer. The knight, like the Ancient Mariner, is changed, and cannot be otherwise. Whatever the poem suggests to us, it itself enchants us.

To conclude with Keats's Odes is to turn to a world of poetry rich with appropriate controversy. It is not their greatness that is in doubt, but the enlivening attempt by critics to chart the minute course of the arguments that run within these great musical structures. Keats, in the Odes, has a power to speak through his masterly and dense control of patterns of imagery, of rhyme, of words, of themes. His words can sing in a musical phrase, and at the same time be very dramatic. Keats could be light-hearted about these achievements: one remembers the 'Ode to a Nightingale' and Keats's mocking phrase about it – when his brother George was writing out a copy in January 1820, he notes that the poem 'is like reading an account of the Black Hole of Calcutta on an icebergh'. Here is that arresting beginning, with its suggestion of a descent into some lower darkness, drugged and debased:

> My heart aches, and a drowsy numbness pains
> My sense, as though of hemlock I had drunk,
> Or emptied some dull opiate to the drains
> One minute past, and Lethe-wards had sunk:

The pain in the heart has to do with the poet's intensity of happiness as he responds to the happiness of the bird, and so the second half of the stanza rises from thoughts of pain and discovers the freedom of trees in movement,

> In some melodious plot
> Of beechen green, and shadows numberless . . .

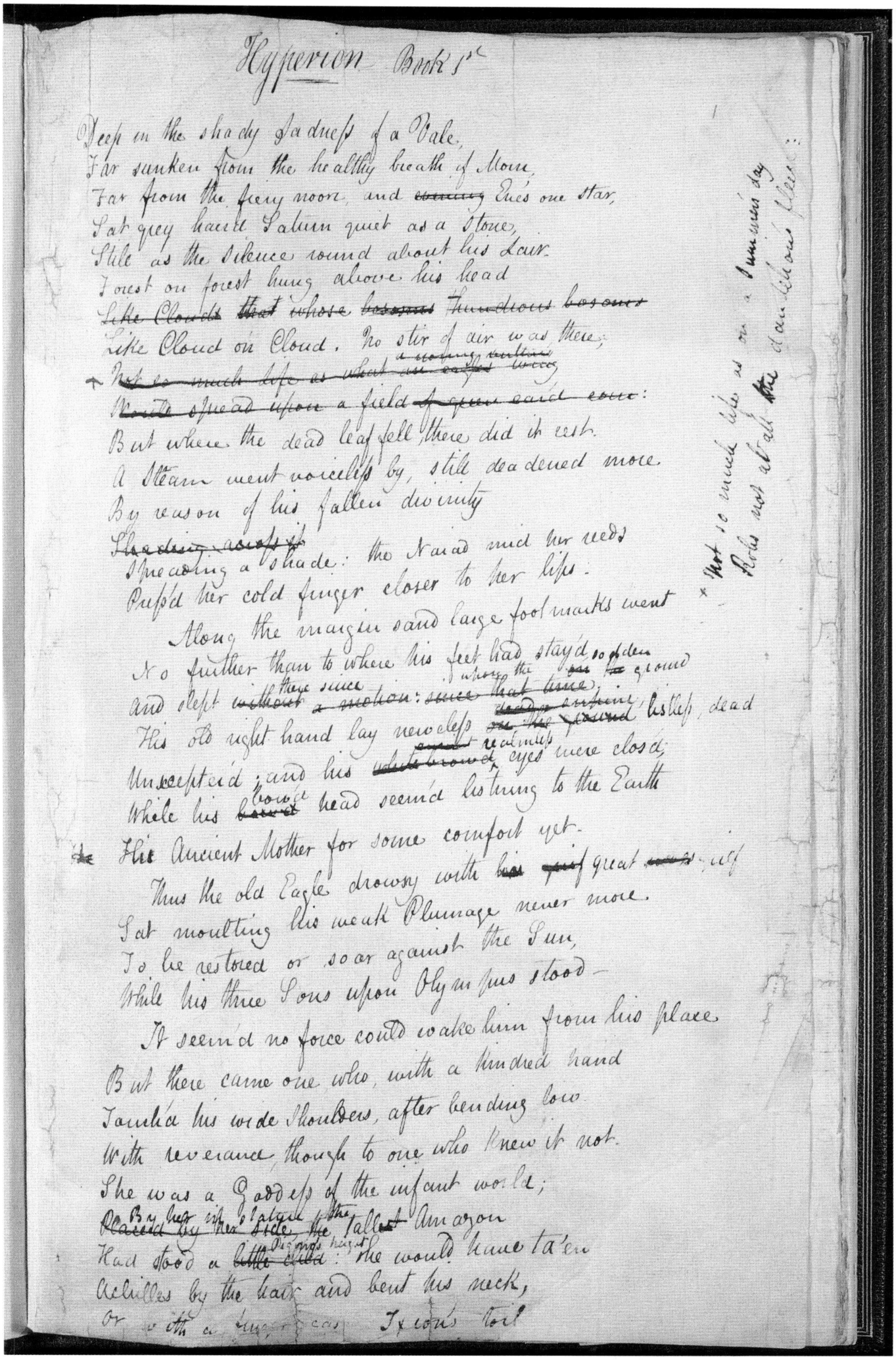

Hyperion Book 1st

Deep in the shady sadness of a Vale,
Far sunken from the healthy breath of Morn,
Far from the fiery noon, and ~~evening~~ Eve's one star,
Sat grey hair'd Saturn quiet as a Stone,
Still as the silence round about his Lair;
Forest on forest hung above his head
~~Like Clouds that whose bosoms thunderous bosoms~~
Like Cloud on Cloud. No stir of air was there,
~~Not so much life as what an eagle there,~~
~~Would spread upon a field of green said corn:~~
But where the dead leaf fell, there did it rest.
A Stream went voiceless by, still deadened more
By reason of his fallen divinity
~~Shading~~ ~~across if~~
Spreading a shade: the Naiad mid her reeds
Pres'd her cold finger closer to her lips.

Along the margin sand large foot marks went
No further than to where his feet had stay'd
and slept without a motion: since ~~upon the ground~~
His old right hand lay nerveless ~~on the ground~~ listless, dead
Unsceptered; and his ~~brows~~ eyes were clos'd,
While his ~~bow'd~~ brow'd head seem'd listening to the Earth
His Ancient Mother for some comfort yet.

Thus the old Eagle drowsy with his great ~~self~~
Sat moulting his weak Plumage never more
To be restored or soar against the Sun,
While his three Sons upon Olympus stood—

It seem'd no force could wake him from his place
But there came one who, with a kindred hand
Tamh'd his wide Shoulders, after bending low
With reverance, though to one who knew it not.
She was a Goddess of the infant world;
~~By her in stature the tall Amazon~~
Had stood a little ~~child~~: she would have ta'en
Achilles by the hair and bent his neck,
Or with a ~~finger~~ ~~stay Ixion's toil~~

Cat. 131 John Keats, original manuscript of 'Hyperion'

where a living creature, not numb at all, sings out 'in full-throated ease.' Such contrasts as are within this stanza form the structure of the whole poem, with its alternating positions.

The second stanza takes up the idea of drinking, not of hemlock, but of something recognisably alcoholic; but then, as the lines advance, something ancient, classical, communal, medieval is added to the imagined vintage that will transport the mind:

> O, for a draft of vintage! that hath been
>   Cool'd a long age in the deep-delved earth,
> Tasting of Flora and the country green,
>   Dance, and Provençal song, and sunburnt mirth!

And then the verse takes on 'the warm South', and among the Mediterranean tones comes the red stream of Hippocrene at Delphi. 'The blushful Hippocrene' was thought of as the ancient fountain of inspiration for poets, but in Keats's 'narrative', suddenly it turns into a definite wine, like one of those clarets he and Brown so frequently drank together (sometimes after dressing the tongue with a little cayenne pepper to emphasise the contrasting relief that the claret could give).

The escape is not ultimately alcoholic. Keats, however, makes it clear that there is much to escape from:

> The weariness, the fever, and the fret
>   Here, where men sit and hear each other groan;
> Where palsy shakes a few, sad, last gray hairs,
>   Where youth grows pale, and spectre-thin, and dies;
>   Where but to think is to be full of sorrow . . .

He goes on to the world of loss, the assault of time, of illness, the losing of beauty, and the fickleness of love.

Rather than fly with Bacchus, the god of wine, Keats takes the alternative guide, poetry: the imagination will chariot him to the desired presence and song. By the next line, he is there; the imagination moves swiftly. Keats can even imagine the moon and starlit heavens above the trees contrasting with the verdurous glooms below them:

> Already with thee! tender is the night,
>   And haply the Queen-Moon is on her throne,
>   Cluster'd around by all her starry Fays;
>   But here there is no light,
> Save what from heaven is with the breezes blown
>   Through verdurous glooms and winding mossy ways.

The only light is rather wonderfully 'blown' into the darkness.

And imagination is never more strong than in the half-funereal tones of the next stanza, which at once declares that nothing can be seen, and, at the same time, triumphantly displays the whole of the natural world in its ordered change. Here Keats's knowledge of botany emphasises the world of process: the flowers are picked out for their flowering over time, from the time of white hawthorn to that of the coming musk-rose, ripening and becoming the abode of flies on summer eves. This is all presented as a matter-of-fact truth, a mingled celebration, the undercurrent of lamentation suppressed by the parade of new flowers:

> I cannot see what flowers are at my feet,
>   Nor what soft incense hangs upon the boughs,
> But, in embalmed darkness, guess each sweet
>   Wherewith the seasonable month endows
> The grass, the thicket, and the fruit-tree wild;
>   White hawthorn, and the pastoral eglantine;
>   Fast fading violets cover'd up in leaves;
>   And mid-May's eldest child,
>   The coming musk-rose, full of dewy wine,
>   The murmurous haunt of flies on summer eves.

At this point in the poem, Keats loses his indifference, and confesses, as he listens to the music, to the seductive qualities of death itself. But as his skill in argument moves antithetically, his self-persuasion of being half in love with a death that is easeful leads to the brutal fact of death itself, a bitter contrast to the endless vitality of the nightingale: 'To thy high requiem become a sod.' From that dismaying discovery, Keats's rhetoric brings in a massive leap of energy and the bird is invested with an immortality. It is addressed in the emphatic vocative:

> Thou wast not born for death, immortal Bird!
>   No hungry generations tread thee down . . .

and the nightingale is defended from the very process that the world of flowers exemplified: Keats's phrasing echoes Wordsworth in Book IV of *The Excursion*:

> While man grows old, and dwindles, and decays,
> And countless generations of mankind
> Depart; and leave no vestige where they trod.

Wordsworth perhaps had a more kindly view of 'generation' than Keats had, and he, incidentally, thought that it was Spenser who best understood the word and its implication of marriage and the gift of progeny. Keats sees generations as hungry threats. The voice of the nightingale has been the same voice, whether heard in the ancient days of Rome perhaps, by the powerful or the humble, 'emperor and clown'; it is the same indifferent, beautiful voice that might have brought comfort to those in trouble –

Cat. 142 John Keats, original manuscript of 'Ode to a Nightingale'

Ruth, perhaps, as she stood in tears amid the alien corn; and at once we see that beside the biblical story, Keats must have recalled that rich design of Nicolas Poussin in the Pesne print, *Ruth and Boaz*. The last lines return to the image of 'the enchanted castle' by Claude Lorrain, the picture that Keats had described in his letter to Reynolds, in the hope that it could be a comfort to his sick friend. Here, the bird's singing is possibly not heard at all; no-one is mentioned, and the faery lands are forlorn. Of course, in the epistle to Reynolds, Keats ends with a sudden plunge into a more tragic world, where romance is not possible:

> but I saw
> Too far into the sea; where every maw
> The greater on the less feeds evermore:—
> But I saw too distinct into the core
> Of an eternal fierce destruction,
> And so from happiness I far was gone.

A similar plunge takes place in the last stanza of the Ode. Keats falls away back into the world that is without romance. The nightingale's music has become a mere plaintive anthem, fading and growing distant as it moves over a local landscape; our eye and ear travel with it, negotiating the different terrains and their prepositions:

Cat. 143 Claude Lorrain, *Landscape with Psyche outside the Palace of Cupid, 'The Enchanted Castle'* (1664)

> Past the near meadows, over the still stream,
>   Up the hill-side; and now 'tis buried deep
>   In the next valley-glades:

29

The stream has become still with distance, and the wonderful voice cannot be kept. It is quietly buried deep. We live in this world, and must return to it. But Keats leaves us with questions. Was it a vision, some glimpse into another world of high intensity? Was that the real perception, the being awake? Or, is what we call being awake being really blind and deaf, sleeping? It hardly matters. We have been through the poem with Keats, through the meditation. Whatever possibilities at any one moment a nightingale might offer to a responding mind, the voice of Keats remains. He will himself comment about a Grecian urn that provokes him into thinking that it will itself 'remain, in midst of other woe / Than ours, a friend to man'. We listen to his 'Ode to a Nightingale', its patterning and its music surely rivalling the song of any bird; and however we interpret it, and because we interpret it, it is a friend to man. Three times the poet says to the disappearing bird, 'Adieu! . . . Adieu! adieu!' The next words of Hamlet's father's ghost, after his three adieus as he fades and vanishes across the border back into the world of the dead are: 'Remember me.' Like Hamlet recalling the ghost of his father, the reader and the poet will not fail to remember the voice of the bird and to puzzle over its possible visionary significance.

It is not surprising that Keats should turn from the philosophic considerations of music and time in the 'Nightingale' to a meditation on time and the visual arts in the 'Grecian Urn'. Music has the purity (or limitation) of being a non-verbal art; it cannot tell a story. Nor is the urn verbal (though Keats gives it words at the end of the poem), but it can, if not tell, at least suggest stories. It allows possibilities, and Keats, in his quest for meaning, sets off to explore. He addresses the urn, undamaged, intact, perfect, as though the bride of quietness and the protected foster-child of time. It is a historian, but an imperfect one. The poet, looking at its sculptured scenes, has by questions to suggest its stories. The first is excited, frantic, sexual, communal, involving possibly both men and gods in pursuit of maidens loth; a fertility rite perhaps. The second, as the poet interprets other unheard and purely visual melodies, is calmer. It is a gentler, individual wooing scene, and it speaks to the spirit. The longing depicted in it can never be satisfied, 'Bold Lover, never, never canst thou kiss', but Keats is prepared and enters the scene to offer consolations. Winter can never come; he can even stop the leaves from dropping – 'nor ever can those trees be bare' – and she, the desired, 'cannot fade, though thou hast not thy bliss'. The verse moves from benefits to disadvantages, back and forth, as Keats envisages a normal world of process frozen in time. It becomes eternity, an intense world of ever-lasting anticipation, perpetual desire, preferable, indeed 'far above' – 'All breathing human passion'

> That leaves a heart high-sorrowful and cloyed,
> A burning forehead, and a parching tongue.

Ode on a Grecian Urn 1819.

1

Thou still unravish'd bride of quietness,
Thou foster child of silence and slow time,
Sylvan Historian, who can'st thus express
A flowery tale more sweetly than our rhyme,—
What leaf-fring'd legend haunts about thy shape,
Of Deities, or mortals, or of both
In Tempe, or the Dales of Arcady?
What men or Gods are these? what maidens loth
What love? what dance? what struggle to escape?
What pipes and timbrels? what wild extacy?

2

Heard melodies are sweet, but those unheard
Are sweeter,—therefore ye soft pipes play on;
Not to the sensual ear, but, more endear'd,
Pipe to the spirit-ditties of no tone;
Fair Youth, beneath the trees thou can'st not leave
Thy song, nor ever can those trees be bare,—
Bold lover, never, never can'st thou kiss
Tho' winning near the goal,—O, do not grieve!
She cannot fade, tho' thou hast not thy bliss
For ever wilt thou love, and she be fair!

Cat. 148 John Keats, earliest known manuscript (in the hand of George Keats), of 'Ode to a Grecian Urn'

And no doubt Keats's emphasis on these physical conditions came from a medical man's observation. Quickly leaving the painful, actual world, Keats moves into his third scene on the urn, again a social one, this time a ritual sacrifice. By questions he suggests the action – the procession, the priest, the heifer, and then he envisages a scene that is not even on the urn at all, so entirely has he become caught up in its 'life':

> And, little town, thy streets for evermore
> Will silent be; and not a soul to tell
> Why thou art desolate, can e'er return.

The little town, wherever it is built, will evermore be silent and desolate, for its people are all at the sacrifice; its men and maidens are marble on a marble urn; they can never go back. Keats feels tender about the town's desolation; it suffers a kind of death. And so, alternating between a rich, imagined life and a terrible non-life, the marble medium of the urn that continually brings us up short, Keats closes the poem. He is teased out of thought, as are we, bringing ourselves with the poet to swing in and out of life and in again, and finally to think about this cold mysterious 'pastoral'. An urn has to do with death; its full round shape and the sexual ritual on it has to do with birth; it has lovers, and people in a procession coming from somewhere out of sight and going to some green altar likewise not in sight. It suggests origins and endings, and a sense of the gods beyond us. Its medium suggests death as well as permanence. It teases us out of thought. And that it is why it is a friend to man, and always will be. Its own beauty of form and the beautiful, tender feelings it evokes for human process are real and true – 'Beauty is truth'. At the same time, as philosophical meditation on the cold, unliving art form, its deadness, our frustrations at the world of process and our inevitable mortality, our search for meaning, our awareness itself, our consciousness – these are aspects of truth; and there is a beauty in the way we struggle to find meaning: 'Truth is Beauty'. The urn is right. All we need is an imagination and a thinking mind. The urn and the poem, itself an 'Attic shape! Fair attitude!', together exercise and reward these faculties. It is what enriches us as human beings.

No one urn, incidentally, is behind Keats's urn. The scenes on his created urn are rich in significance beyond those of any known object. He knew several actual urns, and would both gather precise and anachronistic details of Grecian life from these and from, say, the paintings of Claude Lorrain, which he might have seen; most of his knowledge would come from the prints in Earlom's *Liber Veritatis*, 1777, published by Boydell. Here he would find depictions of ceremonious groups going to and fro between little towns.

And finally, 'To Autumn'. It is the richest poem in all Keats's achievements. Its final reference to the spring enlarges the scale of the poem to comprehend all four seasons turning beneath the god-like sun. That the autumn should be 'Close bosom-friend of the maturing sun' means that we are thinking on a heroic scale; there is not the domesticity of harvest fields as depicted by, say, George Stubbs, where the whole village hierarchy comes together in a community. The imagery of the first stanza is of forces at work, mysteriously swelling the plants and pressing goodness upon them until growth itself becomes a kind of excess. In the second stanza the figure of Autumn is allegorical, perhaps feminine with suggestions of Ceres, but not assertively so. The four vignettes of autumn – the figure on the granary floor, asleep in the furrow, a gleaner balancing a pitcher on the head, or simply watching the cider-press,

> with patient look,
> Thou watchest the last oozings hours by hours

– all these suggest a passivity, yet at the same time a vital omnipresence. That passivity nevertheless allows the powers to complete the harvest in their own slow-time: all is being perfected for the final gleaning. Then, in the final stanza, there is one of those subtle outbursts of vigour that we have come to expect from Keats at his very best. There is a questioning search for the sounds of spring, and a sense, despite their absence, that there is a more important music to be found in every corner of this autumnal scene, a music that often refers to the spring ('full-grown lambs') but, at the same time, is rich in the sudden discovery of its own music – thin sounds of small creatures borne on a light wind. All the sensuality of the first stanza has disappeared; there is a patient acceptance of the whole process of the seasonal cycle, made bearable because it will begin again. There is no pathos, no self-pity. If the swallows flying away echo Book VI of the *Aeneid* with Virgil's image of the dead crossing the river Styx, Keats has stripped the image of its primary allegorical meaning, translating it into an appropriate diminuendo for a close; and if the 'hilly bourn' reminds us of Hamlet's 'bourn from which no traveller returns', Keats strips out the idea of Hamlet's life-and-death drama, simply emphasising that Autumn's detailed and delicate processes are in effect a kind of music, an harmonious ending.

> Where are the songs of Spring? Ay, where are they?
>   Think not of them, thou hast thy music too—
> While barrèd clouds bloom the soft-dying day,
>   And touch the stubble-plains with rosy hue:
> Then in a wailful choir the small gnats mourn
>   Among the river sallows, borne aloft
>   Or sinking as the light wind lives or dies;
> And full-grown lambs loud bleat from hilly bourn;
>   Hedge-crickets sing; and now with treble soft
>   The red-breast whistles from a garden-croft;
>   And gathering swallows twitter in the skies.

CHRONOLOGY
1795-1821

1795

31 October John Keats is born at the Swan and Hoop Livery Stables, 24 Moorfields Pavement Row, London, the son of Thomas and Frances Keats. His brothers, George and Tom, are born in 1797 and 1799 respectively. A sister, Frances ('Fanny') is born in 1803.

18 December He is baptised at St. Botolph's, Bishopsgate.

1803-11

Keats attends John Clarke's school at Enfield. He befriends the headmaster's son, Charles Cowden Clarke, who encourages his interest in poetry.

1804

16 April His father dies in a riding accident.

27 June His mother remarries. With his brothers Keats lives with his grandparents at Ponders End, Enfield.

1810

March His mother dies of tuberculosis. She is buried on 20 March. In July Richard Abbey and John Sandell are appointed guardians of her children.

1811

Summer Keats leaves Enfield School. Having decided upon medicine as a career he is apprenticed to Thomas Hammond, a surgeon at Edmonton, for five years. During this time he meets regularly with Cowden Clarke, who later calls it 'the most placid period in his painful life'.

1814

Keats writes his first known poem, 'Imitation of Spenser'.

1815

1 October Keats enters Guy's Hospital as a student, lodging with other students (including Henry Stephens) in St. Thomas's Street. His rise is rapid; the following March he is entered as 'a dresser to the surgeons'. As such he performs his own operations. He befriends George Felton Matthew, to whom he writes an epistle in November.

1816

5 May His first published poem, 'O Solitude', appears in *The Examiner*. In the spring and summer he befriends Joseph Severn and Charles Jeremiah Wells.

25 July He passes the examination at Apothecaries' Hall, thus becoming eligible to practise as an apothecary. By this time, however, he has decided not to pursue medicine as a career.

August He goes with Tom Keats to Margate, where he writes epistles to George Keats and to Charles Cowden Clarke. Returning to London in September, he takes lodgings with his brothers at No. 8 Dean Street.

October After reading a folio copy of Chapman's translation of the *Iliad* and *Odyssey* with Cowden Clarke, Keats writes his first great sonnet, 'On First looking into Chapman's Homer'. Over the next few months he meets most of his future circle, including Leigh Hunt, Benjamin Robert Haydon, Benjamin Bailey, James Rice, Charles Brown and John Hamilton Reynolds. He pays his first visit to Haydon's studio on 3 November, by which time he has moved to No 76 Cheapside. After an evening with Haydon he writes the sonnet, 'Great Spirits now on Earth are Sojourning', praising Haydon, Hunt and Wordsworth. Haydon forwards the sonnet to Wordsworth.

November-December He is writing two longer poems, 'I stood tip-toe upon a little hill' and 'Sleep and Poetry'.

1 December The 'Chapman's Homer' sonnet appears in an *Examiner* article (by Leigh Hunt) on 'Young Poets' (Shelley, Reynolds and Keats). Around this time Haydon makes a lifemask of Keats and a sketch of him for his painting *Christ's Entry into Jerusalem*. Also at this time Joseph Severn makes his first sketch of the poet.

1817

January-February Keats is dining regularly at Leigh Hunt's cottage at the Vale of Health, Hampstead. There he meets Horace Smith, Percy Bysshe Shelley and William Godwin. Two sonnets, 'To Koskiusco' and 'After dark vapours' are published in *The Examiner*.

27 February Keats writes the sonnet 'This pleasant tale is like a little copse'.

1/2 March Haydon shows Keats the Elgin Marbles; he writes the two Elgin Marbles sonnets.

3 March His first volume, *Poems*, is published by C. and J. Ollier. The 'Elgin Marbles' sonnets appear in *The Examiner*.

25 March By this time he has moved with his brothers to No. 1 Well Walk, next to Hampstead Heath. Also this month he meets the publisher, John Taylor, who decides to publish his future books.

14 - c. 23 April Keats travels alone to the Isle of Wight, visiting Shanklin and lodging at Carisbrooke. Here he writes the sonnet, 'On the Sea', and begins his long poem, *Endymion*.

c. 24 April He moves to Margate, where he is joined by Tom. While there he is loaned £20 by Taylor (and his partner James Hessey), and is writing Book I of *Endymion*.

10 June Keats is back at Well Walk, where he continues with *Endymion*. By the end of August he has completed Books I and II.

3 September He goes to Oxford to stay with Benjamin Bailey. There he visits Stratford-on-Avon, and completes Book III of *Endymion*. He returns to Hampstead on 5 October.

28 November The first draft of *Endymion* is finished.

c.12 December Goes with Haydon to meet Wordsworth who is visiting London. This month and the next he is seeing Wordsworth 'frequently'.

15, 18 December He sees Edmund Kean perform at Drury Lane in *Riches* and *Richard III*. His review of Kean appears in *The Champion* on the 21st.

28 December He attends Haydon's 'immortal dinner'; Charles Lamb, Wordsworth and Landseer are also among the guests.

1818

January-February He revises *Endymion* and prepares it for the press. He regularly goes to hear Hazlitt lecture on the English poets at the Surrey Institution. Tom Keats begins to show signs of having tuberculosis

February He begins to write 'Isabella, or The Pot of Basil', and visits an exhibition at the British Gallery.

6 or 7 March He joins Tom Keats at Teignmouth. Here he writes a preface to *Endymion*, which, on Taylor's insistence, he revises. Tom has a haemorrhage.

27 March *Endymion* is published about this time. He has finished 'Isabella'.

4 or 5 May Keats leaves Teignmouth with Tom, reaching Hampstead before the 11th.

c.28 May George Keats marries Georgiana Wylie, and presently decides to emigrate to America.

May-September *Endymion* is savagely reviewed in the Tory periodicals.

23 June Keats, with Charles Brown, goes to Liverpool, where they see off George and Georgiana Keats. Keats and Brown continue north on a walking tour of the Lake District and Scotland.

24 - 30 June Arriving at Lancaster they walk through the Lake District. Their route takes them through Kendal, Bowness, Ambleside, Rydal, Wythburn and Keswick, where they walk around Derwentwater and climb Skiddaw. At Rydal they call on Wordsworth, who is not at home. They arrive at Carlisle on the 30th.

1 - 6 August Keats and Brown walk from Dumfries to Inverness. On the way they visit Burns's grave and cottage, spend two days in northern Ireland, visit Iona and Staffa, and climb Ben Nevis.

8 August Exhausted, Keats sails for London, while Brown continues north. He reaches Well Walk on the 18th, and finds Tom extremely ill. About this time he meets Fanny Brawne.

September-November He is nursing Tom at Well Walk. Reynolds urges him to publish 'Isabella'. Between November 1818 and April 1819 he writes 'Hyperion', which remains unfinished.

1 December Tom Keats dies. Keats accepts Brown's invitation to live with him at Wentworth Place, Hampstead. Tom is buried on the 7th.

27 December He visits Haydon, and sees a book of engravings of the frescoes at the Campo Santo, Pisa.

1819

18 or 19 January Keats joins Charles Brown at Chichester, where he visits Stansted Chapel, and writes 'The Eve of St. Agnes'. He returns to Wentworth Place at the beginning of February.

13-17 February He writes 'The Eve of St. Mark'.

Later in the month he writes the 'Bright Star' sonnet. Fanny Brawne transcribes it in her copy of Dante.

1 March He visits the British Museum with Severn.

11 April He walks with Coleridge and Joseph Green on Hampstead Heath.

21 April He reviews Reynolds' parody of Wordsworth, *Peter Bell*, and writes 'La Belle Dame sans Merci'

30 April He writes the 'Ode to Psyche'

May He writes the odes on Indolence, Nightingale, Grecian Urn and Melancholy.

28 June - 12 August Keats is at Shanklin, Isle of Wight, with James Rice and later Charles Brown. With Brown he writes the tragic drama *Otho the Great*, and completes half of 'Lamia'

July The 'Ode to a Nightingale' is published in *Annals of the Fine Arts*.

September He is at Winchester with Brown. There he works on a revision to 'Hyperion' ('The Fall of Hyperion: A Dream'), finishes 'Lamia', revises 'The Eve of St. Agnes', and writes 'To Autumn'

October - December Keats and Brown send *Otho the Great* to Drury Lane, and the play is accepted for the next season. He continues with 'The Fall of Hyperion' and starts a comic poem, 'The Cap and the Bells'.

1820

January The 'Ode on a Grecian Urn' is published in *Annals of the Fine Arts*.

9-29 January George Keats is in the country on business. He copies Keats's poems into one of the poet's old notebooks, taking it with him to America.

3 February After travelling on the outside of a coach in rough weather, Keats has a severe haemorrhage. From this time his health steadily declines, and by the end of the year he is seriously ill with tuberculosis. By this time he is engaged to Fanny Brawne.

25 March He attends a private view of Haydon's *Christ's Entry into Jerusalem*, which contains portraits of Keats, Wordsworth, Hazlitt and Voltaire.

27 April Keats sends the manuscripts for a new volume to Taylor and Hessey. He corrects the proofs the following month.

10 May 'La Belle Dame sans Merci' is published in *The Indicator*.

1 or 3 July *Lamia, Isabella, The Eve of St. Agnes and Other Poems* is published. By this time Keats has been ordered to spend the winter in Italy.

12 August He receives an invitation to visit Shelley in Italy. He declines on the 16th. About this time a subscription is held by his friends to finance his trip to Italy.

17 September Keats, accompanied by Severn, boards the *Maria Crowther* in London Docks. It sails from Gravesend the following night.

c. 1 October After heavy storms the *Maria Crowther* lands, perhaps at Lulworth Cove, and Keats copies the 'Bright Star' sonnet in Severn's copy of Shakespeare.

21 October The *Maria Crowther* reaches Naples, but is held in quarantine until the 31st.

7-8 November Keats and Severn start for Rome, which they reach on the 15th. They lodge on the Piazza di Spagna, and Keats is attended by a British physician, Dr. James Clark.

30 November Keats writes his last known letter, to Charles Brown. On 10 December he has a relapse.

1821

23 February John Keats dies at 11 pm. A death mask is made the following day.

26 February He is buried at the Protestant Cemetery in Rome. News of his death finally reaches London on 17 March.

CATALOGUE

John Keats by Joseph Severn

Fanny Keats by Juan Llanos

George Keats by Joseph Severn

Tom Keats by Joseph Severn

1. Enfield 1795-1816

John Keats was born in London on 31 October 1795. His mother, Frances, was the daughter of a prosperous property-owner, and his father, Thomas, the head livery man of the Swan and Hoop inn and stables on London Wall. In 1804, Thomas Keats died in a riding accident. Frances Keats quickly remarried, but separated from her new husband after a year. In March 1810 she died of tuberculosis. Keats was then fourteen. With his two younger brothers, George and Tom, and his younger sister Fanny, he was left in the care of two guardians, one of whom was the unsympathetic solicitor Richard Abbey.

Keats rarely spoke about these earliest years and their many misfortunes, and it is only when the main course of his life, that of poetry, begins to emerge, that a witness appears. Charles Cowden Clarke was the son of the headmaster of Enfield School, the liberal establishment that Keats attended between 1803 and 1811. In his company Keats first encountered what, as he said to Cowden Clarke, would be 'all that my life now endears'. From hereon, poetry would be his first passion: 'I find that I cannot exist without poetry,' he later wrote to J.H. Reynolds, 'without eternal poetry—half the day will not do—the whole of it—I began with a little, but habit has made me a Leviathan.' In this respect Keats was single-minded. As his ambition grew, so the trials of his experience could be vicariously faced and transcended only through his poetic vision. And as this vision widened and matured, the more it was able to embody, as he put it in a letter to Charles Brown in November 1821, the last letter he ever wrote, 'the knowledge of contrast, feeling for light and shade, all that information (primitive sense) necessary for a poem'.

Looking back to 'that hallowed old arbour' where he and Keats would meet, read and talk, Cowden Clarke recalled some of the authors to which, in 'teeming wonderment', Keats was introduced. Spenser he read 'as a young horse would through a summer meadow—ramping'; reading aloud Shakespeare's *Cymbeline* 'his eyes filled with tears, and his voice faltered'; Lemprière's *Classical Dictionary* 'he appeared to *learn*', and, in October 1816, Chapman's translation of Homer's *Iliad* and *Odyssey* inspired his first great poem, 'On First Looking into Chapman's Homer'. Now a medical student in the city, Keats in this sonnet remembers the 'realms of gold', 'the many goodly States and Kingdoms' through which he had travelled in Enfield, and, like 'stout Cortez, when with wond'ring eyes / He first saw the Pacific', he sees the 'new Planet' of his own poetry before him.

G. HAWKINS AFTER A.P. MOORE

I   *A View of St. Botolph's Church, Bishopsgate*
Published London: 2 August 1802
Stipple engraving, 50.2 x 39.5 cms
Guildhall Library, City of London

Keats was baptised at St. Botolph's Church, Bishopsgate, near to his parents' livery stables at Finsbury, on 18 December 1795. Born within sound of Bow Bells (the bells of St. Mary-le-Bow in Cheapside), he was, technically, a Cockney. The popular idea, however, that he spoke with a kind of stage cockney accent, is extremely unlikely. His younger sister, Frances ('Fanny') was also baptised here, on 17 June 1803.

FREDERICK LEWIS (1779-1856)

2   *Forty Hill, Enfield*
Watercolour, 26.7 x 24.2 cms
*By Courtesy of the Board of Trustees
of the Victoria & Albert Museum*

Illustrated in colour on p. 2

3   *View at Enfield*
Watercolour, 22.9 x 30.5 cms
*By Courtesy of the Board of Trustees
of the Victoria & Albert Museum*

John Clarke's school at Enfield formed a refuge from the tragedies at home. Its teaching was sympathetic, its scale small and its curriculum progressive. Enfield itself, which Keats also knew as his grandparents' home, was then a hamlet of fields, woods and streams, and despite subsequent trips to the Lake District, Scotland, and the Isle of Wight, Keats always felt closest to this more intimate landscape. 'Nothing seemed to escape him,' remembered Joseph Severn, 'the song of a bird and the undernote of response from covert or hedge, the rustle of some animal, the changing of the green or brown lights and furtive shadows, the motions of the wind—just how it took certain tall flowers and plants—and the wayfaring of the clouds . . . Certain things affected him extremely, particularly when "a wave was billowing through a tree," as he described the uplifting surge of air among swaying masses of chestnut or oak foliage; or when, afar off, he heard the wind coming across woodlands'. The absence of trees, in particular, he seems to have felt keenly: 'I like my old lodging here', he wrote to Leigh Hunt from 'this treeless affair', Margate, in May 1817, '[if I] could contrive to do without trees'.

Frederick Lewis also spent his early years at Enfield. Here he shows it as a rural idyll of trees, picnicing children and farm wagons.

After his father's death, Keats spent time at Ponders Green, Enfield, with his maternal grandmother Alice Jennings, his 'Granny good' as he calls her in the third stanza of his 'There was a Naughty Boy' where he refers to keeping goldfish in her washing tub. An Enfield idyll is evoked in a letter to Fanny of 13 March 1819, where he remembers 'how fond I used to be of Goldfinches, Tomtits, Minnows, Mice, Ticklebacks, Dace, Cock salmons and all the whole tribe of the Bushes and the brooks: but verily they are better in the trees and the water – though I must confess even now a partiality for a handsome Globe of goldfish'.

UNKNOWN ARTIST

4 *Charles Cowden Clarke (1787-1877)*
Watercolour on marble, 30.2 x 25.1 cms
National Portrait Gallery, London

Illustrated on p. 3

Outside the complexities of his relations with his own immediate family, Charles Cowden Clarke was perhaps the single most important figure in Keats's life between the death of his mother and his first meeting with Leigh Hunt. That Keats should address him in a letter, most unusually for him, by his Christian name, is a sign of their intimacy.

Through their years together at Enfield, and then during Keats's apprenticeship to Thomas Hammond at nearby Edmonton, this 'reader of genuine discernment', as Leigh Hunt called him, encouraged Keats's ever-growing love of and enthusiasm for literature. It was Cowden Clarke who introduced him to his future 'presiders', Homer, Spenser, Shakespeare and Milton, and then, in the figures of Leigh Hunt and Benjamin Robert Haydon, contemporary literary and artistic London. Keats gratefully and affectionately acknowledges this legacy, 'the most placid period of his painful life', in his epistle addressed to Cowden Clarke (published in the 1817 *Poems*):

> Ah! had I never seen,
> Or known your kindness, what might I have been?
> What my enjoyments in my youthful years,
> Bereft of all that now my life endears?
> And can I e'er these benefits forget?
> And can I e'er repay the friendly debt?
> No, doubly no;—yet should these rhymings please,
> I shall roll on the grass with two-fold ease:
> For I have long-time been my fancy feeding
> With hopes that you would one day think the reading
> Of my rough verses not an hour misspent;
> Should it e'er be so, what a rich content!

Clarke lost touch with Keats after 1817, 'I have not seen . . . C.C.C. for God knows when' the latter wrote in February 1819; yet this formative friendship left a lasting impression on both men, and Clarke's recollections of the poet during their years of intimacy in his *Recollections of Writers* (1861), are particularly vivid. After Keats's death Clarke turned to publishing, moving easily in many literary circles. From 1834 to 1856 he was a popular lecturer on literary subjects,

and with his wife, Mary, he collaborated on a *Shakespeare-Key* (1879) and an edition of Shakespeare's works. Always ready to defend Keats from posthumous attacks, and quick to correct biographical inaccuracies, his good intentions of writing a larger memorial of the poet were still unfulfilled when he died in his ninetieth year.

CHARLES COWDEN CLARKE

5 *Commonplace Book*
Leeds University Library, Brotherton Collection

Evidence of Clarke's own reading, while he tutored Keats, is provided by this well-maintained and carefully indexed commonplace book. The quotations range from the classical to the radical, from eighteenth-century poets (Cowper, Collins, Chatterton) to the contemporary (Beattie, Blake, Wordsworth). His own poetry, though minor, sometimes anticipates Keats's mature verse. The poem 'The Nightingale' (dated 1813) ends with the lines:

> Sweetest warbler! Say
> What sorrows can afflict thy breast!—
> Thou hast no shining friend to spoil
> Thee of thy mate;—no oily villain thou
> To lure thy little partner from her home.—
> Senseless of these woes—happy bird!
> Happy bird!—thou'rt in Paradise'

RICHARD MONCKTON MILNES (1809-1885)

6 *Life, Letters, and Literary Remains*
of John Keats
London: Edward Moxon, 1848
Leeds University Library, Brotherton Collection

Clarke's opinion of Milnes's Life of Keats was mixed. '[It has] all I could have wished for his monumental fame' he commented when it first appeared, though later, in 1864, he remarked privately to Joseph Severn, 'there ought to be a better life of him'. This, his own copy, contains some vigorous annotations that, in general, are concerned with making Keats a stronger and more virile figure than the then current image of a fragile spirit destroyed by an unsympathetic world. Against a quote from Keats's letter to Woodhouse of 27 October 1818, he marks: 'This not the man to be "snuffed out by an article"—my overweening, egotistical Lord Byron. C.C.C.'; his comment upon a part of Shelley's preface to *Adonais* ('it was by assiduous watching that he was restrained from effecting purposes of suicide') is simply 'No! No! No!', and he corrects the following anecdote: 'His bodily vigour too must, at this time, have been considerable, as he signalised himself, at Hampstead, by giving a severe drubbing to a butcher, whom he saw beating a little boy.' Clarke writes beside Milnes's account: 'not accurate. He was torturing a kitten, Keats told it me. They fought for nearly an hour. And the fellow was bled, or carried home.—'

RICHARD MONCKTON MILNES (ED.)

7 *The Poetical Works of John Keats*
London: Edward Moxon & Co., 1868
The Wordsworth Trust

Beneath the frontispiece portrait of Keats (based upon the posthumous medallion by Girometti), Clarke has written in pencil: 'A walrus would quite as well have answered the purpose for a portrait of John Keats. C.C.C.' He himself thought Severn's first portrait (see cat. 39) the best likeness.

EDMUND SPENSER (C. 1552-99)

8 *The Works of that Famous English Poet Mr. Edmund Spenser*
London: Henry Hills for Jonathan Edwin, 1679
The British Library Board

'It were difficult', recalled Cowden Clarke, 'at this lapse of time, to note the spark that fired the train of his poetical tendencies; but he must have given unmistakeable tokens of his mental bent; otherwise, at that early stage of his career, I never could have read to him the "Epithalamium" of Spenser; and this I remember having done, and in that hallowed old arbour, the scene of many bland and graceful associations—the substances having passed away. At that time he may have been sixteen years old; and at that period of life he certainly appreciated the general beauty of the composition, and felt the more passionate passages; for his features and exclamations were ecstatic . . . like a true poet, too—a poet "born, not

manufactured," a poet in grain, he especially singled out epithets, for that felicity and power in which Spenser is so eminent.'

His first poem, 'Imitation of Spenser' is thus a tribute to his first poet, and he later put Spenser's portrait on the title page of his first published volume of verse. Keats would employ the stanza form of *The Faerie Queene* to great effect in 'The Eve of St. Agnes', though in that poem Spenserian romance is translated into his own, darker vision. For it became increasingly difficult, for him, 'an inhabitant of wintry earth', to feel at home in Spenser's world of romance. He wrote in 1818, *apropos* of a suggestion by Reynolds:

Spenser, a jealous honourer of thine,
　A forester deep in thy midmost trees,
Did last eve ask my promise to refine
　Some English that might strive thine ear to please.
But Elfin-Poet, 'tis impossible
　For an inhabitant of wintry earth
To rise like Phoebus with a golden quell,
　Fire-wing'd, and make a morning in his mirth:
It is impossible to escape from toil
　O' the sudden, and receive thy spiriting:—

JOHN LEMPRIÈRE (D. 1824)

9 *Classical Dictionary*
Imperfect copy (octavo) belonging to Wordsworth
The Wordsworth Trust

'I hope' wrote Keats in the preface to *Endymion*, 'I have not in too late a day touched the beautiful mythology of Greece, and dulled its brightness'. Greek myth informs much of Keats's poetry, and Lemprière's *Dictionary* introduced him to the subject. Cowden Clarke recollected: 'the books . . . that were his constantly recurrent sources of attraction were Tooke's "Pantheon", Lemprière's "Classical Dictionary," which he appeared to *learn*, and Spence's "Polymetis." This was the store whence he acquired his intimacy with the Greek mythology; here was he "suckled in that creed outworn"'.

Finis.

This pleasant Tale is like a little copse
The honied lines do freshly interlace
To keep the Reader in so sweet a place
So that he here and there full-hearted stops
And oftentimes he feels the dewy drops
Come cool and suddenly against his face
And by the wandering Melody may trace
Which way the tender-legged linnet hops
O what a Power hath white Simplicity!
What mighty Power has this gentle Story!
I that for ever feel athirst for glory
Could at this Moment be content to lie

JOHN KEATS

10 'On the Floure and the Leafe'
Manuscript written into Charles Cowden
Clarke's copy of Chaucer's poems
The British Library Board

Underneath the poem 'The Flower and the Leaf'
Keats has written the sonnet beginning 'This pleasant
tale is like a little copse'. Cowden Clarke was remind-
ed of the incident when, in 1835, he was editing his
Riches of Chaucer:

It happened at the period when Keats was about
publishing his first little volume of poems (in the
year 1817); he was then living in the second floor
of a house in the Poultry, at the corner of the
court leading to the Queen's Arms tavern—that
corner nearest to Bow church. The author had
called upon him here, and finding his young
friend engaged, took possession of a sofa, and
commenced reading, from his then pocket-com-
panion, Chaucer's "Flower and the Leaf." The
fatigue of a long walk, however, prevailed over the
fascination of the verses, and he fell asleep. Upon
awaking, the book was still at his side; but the
reader may conceive the author's delight, upon
finding the following elegant sonnet written in his
book at the close of the poem. During my sleep,

Keats had read it for the first time; and, knowing
that it would gratify me, had subjoined a testimo-
ny to its merit, that might have delighted Chaucer
himself.

Stimulated perhaps by Cowden Clarke's company
and the once-familiar act of joint reading, the sonnet
recalls earlier days when, in Cowden Clarke's words,
'we always sat in an arbour at the end of a spacious
garden, and—in Boswellian dialect—"we had a good
talk."'

This pleasant tale is like a little copse:
    The honied lines do freshly interlace,
    To keep the reader in so sweet a place,
So that he here and there full hearted stops;
And oftentimes he feels the dewy drops
    Come cool and suddenly against his face,
    And by the wandering melody may trace
Which way the tender-legged linnet hops.

Oh! What a power hath white simplicity!
    What mighty power has this gentle story!
    I, that for ever feel athirst for glory,
Could at this moment be content to lie
    Meekly upon the grass, as those whose sobbings
    Were heard of none beside the mournful robbins.

February, 1817

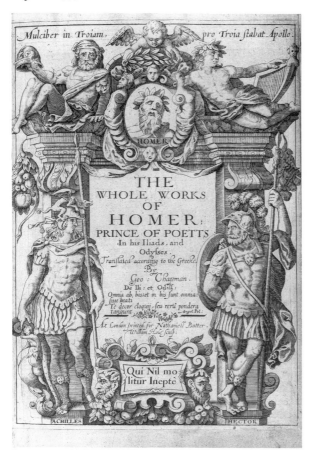

GEORGE CHAPMAN (?1559–1634)

II   *The Whole Works of Homer; Prince of Poets*
London: John Bull [1632?]
The British Library Board

The high-point of Keats's and Cowden Clarke's reading was, of course, the evening in October 1816 when they read passages from and delighted in the superb folio edition of George Chapman's translation of the *Iliad* and *Odyssey*. Cowden Clarke recalled the episode:

> A beautiful copy of the folio edition of Chapman's translation of Homer had been lent me. . . . and to work we went, turning to some of the "famousest" passages, as we had scrappily known them in Pope's version. . . . Chapman supplied us with many an after-treat; but it was in the teeming wonderment of this his first introduction, that, when I came down to breakfast the next morning, I found upon my table a letter with no other enclosure than his famous sonnet, "On First

Looking into Chapman's Homer." We had parted, as I have already said, at day-spring, yet he contrived that I should receive the poem from a distance of, may be, two miles by ten o'clock.

On the verso of the engraved title page is a portrait of Chapman, with an inscription dated 1616; and on the next page is an engraving of two Corinthian columns surmounted by the Prince of Wales's plume and motto. The translation itself (in rhymed lines of fourteen syllables in the case of the *Iliad* and of ten syllables in the *Odyssey*) despite its mistranslations and clumsy metre, was greatly preferred by Keats to Pope's smoother version; he enjoyed Chapman's rougher tone and energy:

> Then forth he came, his both knees falt'ring, both
> His strong hands hanging down, and all with froth
> His cheeks and nostrils flowing, voice and breath
> Spent to all use, and down he sank to death.
> The sea had soak'd his heart through; all his veins
> His toils had rack'd t' a labouring woman's pains.
> Dead weary was he.

WILLIAM ROBERTSON (1721–93)

12   *The History of America*
London: S.A. & H. Oddy, 1808
The Wordsworth Trust

As well as on Homer, the sonnet 'On First Looking into Chapman's Homer' draws on William Robertson's *History of America*, specifically the episode in Book III where Balboa discovers the Pacific (in the sonnet Keats confuses him with Cortez):

> At length the Indians assured them, that from the top of the next mountain they should discover the ocean which was the object of their wishes. When with infinite toil they had climbed up the greater part of that steep ascent, Balboa commanded his men to halt, and advanced alone to the summit, that he might be the first who should enjoy a spectacle which he had so long desired. As soon as he beheld the South Sea stretching in endless prospect below him, he fell on his knees, and lifting up his hands to heaven, returned thanks to God, who had conducted him to a discovery so beneficial to his country, and so honourable to himself.

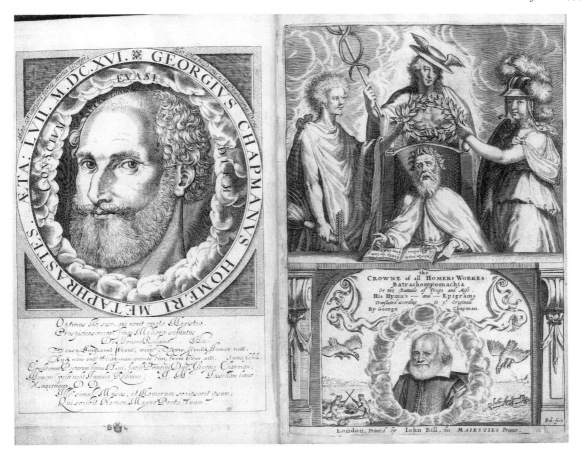

On First looking into Chapman's Homer

MUCH have I travell'd in the realms of gold,
  And many goodly states and kingdoms seen;
  Round many western islands have I been
Which bards in fealty to Apollo hold.
Oft of one wide expanse had I been told
  That deep-brow'd Homer ruled as his demesne;
  Yet did I never breathe its pure serene
Till I heard Chapman speak out loud and bold:
Then felt I like some watcher of the skies
  When a new planet swims into his ken;
Or like stout Cortez when with eagle eyes
  He star'd at the Pacific—and all his men
Look'd at each other with a wild surmise—
  Silent, upon a peak in Darien.

2. Medical Student, 1815-16

In 1811 Keats left Enfield to begin an apprenticeship to an apothecary, Thomas Hammond, in nearby Edmonton. Five years later, in October 1815, he enrolled as a medical student at Guy's Hospital, there completing his medical training. On 25 July 1816 he sat, and passed the examination at Apothecaries' Hall, thereby becoming eligible, under the new Apothecaries Act of 1815, to practice as an apothecary. Almost immediately, however, he gave up his medical career in favour of poetry.

'The Borough is a beastly place in dirt, turnings and windings' he wrote to Cowden Clarke in October that year, and life at Guy's was indeed very different from 'the lawny fields, and pebbly water' of Enfield. Almost daily, he would have worked in the foetid stench of the dissecting room, witnessed the cries of patients in the pre-anaesthetic operating theatre, and stood by as Ben Crouch and his team of 'resurrection-men', or bodysnatchers, plied their wares. Later, as a dresser, he not only would perform his own, simple operations, but watch his surgeon, William 'Billy' Lucas, 'the butcher of Guy's', bungle the others. Such experiences would always make the physical aspects of his poetry uniquely vivid. What is more, the Hippocratic ideals of the medical profession left in his mind a tension between 'fine writing' and 'fine doing'.

Then there was the example of his lecturers – surgeons, chemists and botanists who rejected theoretical speculation for empirical research and personal experience, the diligent observation of natural processes and the contemplation of minutiae. 'Axioms in philosophy are not axioms until they are proved upon our pulses', Keats wrote to Reynolds on 3 May 1818, 'We read fine things but never feel them to the full until we have gone the same steps as the Author.' His lecturers also emphasised a necessary calmness of mind, what Keats called 'disinterestedness'. Surgery, Astley Cooper told his students, 'requires a good Eye, a steady hand, and above all a Mind which is not easily ruffled by circumstances'. 'This is the world', Keats wrote to his brother and sister-in-law on 19 March 1819, 'we cannot expect to give way many hours to pleasure—Circumstances are like Clouds continually gathering and bursting . . . very few men have ever arrived at a complete disinterestedness of Mind'. Responding to Sarah Jeffrey's suggestion that he become a ship's surgeon he mused, 'To be thrown among people who care not for you, with whom you have no sympathies forces the Mind upon its own resources, and leaves it free to make its speculations of the differences of human character and to class them with the calmness of a botanist.'

T. HIGHAM AFTER THOMAS SHEPHERD

13 *Guy's Hospital and Statue of Thomas Guy, the Founder*
Stipple engraving, 10.3 x 14.8 cms
Guildhall Library, City of London

Guy's Hospital was nearly a hundred years old when Keats enrolled there. It was founded in 1724 by Thomas Guy, a successful bookseller and financier, who was a Governor of St. Thomas's Hospital, and supported that institution, financing, among other things, three new wards. Guy, who had made his vast fortune in the South Sea Bubble, founded Guy's to provide for the numerous patients who either could not be received in St. Thomas's, or had been discharged from there as incurable.

J. PASS

14 *North Front of Guy's Hospital*
Colour stipple engraving, 10.2 x 15.9 cms
Guildhall Library, City of London

Illustrated on p. 8

The engraving shows an amputee standing outside the gates, while another patient, perhaps about to be rendered the same service, is being stretchered inside. As one of the big voluntary hospitals founded less than a century earlier, Guy's would have been a new opportunity for the sick poor, who formerly had known no middle-ground between the quack doctor and the resplendent, carriage-borne physician (the ancient institutions of St. Bartholo-mew's and St. Thomas's being usually overflowing). It became not only a source of prestige for the physicians to be associated with such hospitals, it was also an opportunity for the more conscientious physician to study and relieve, as he walked the wards, an unending series of fevers and diseases. The hospitals also enabled the relatively new science of surgery to develop, and inevitably they became the main centres of research, education and training for the profession. So much so that by Keats's time it was compulsory for a would-be apothecary to gain six months practical experience at a hospital.

UNKNOWN ARTIST

15 *The Middle Court of St. Thomas's Hospital Borough*
Pencil, 22.7 x 17.1 cms
Guildhall Library, City of London

St. Thomas's, a development from a thirteenth-century lazar house, was on the other side of the road from Guy's. After the foundation of Guy's an informal arrangement quickly grew up whereby the teaching offered by one hospital was made open to the students from the other, until in 1760 there occurred a quarrel between Guy's and St. Thomas's about reciprocal attendance of students. Six years later the Governors of Guy's resolved 'that the barrier between this hospital and St. Thomas's be taken down and that the pupils of St. Thomas's have free leave to see not only operations, but also all other practice of this hospital'. St. Thomas's agreed, and the two hospitals were known generally as the 'United Hospitals'.

By this arrangement, Keats fought his way into the packed lectures on anatomy, surgery and dissection at St. Thomas's, and into those on the theory and practice of medicine, therapeutics and materia medica, chemistry, midwifery, physiology and experimental philosophy at Guy's.

Middle Court of St Thomas's Hospital Borough

RICHARDSON OF EDINBURGH

16   *General Operations Set*
      Pre-1850
      49.5 x 22.2 x 9.5 cms
      Science Museum, London

External diseases, injuries and operations were historically the concern of surgeons. Most surgeons were busy carrying out such relatively simple operations as amputations; pioneers, like Astley Cooper, were experimenting and extending medical knowledge. The horrors of the pre-anaesthetic operating theatre are vividly described by John Flint South in his *Memorials* (1884):

> The operating theatre was small, and the rush and scuffle to get a place was not unlike that for a seat in the pit or gallery of a dramatic theatre; and when one was lucky enough to get a place, the crowding and squeezing was oftentimes unbearable, more especially when any very important operation was being performed . . . behind a second partition stood the pupils, packed like herrings in a barrel, but not so quiet, as those behind were continually pressing on those before, often so severely that several could not bear the pressure, and were continually struggling to relieve themselves of it, and not infrequently to be got out exhausted. There was also a continual calling out of "heads, heads," to those about the table, whose heads interfered with the sightseers, with various appellatives, in a small way resembling the calls at the Sheldonian Theatre during Commemoration . . . I have often known even the floor so crowded that the surgeon could not operate till it had been partially cleared . . . I soon got over the blood-shedding which necessarily ensued; and so long as the patient did not make much noise I got on very well, but if the cries were great, and especially if they came from a child, I was quickly upset, had to leave the theatre, and not infrequently fainted.

17   *Set of Apothecary's Scales*
      Science Museum, London

18   *Apothecary's Pestle & Mortar*
      Science Museum, London

RICHARD POWELL

19   *The Pharmacopoeia of the Royal College*
      of Physicians of London
      London: Longman, Hurst, Rees, Orme
      and Brown, 1815
      The British Library Board

The apothecary's traditional role in the medical world was the compounding and selling of drugs from botanical and mineral sources; their application was the province of the physician. The apothecary prepared, and the physician prescribed, and it was only with the 1815 Apothecaries Act that the apothecaries gained formal recognition as people of practical medical knowledge, and ceased to be seen as 'mere tradesmen'.

Two centuries before, in 1618, alarmed by the growth of adulterated and over-priced drugs, the Royal College of Physicians had published the first *Pharmacopoeia*. This contained details of the correct measurements and mixing and application of all bona fide drugs, and, through constant enlargement and improvement, it was still a basic source of reference in Keats's time. Its immediate result was, in fact, a growth in the apothecary's power, as South's *Memorials* records:

> As there were now medicines to be had authorised by the College as fit for treating "all the ills which flesh is heir to," and as there was no restriction to any one physicking himself therewith to his heart's content, and it was very natural for common people to think that those who made medicines were very likely to know what they were good for and ready to give them accordingly, it is not at all surprising that the lower class, and even many of those above it, should have resorted to the apothecary rather than continue putting themselves under old women and quacks, for which the public had long had great propensity . . .

Originally written in Latin, this copy is one of the translations available to students and practitioners in 1815. Keats was required to learn large parts of it in Latin for his examination.

20   *Medicine Chest*
      1813
      Wood, glass & pewter, 14.7 x 14.8 x 11.3 cms
      Science Museum, London

The chest contains the following common medicines: Laudanum (by W.B. Hudson, Chemist & druggist, 27 Haymarket, London); Paregoric Elixir (by Savory, Moore & Co., Chemists to the Royal Family, 136 New Bond St; 220 Regent Street, London); Essence of Peppermint (by Savory, Moore & Co.); Antimonial Wine (by Grindle, Chemist & Druggist, 122 Pall Mall); and Spirit of Lavender (by B. Langley, Chemist & Druggist, High Street, Dorking Est 1760). This last has written on the bottle: 'medicines from Apothecaries' Hall, Physicians Prescriptions Strictly attended to'.

      S. WODEHOUSE
21   *Lancets and Case*
      Silver mounted tortoiseshell case fitted with four steel lancets, 6.5 x 3 x 1.4 cms
      Science Museum, London

The lancet could be used, among many things, for tapping the vein in order to release blood. Blood letting, by lancet, cupping glass or leech, was a standard, almost ubiquitous treatment for all kinds of diseases in Keats's time. On 17 December 1820, during his final illness in Italy, Keats had a haemorrhage, vomiting two cupfuls of blood. 'In a moment I got Dr Clarke', wrote Severn to Charles Brown, 'who saw the manner of it, and immediately took away about 8 ounces of blood from the Arm.' Four years later in Greece, Byron's doctor persuaded his reluctant patient to submit to bleeding, and probably hastened his patient's death.

22   *Cupping Set*
      Mid 19th Century
      Wood, glass & brass, 27.5 x 15.2 x 9.2 cms
      Science Museum, London

Cupping was a particularly painful way of blood letting, whereby it was drawn from the patient by scarifying the skin and applying a 'cup' or cupping glass, the air in which had been rarefied by heat or suction.

23   *Leech Jar (with Cage)*
      Made Staffordshire, 23 x 29 cms
      Science Museum, London

Where lances or cupping glasses could not be applied, a leech would serve to draw off the blood. Leeches are still occasionally used in modern surgery to remove excess blood in, for instance, eye operations, or plastic surgery.

24   *Forceps*
      30 x 10 cms
      Science Museum, London

The idea of a 'man-midwife', with its threat to traditional morals, took some time to be accepted. By Keats's time, however, midwifery, and the use of the obstetrical forceps, was a standard part of medical training. For three generations this device had been the secret instrument of the seventeenth-century Chamberlen family. Peter Chamberlen, for a period a fellow of the Royal College of Physicians, justified secrecy on strictly commercial grounds, though Hugh Chamberlen eventually divulged the secret, at a price, to the Dutch, after he had failed to sell it to the French. For some years afterwards it was improperly and dangerously used. Sterne's Dr Slop, for instance, memorably knocks out three of his own front teeth while manipulating the device in *Tristram Shandy*.

      FRANCIS CHANTRY (1781-1841)
25   *Sir Astley Cooper (1768-1841)*
      1825
      Two pencil sketches, 50.8 x 68.6 cms
      National Portrait Gallery, London

Astley Cooper was the greatest and most innovative surgeon of his day; anatomy, he said, was 'our polar star'. For twenty-five years, between 1800 and 1825, Cooper was a lecturer and demonstrator at St. Thomas's. There his brilliant surgery put him in the public eye; he developed an enormous private practice, and in 1828 was appointed surgeon to the king. His strongly-held principle was that all medical knowledge (past and future) was based on documented experience and careful observation. John Flint South writes:

The strength and modernity of Astley Cooper's medical knowledge, philosophy and character could only have had a profound influence upon Keats. Cooper was among the most admired medical men of his day, and, as Flint South concludes: 'all those who . . . enjoyed the privilege of his instruction and his intercourse . . . held it in the highest honour to be able to say— "I was a pupil of Astley Cooper"'.

Interestingly, Keats was appointed a dresser within a few weeks of his arrival, perhaps through the influence of John Henry Green, the son-in-law of Thomas Hammond, the doctor to whom Keats was apprenticed, and an esteemed younger colleague of Cooper.

FREDERICK TYRELL (ED.)

26   *The Lectures of Sir Astley Cooper on the Principles and Practice of Surgery*
London: Thomas and George Wedgewood, 1824
The British Library Board

Cooper was, in addition, a teacher of considerable talent. The notes that Keats took at Cooper's lectures are the only lecture notes of Keats that have survived (they are now kept at Keats House, Hampstead). The volume here of transcribed lectures was made by Frederick Tyrell, apprentice to Cooper and for a while (with George Cooper) a fellow-lodger of Keats at 28 St. Thomas's Street. John Flint South describes Cooper's lectures, where the usually rowdy audience was, for once, subdued:

He rarely endeavoured to tell more than he knew from his own personal work and knowledge, and when he had to refer to any particular matter which was beyond it, he pulled a little red book out of his pocket and read from it. . . . as he only talked of what he really knew from his own experience, what he taught was to be implicitly trusted . . . . His teaching was empiric, in the true sense of the word; facts almost entirely his own, and more or less sequentially put together, made up his lectures . . . He was content to give his pupils the results of his own experience and observation, the latter of which was most diligently maintained throughout his long and laborious life.

This dedication to observation and personal knowledge depended upon constant dissection: 'if I laid my head upon my pillow at night' Cooper is said to have remarked, 'without having dissected something in the day, I would think that a wasted day.' It also had to be supported by a steady, unruffable intellect:

the quality which is considered of the highest order in surgical operations, is self-possession; the head must always direct the hand, otherwise the operator is unfit to discover an effectual remedy for the unforeseen accidents which may occur in his practice.

Almost to a minute he was in the theatre, where loud and continued greetings most truly declared the affectionate regard his pupils had for him. His clear silvery voice and cheery conversational manner soon exhausted the conventional hour devoted to the lecture; and all who heard him hung with silent attention on his words, the only sounds which broke the quiet being the subdued pen-scratching of the note-takers. . . .

W.T. Fry after J. Tannock

27   *William Babington (1765-1833)*
     Stipple engraving, 21.3 x 16.5 cms
     Wellcome Institute Library, London

Dr Babington lectured with Dr Curry at Guy's on 'Chemistry' and 'Practice of Medicine'. Successively a student, apothecary, lecturer and physician at Guy's, he gave up as physician in 1811 to concentrate his energies upon chemistry and mineralogy, his abiding passions. He was eventually co-founder and President of the Geological Society. Dr Munk wrote that 'History does not supply us with a physician more loved or more respected than was Dr Babington', and John Flint South gives an equally pleasing description:

> Dr. Babington, [was] a good-tempered, kindly Irishman. . . . He had no pretensions to oratory, but he was a very excellent practical teacher, who was listened to with great pleasure and advantage, as his lectures were full of experience and practical good sense which the simplest mind could receive and understand. He used to wear black, with silk stockings, was a very untidy dresser, and rejoiced in dirty hands, but he was gentle and pleasant with every one, and always ready with some funny anecdote, and always in a hurry, for which his large and well-earned practice was a just excuse.

Unknown Artist

28   *William Allen (1770-1843)*
     Lithograph, 40.8 x 33.2 cms
     Wellcome Institute Library, London

William Allen was a lecturer at Guy's in chemistry and experimental philosophy. In his and Babington's introduction to their Syllabus, there is a recognition of the pace of developments:

> Upon taking a retrospect of the last five and twenty years it will appear, that the discoveries within that period are so numerous and important,—the change which the Nomenculture has lately undergone is so essential and entire, that the Chemistry of the present day, compared with that of former times, may not improperly be considered as a new science expressed in a new language.

Allen was looking at broad principles and new approaches, rather than sticking to old remedies. At Guy's from 1802 to 1826, Allen, like his colleague Astley Cooper, was keen on experiment and observation to arrive at new knowledge. He was a Fellow of the Royal Society, and lectured at the Royal Institution at the request of his friend Humphrey Davy.

His activities were not confined to science – a well-known philanthropist he believed in public education, and he campaigned for the abolition of both the slave trade (he was a friend of William Wilberforce and Thomas Clarkson) and capital punishment. In 1811 he started the quarterly journal, *The Philanthropist*, which ran until 1817.

Joseph Henry Green

J.H. LYNCH AFTER J.F. TENNISWOOD

29   *Joseph Henry Green (1791-1863)*
Lithograph, 32.7 x 26 cms
Wellcome Institute Library, London

'Last Sunday I took a Walk towards highgate' wrote
Keats to his brother and sister-in-law on 15 April 1819,
'and in the lane that winds by the side of Lord
Mansfield's park I met Mr Green our Demonstrator
at Guy's in conversation with Coleridge'. In 1813
Green had married Eliza Hammond, the daughter of
Thomas Hammond, while Keats was Hammond's
apprentice. The same year, Green was appointed
demonstrator in anatomy at St. Thomas's Hospital
continuing that office during Keats's pupillage there.
Only four years older than Keats, he must have been
a social acquaintance as well as a former teacher when
they met near Hampstead Heath.

Green's medical career was distinguished. In 1820 he
was elected surgeon to St. Thomas's Hospital; in 1824
he became Professor of Anatomy at the College of
Surgeons; in 1825 he was elected into the Royal
Society, and in the same year became Professor of
Anatomy at the Royal Academy (where he gave six
lectures a year on anatomy and its relation to the fine
arts). In 1830 he accepted the chair of surgery at the
newly-established King's College, London. As an
'operator' he was held in high repute, particularly in
lithotomy (the removal of stones from the bladder),
and was known for his cool judgement. Like Astley

Cooper, he saw dissection as an essential part of a
surgeon's education, writing:

> It must be recollected that lectures, however
> necessary, are only calculated to give general ideas;
> whereas it is required of the practitioner, that his
> knowledge should be particular and even minute.
> It is not sufficient that he is merely acquainted
> with the presence of certain parts, but he must
> know precisely their situation and extent. The sur-
> geon's knife may give health or death within the
> space of one hour's breadth. This kind of knowl-
> edge is to be acquired by actual dissection alone.

Green also replaced the old *Dissector's Manual* with
a new edition in 1820, containing plates and said to
be the first of its kind and scope yet published.

Samuel Taylor Coleridge had been an acquaintance
of Green in 1817, and the relationship gradually developed into friendship, even discipleship. Green was so
impressed by Coleridge's philosophical teaching that
in 1817 he went to Germany to study philosophy
under Professor Solgar, of Berlin; later both of his
Hunterian Orations were devoted to philosophical
subjects, in 1840 on 'Vital Dynamics' and in 1847 on
'Mental Dynamics or Ground Work of Professional
Education'. Not only did Coleridge appoint Green
his executor on his death, to him fell the enormous
(and unfulfilled) task of giving Coleridge's many
words and thoughts a coherency and structure.

ISAAC MILLS AFTER FRANCIS SIMONAN

30   *James Curry*
Published Chichester, 1819
Line engraving, 10.7 x 9.5 cms
Wellcome Institute Library, London

Curry shared the course in 'Chemistry' with Dr.
Babington, and in 'Theory of Medicine, and Materia
Medica' with Doctor Cholmeley during the autumn
lecture series at Guy's. In his introductory lecture on
the latter he stressed that 'true knowledge and successful treatment of disease' involves 'a diligent inves-
tigation of the History of Diseases in general', together with 'a knowledge of the patient's constitution,—
idiosyncrasies,—and mode of life', and 'an intimate
acquaintance with the Materia Medica.' Curry's own
preferred remedy, which he raised to the level of a
general elixir, was calomel (mercurous chloride); John

JAMES CURRY, M.D. & F.A.S.
LECTURER,
on the Theory and Practice of Medicine
at Guys Hospital etc.

ALEXANDER MARCET, M.D., F.R.S.
late Prof.r of Chemistry in Geneva
Born Augt. 1770. Died Oct.g. 1822.

Flint South gives a lively description of 'Calomel Curry' in his *Memorials*:

> He was a man of very extensive reading and of very observant habits; his lectures went into the very bottom of things; he told all that had been said and written by every one who had handled the subjects on which he treated, but he dearly loved theorising and criticising, and the greater part of his portion of the course was occupied with the discussion of the various doctrines of fever, other and equally important subjects being generally very cursorily treated. He was very fierce and uncompromising in his criticism on the experience and views of other physicians, but the whole of his treatment consisted in calomel, or calomel and opium, and this to such extent that he acquired the nickname "Calomel Curry".

H. MEYER AFTER SIR HENRY RAEBURN

31 *Alexander Marcet (1770-1822)*
Stipple engraving, 41.3 x 30 cms
Wellcome Institute Library, London

Alexander Marcet, who with Babington and Allen was Keats's lecturer in chemistry, was a distinguished chemist who had been made a fellow of the Royal Society that year (1815). Born in Geneva, he received his medical doctorate from Edinburgh University in

1797 with a thesis on diabetes. In 1799 he became a licentiate of the London College of Physicians, and in 1804 a physician at Guy's Hospital, where he also became a lecturer in chemistry. In 1817 he published 'An Essay on the Chemical History and Medical Treatment of Calculus Disorders'. Extremely successful, he became less inclined towards medical practice in later life, but during his lectureship in Keats's student days he embodied the altruistic motives behind the foundation of the voluntary hospitals, saying:

> But in thus enforcing a salutary discipline, let us never lose sight of the primary object of this, and all other hospitals, which is—the relief of suffering humanity. The Medical Schools which have been grafted upon these establishments, however useful and important, are but secondary objects; we must therefore always consider the comfort and well-doing of our patients as the first and principle aim in all our proceedings.

J. KENNERLY AFTER H. ASHBY

32 *John Haighton (1755-1823)*
Published London: 1 July 1818
Mezzotint, 50.5 x 39.5 cms
Wellcome Institute Library, London

The Autumnal Course of Lectures at the United Hospitals in 1815, as advertised in the London Medical and Physical Journal, contains two courses of lectures by Haighton, namely 'Midwifery, and

responsible for preparing them, botany was an essential part of medical training. 'It is therefore high time', Salisbury told his pupils, 'that those persons who are engaged in the business of pharmacy should be obliged to become so far acquainted with plants, as to be able to distinguish at sight all such as are useful in diet or medicine.' Later Keats would express a desire to study human nature 'with the calmness of a botanist', and he retained a fondness for the familiar flora of Enfield and Hampstead. 'I muse with the greatest affection on every flower I have known from my infancy' he wrote to James Rice on 14 February 1820, 'I have seen foreign flowers in hothouses of the most beautiful nature, but I do not care a straw for them. The simple flowers of our spring are what I want to see again.' Leigh Hunt wrote in his *Recollections of Byron and his Contemporaries* that Hampstead was 'rich in the botany for which this part of the neighbourhood has always been celebrated.'

J. HINCHCLIFFE AFTER THOMAS SHEPHERD

34 *Apothecaries' Hall, Pilgrim St., Blackfriars*
    Published London: 1831
    Stipple engraving, 9.7 x 14.6 cms
    Guildhall Library, City of London

35 *Apothecaries' Hall, Pilgrim St., Blackfriars*
    Pencil sketch for the above, 11.4 x 16.8 cms
    Guildhall Library, City of London

The apothecary was originally a member of the medieval Guild of Grocers, until, in 1617, the Worshipful Society of Apothecaries was granted a charter by James I. As it gradually gained the knowledge to examine patients, diagnose diseases and administer remedies, the Society sought for respect and recognition against the disdain of the physicians. To rid its profession of quacks, it ceased simply to police the administering of drugs, and began to see the education of apprentices as its chief duty. The aim of the 1815 Apothecaries Act was to seek 'a legislative enactment that would, by its gradual operation, secure for the service of the public properly educated practitioners'. With the support of the College of Physicians, the bill gave the Apothecaries Society the right to examine 'all persons applying for certificates to practise . . . in the science and practice of medicine, pharmacy, chemistry, materia medica, and medical botany'. Subsequent to this act, a would-be

Diseases of Women and Children' and 'Physiology, or Laws of the Animal Oeconomy'. There is no actual evidence that Keats attended these courses, but nevertheless Haighton was one of the central figures of Guy's and Thomas's while he was a student.

Himself a former student of St. Thomas's, Haighton began his career as a demonstrator of anatomy under Henry Cline, as a colleague (and rival) of Astley Cooper. Perhaps as a reaction to this, he resigned his demonstratorship in 1789 and turned to physiology and midwifery, soon becoming an excellent 'operator' and lecturer in obstetrics. A fellow of the Royal Society, he was also known for his research in the fields of the nervous system, mathematics and astronomy. Personally, he was argumentative, irritable, and quite ruthless in his physiological experiments; 'the Merciless Doctor', as his opponents knew him, once killed a favourite spaniel to prove Cooper wrong over a disputed point.

WILLIAM SALISBURY (D. 1823)

33 *Hints addressed to Proprietors of Orchards
    and to Growers of Fruit in General*
    London: Longman, Hurst, Rees, Orme
    and Brown, 1816
    Royal Horticultural Society

William Salisbury was Keats's teacher of botany at Guy's, and his instruction was in the form of regular field trips. With a large proportion of remedies then being botanical, and the apothecary being specifically

Drawn by Tho. H. Shepherd.

Engraved by J. Hinchliff.

APOTHECARIES' HALL, PILGRIM ST.

Cat. 34

July. 25th 1816. —

189 MR. *John Keats. of full age* — CANDIDATE for a CERTIFICATE to practise as an APOTHECARY in *the Country.*

An APPRENTICE to MR. *Thomas Hammond of Edmonton* APOTHECARY for 5 Years.

TESTIMONIAL from *Mr. Thos. Hammond.*

LECTURES.

2 COURSES on ANATOMY and PHYSIOLOGY.
2 ——— THEORY and PRACTICE of MEDICINE.
2 ——— CHEMISTRY.
1 ——— MATERIA MEDICA.

HOSPITAL ATTENDANCE.

6 MONTHS at *Guy's & St. Thomas's.* ———
as
MONTHS at

168 *Examined by Mr. Brande & approved*

Cat. 37

apothecary such as Keats required the following train-ing: firstly, a five-year apprenticeship with an apothe-cary; secondly, at least six months 'suitable attendance on the practice of a hospital' and the production of 'testimonials of a sufficient medical and classical education, and of good moral conduct'; and thirdly, an examination held at Apothecaries' Hall. The exam-ination was no formality, and people did well to pass.

With the surgeons serving the hospitals, and the physicians serving the rich, the Act meant that, in effect, the apothecary became the general practitioner of the day.

T. BRIDGFORD
36   *William Thomas Brande (1788-1866)*
      Lithograph, 26.2 x 19.5 cms
      Wellcome Institute Library, London

'Examined by Mr Brande and approved' reads Keats's Apothecary Certificate, and William Brande, Lon-don's leading chemist, fellow of the Royal Society, one-time assistant of Michael Faraday and friend of Humphrey Davy, would have been a tough examiner. He was also particularly concerned with the training of students: in 1812, he was appointed professor of chemistry and superintending chemical operator to the Apothecaries Company, in 1836 one of the origi-nal fellows of the University of London, and in 1846 an examiner and fellow of the Royal Society of Edin-burgh. He also tidied up and greatly improved *The London Pharmacopoeia* and was the author of two standard textbooks, *The Manual of Chemistry* and *The Dictionary of Pharmacy and Materia Medica*. Again, like all Keats's lecturers, he possessed a passion

for his subject and a forward-looking mind, best illus-trated in his own recollection of his time as a boy in about 1804:

> I was now full of ardour in the prosecution of chemistry, and although my brother—with whom I still lived, whose apprentice I was, and in whose shop, notwithstanding all other associations, I still worked, and passed a large part of my time— threw every obstacle in the way of my chemical progress that was decently in his power, I found time, however, to read, and often to experiment, in my bedroom late in the evening. I thus collect-ed a series of notes and observations which I fondly hoped would at some future period serve as the basis of a course of lectures, and this in time they actually did.

37   *Keats's Apothecary Certificate*
      The Worshipful Society of Apothecaries of London

The certificate (illustrated opposite) gives a full record of Keats's studentship – his term of appren-ticeship, his attendance at lectures, and his hospital experience.

JOHN KEATS

38 *'Give me women, wine and snuff'*
Autograph manuscript
*The Master & Fellows of Trinity College,
Cambridge*

Henry Stephens, a fellow student and lodger of Keats,
and later the inventor of blue-black ink, gave an
account of this poem to Richard Monckton Milnes:

> Whilst attending lectures, he [Keats] would sit &
> instead of Copying out the lecture, would often
> scribble some doggerel rhymes, among the Notes
> of Lecture, particularly if he got hold of another
> Student's Syllabus—In my Syllabus of Chemical
> Lectures he scribbled many lines on the paper
> cover, This cover has been long torn off, except
> one small piece on which is the following frag-
> ment of Doggerel rhyme

> > "Give me wine & snuff
> > Until I cry out, hold! enough"
> > You may do so, sans objection
> > Until the day of resurrection,"

> This is all that remains, & is the only piece of his
> writing which is now in my possession.

Stephens, we see, has censored the verses, omitting
the reference to women, one third of Keats's Trinity.
The full text reads:

> Give me women, wine and snuff
> Until I cry out "hold, enough!"
> You may do so sans objection
> Till the day of resurrection;
> For, bless my beard, they aye shall be
> My beloved Trinity.

Henry Stephens by an
unknown artist

3. HAMPSTEAD 1816-17

When Cowden Clarke introduced Keats to Leigh Hunt in October 1816 it began, as Keats foresaw, 'an era in my existence'. For the meeting placed him in a circle of writers, critics and artists that stimulated his own endeavours, and provided him with most of his friends, among them Benjamin Robert Haydon, John Hamilton Reynolds, Percy Bysshe Shelley, Benjamin Bailey, Charles Wentworth Dilke, William Hazlitt, his first publisher, Charles Ollier, his next and final publisher John Taylor, and his 'capital friend' Charles Brown. For the young poet they were an encouraging group; without exception, they saw him as a poet of high promise, possibly of future greatness. Hunt introduced him to the public as one of the three most promising young poets of the day; Haydon put 'Keats's genius' on a par with Wordsworth's, and Bailey wrote to the *Oxford Herald* to say that his poetry had 'the richest promise I ever saw of an etherial imagination maintained by vast intellectual power'. Shelley saw him as 'a rival who will far surpass me'.

More importantly for Keats, who never proclaimed genius for himself, the circle opened up new areas of interest and insight. From Hunt and Haydon he learned of the visual arts, particularly of the Renaissance and Classical antiquity, and of their close relationship with poetry. Also from Haydon, and other artists like William Hilton, William Bewick and Peter De Wint, he was made aware of current trends in contemporary art. Hazlitt's lectures on the English poets at the Surrey Institution had a deep influence on his own approach to literature and philosophy.

Most of all, he was in the company of men who shared his belief in the significance and high purpose of literature and art. Keats's letters from this time are crowded with some of the most profound thoughts about poetry and poets that have ever been made by an English writer. 'What a time!' he wrote to Bailey in his enthusiasm, 'I am continually running away from the subject'. This very receptive period culminated in March 1817, with the publication by Charles Ollier of Keats's *Poems*. Haydon prophesied: 'It is a flash of lightening that will rouse men from their occupations, and keep them trembling for the crash of thunder that *will* follow.' But it was, the author knew, a minor volume. He had to test his powers to their limit, in a new, large-scale poem. 'I think that I could not be deceived in the Manner that Hunt is,' he wrote to Haydon in May, 'may I die tomorrow if I am to be. There is no greater Sin after the 7 deadly than to flatter oneself into an idea of being a great poet.'

JOSEPH SEVERN

39   *John Keats*
     C. 1816
     Charcoal, 8.6 x 7.3 cms (oval)
     By Courtesy of the Board of Trustees
     of the Victoria & Albert Museum

Severn made this, the earliest surviving portrait of Keats, around 1816. The fervid expression, so evident here, struck the artist particularly. He later described it as 'a peculiarly dauntless expression, such as may be seen on the face of some seamen', recalling 'those falcon-eyes . . . the almost flamelike intensity of Keats's eager glances when he was keenly excited or interested'. His friends seem to have considered it a good likeness. Charles Cowden Clarke described it in his *Recollections* as 'the most perfect and favourite portrait of him . . . which I remember the artist sketching in a few minutes, one evening, when several of Keats's friends were at his apartments in the Poultry.' Certainly it is less affected by the romantic gestures that are found in Severn's later portraits of the poet, where the 'eager glances' tend to become a watery, 'poetic' gaze.

THOMAS CHARLES WAGEMAN

40   *James Henry Leigh Hunt (1784-1859)*
     1815
     Pencil, 21 x 16.5 cms
     National Portrait Gallery, London

     Illustrated on p. 4

'The busy time has just gone by,' Keats wrote to Charles Cowden Clarke on 9 October 1816, 'and I can now devote any time you may mention to the pleasure of seeing Mr Hunt—'t will be an era in my existence'. The friendship that followed was almost immediate. 'We became intimate on the spot,' Hunt recollected, 'and I found the young poet's heart as warm as his imagination.' Even so, Keats's growing independence, both as a man and as an artist, eventually drew him away from his former mentor.

A poet, essayist and editor (of the radical periodical, *The Examiner*) in his own right, Hunt was also a vigorous supporter of younger writers, not only of Keats, but of Byron, Shelley, Reynolds and, later, of Tennyson. His direct literary influence on Keats, particularly the familiar tone, luxuriant southern imagery and suburban 'Greekishness' of *The Story of Rimini* (1816),

was only temporary; and indeed Keats soon developed a strong distaste for it; 'Hunt keeps on in his old way', he wrote to George and Georgiana Keats in December 1818, 'I am completely tired of it all—He has lately publish'd a Pocket-Book call'd the litrrary Pocket-Book—full of the most sickening stuff you can imagine.' What is more, he rightly suspected that his public image as a weak protegée of Hunt, who was well-known for his radicalism, and as a member of Hunt's 'Cockney School' of poetry, would put him in the firing line of the Tory reviewers.

More lasting was Hunt's talent for enjoyment and appreciation, the sheer variety of his interests (literature, fine art, music, drama) and, above all, his gift for friendship. His last letter to Keats has often been quoted for its self-effacing generosity and stoicism:

> tell him—tell that great poet and noble-hearted man—that we shall all bear his memory in the most precious part of our hearts, and that the world shall bow their heads to it, as our loves do . . . Tell him he is only before us on the road, as he was in everything else; or whether you tell him the latter or no, tell him the former, and that we shall never forget that he was so, and that we are coming after him.

LEIGH HUNT

41   *Sonnet: 'To John Keats'*
     Dated 1 December 1816
     Autograph manuscript
     The British Library Board

Tis well you think me truly one of those
Whose sense disarms the loveliness of things;
For surely as I feel the bird that sings
Behind the leaves, or the kiss-asking rose,
Or the rich bee, rejoicing as he goes,
Or the glad issue of emerging springs,
Or, over-head, the glide of a dove's wings,
Or trees, or turf, or midst of all, repose;

And surely as I tell things lovelier still,
The human book – & the harmonious form
Containing woman, & the smile in ill,—
And such a heart as Charles's, wise & warm,—
As surely as all this, I see even now,
Young Keats, a flowering laurel on your brow.'

Cat. 39

To John Keats. Dec. 1. 1816.

'Tis well you think me truly one of those
Whose sense discerns the loveliness of things;
For surely as I feel the bird that sings
Behind the leaves, or the kiss-asking rose,
Or the rich bee, rejoicing as he goes,
Or the glad issue of emerging springs,
Or, over-head, the glide of a dove's wings,
Or trees, or turf, or midst of all, repose;

And surely as I feel things lovelier still,
The human look, — & the harmonious form
Containing woman, — & the smile in it, —
And such a heart as Charles's, wise & warm, —
As surely as all this, I see even now,
Young Keats, a flowering laurel on your brow.

Leigh Hunt's tribute to Keats's poetic promise in the last line of this sonnet was on regular occasions taken literally; after a sonnet competition (a favourite pastime in Hunt's circle), it was the custom for the winner to be crowned with laurel. Keats would in time look back upon these incidents with some embarrassment. 'I put on no laurels till I have finished Endymion' he wrote to Bailey on 8 October 1817, 'and I hope Apollo is not angered at my having made a Mockery at him at Hunt's'.

The result of one such competition between Keats and Hunt, 'On the Grashopper and the Cricket', was published in *The Examiner* in September 1817 (illustrated opposite).

'THE EXAMINER'
42 *'O solitude, if I must with thee dwell'*
    5 May 1816
    Private Collection

43 *'Young Poets'*
    1 December 1816
    The British Library Board

Leigh Hunt set up the weekly *Examiner* with his elder brother John in January 1808. It was named, so Leigh Hunt wrote in his *Autobiography*, 'after the 'Examiner'

of Swift and his brother Tories' in honour of their 'wit and fine writing, which, in my youthful confidence, I proposed to myself to emulate'. The expressed object of the paper was 'to assist in producing Reform in Parliament, liberality of opinion in general (especially in freedom from superstition), and a fusion of literary taste into all subjects whatsoever. It began with being of no party; but Reform soon gave it one'. This tendency towards radicalism and reform led, in February 1813, to the editors being imprisoned for a libel on the Prince Regent. On their release two years later there was a conscious move to develop the paper's literary character. So Keats was no stranger to its pages when, on 5 May 1816, *The Examiner* printed Keats's first published poem, 'O solitude'.

'I shall never forget the impression made upon me by the exuberant specimens of genuine though young poetry that were laid before me', Hunt later wrote of their first meeting in August. He went on to publish seven more of Keats's poems in *The Examiner* (see opposite), and there announced the addition of 'three young writers' (namely Keats, Shelley and J.H. Reynolds) 'to the new school'.

Leigh Hunt's Cottage at Hampstead

UNKNOWN ARTIST
44 *Leigh Hunt's Cottage at Hampstead*
    Watercolour, 10.5 x 13.8 cms
    Guildhall Library, City of London

...tch ...pper ...lete the

...he adds, that the Sister of the deceased was refused admittance to see the remains, till the body was so changed that she with difficulty recognised it to be her brother's, and the blood was then oozing through the shroud.

TO SOLITUDE.

O SOLITUDE! if I must with thee dwell,
  Let it not be among the jumbled heap
  Of murky buildings;—climb with me the steep,
Nature's Observatory,—whence the dell,
Its flowery slopes—its rivers crystal swell,
  May seem a span: let me thy vigils keep
  'Mongst boughs pavilion'd; where the Deer's swift leap
Startles the wild Bee from the Fox-glove bell.
Ah! fain would I frequent such scenes with thee;
  But the sweet converse of an innocent mind,
  Whose words are images of thoughts refin'd,
Is my soul's pleasure; and it sure must be
  Almost the highest bliss of human kind,
When to thy haunts two kindred spirits flee.

J. K.

MINER. 59...

TWO SONNETS ON THE GRASSHOPPER AND CRICKET.

I.

[FROM POEMS BY JOHN KEATS.]

THE poetry of earth is never dead:
  When all the birds are faint with the hot sun,
  And hide in cooling trees, a voice will run
From hedge to hedge about the new-mown mead;
That is the Grasshopper's:—he takes the lead
  In summer luxury,—he has never done
  With his delights; for when tired out with fun,
He rests at ease beneath some pleasant weed.
The poetry of earth is ceasing never:
  On a lone winter evening, when the frost
    Has wrought a silence, from the stove there shrills
The Cricket's song, in warmth increasing ever,
  And seems to one, in drowsiness half lost,
    The Grasshopper's among some grassy hills.

December 30, 1816.

II.

BY LEIGH HUNT;—NEVER BEFORE PUBLISHED.

GREEN little vaulter in the sunny grass,
  Catching your heart up at the feel of June,
  Sole voice left stirring midst the lazy noon,
When ev'n the bees lag at the summoning brass;—
And you, warm little housekeeper, who class
  With those who think the candles come too soon,
  Loving the fire, and with your tricksome tune
Nick the glad silent moments as they pass;—
O sweet and tiny cousins, that belong,
  One to the fields, the other to the hearth,
Both have your sunshine; both though small are strong
  At your clear hearts; and both were sent on earth
To ring in thoughtful ears this natural song,
  —In doors and out,—summer and winter,—Mirth.

December 30, 1816.

ORIGINAL POETRY.

SONNET.

AFTER dark vapors have oppress'd our plains
  For a long dreary season, comes a day
  Born of the gentle SOUTH, and clears away
From the sick heavens all unseemly stains,
The anxious Month, relieving of its pains,
  Takes as a long lost right the feel of MAY:
  The eyelids with the passing coolness play
Like Rose leaves with the drip of Summer rains.

The calmest thoughts come round us; as of leaves
  Budding—fruit ripening in stillness—Autumn Suns
Smiling at Eve upon the quiet sheaves—
  Sweet SAPPHO's Cheek—a smiling infant's breath—
The gradual Sand that through an hour-glass runs—
A woodland Rivulet—a Poet's death.

J. K.

The last of these young aspirants whom we have met with, and who promise to help the new school to revive Nature and

  "To put a spirit of youth in every thing,"—

is, we believe, the youngest of them all, and just of age. His name is JOHN KEATS. He has not yet published any thing except in a newspaper; but a set of his manuscripts was handed us the other day, and fairly surprised us with the truth of their ambition, and ardent grappling with Nature. In the following Sonnet there is one incorrect rhyme, which might be easily altered, but which shall serve in the mean time as a peace-offering to the rhyming critics. The rest of the composition, with the exception of a little vagueness in calling the regions of poetry "the realms of gold," we do not hesitate to pronounce excellent, especially the last six lines. The word *swims* is complete; and the whole conclusion is equally powerful and quiet:—

ON FIRST LOOKING INTO CHAPMAN'S HOMER.

MUCH have I travel'd in the realms of Gold,
  And many goodly States and Kingdoms seen;
  Round many western Islands have I been,
Which Bards in fealty to Apollo hold;
But of one wide expanse had I been told,
  That deep-brow'd Homer ruled as his demesne;
  Yet could I never judge what men could mean,
Till I heard CHAPMAN speak out loud and bold,

---

762 THE EX...

Then felt I like some watcher of the skies,
  When a new planet swims into his ken;
Or like stout CORTEZ, when with eagle eyes
  He stared at the Pacific,—and all his men
Looked at each other with a wild surmise,—
  Silent, upon a peak in Darien.

Oct. 1816. JOHN KEATS.

We have spoken with the less scruple of these poetical promises, because we really are not in the habit of lavishing praises and announcements, and because we have no fear of any pettier vanity on the part of young men, who promise to understand human nature so well.

☞

ORIGINAL POETRY.

TO KOSCIUSKO.

GOOD KOSCIUSKO! thy great name alone
  Is a full harvest whence to reap high feeling;
  It comes upon us like the glorious pealing
Of the wide spheres—an everlasting tone:
And now it tells me that in worlds unknown
  The names of Heroes, burst from clouds concealing,
  Are changed to harmonies, for ever stealing
Through cloudless blue, around each silver throne.

It tells me, too, that on a happy day,
  When some good spirit walks upon the earth,
Thy name, with ALFRED's, and the great of yore,
  Gently commingling, gives tremendous birth
To a loud hymn, that sounds far, far away,
  To where the great GOD lives for evermore.

Dec. 1816. J. K.

Keats's publications in *The Examiner*: clockwise from top left – 'To Solitude', 5 May 1816; 'On First Looking into Chapman's Homer', 1 December 1816; 'To Kosciusko', 16 February 1817; 'After dark vapours', 23 February 1817; two sonnets on the Elgin Marbles, 9 March 1817

GEORGE SHEPHERD (fl. c. 1800 - c. 1830)
45   *The Vale of Health, Hampstead*
     Signed and dated 1825
     Watercolour, 25.3 x 35.4 cms
     By Courtesy of the Board of Trustees
     of the Victoria & Albert Museum

Hunt had transformed his prison cell into a bower of civilised delight – 'Charles Lamb declared there was no other room except in a fairy tale' he said proudly. A piano was installed; bookcases, busts and engravings embellished the walls, and the bars were tastefully concealed by venetian blinds. After his release he fulfilled his dream and moved, in October 1815, into a cottage in the Vale of Health, Hampstead. His natural exuberance quickly turned the house into a hub of literary and artistic life, and here Keats was introduced to the visual arts through Hunt's large collection of sculpture and art, not least his collection of prints depicting old master paintings. The final lines of 'Sleep and Poetry', the poem that concluded the 1817 volume, were composed here; it is one of Keats's first attempts to capture the feeling of a picture in verse:

It was a poet's house who keeps the keys
Of Pleasure's temple. Round about were hung
The glorious features of the bards who sung
In other ages—cold and sacred busts
Smiled at each other. Happy he who trusts
To clear Futurity his darling fame!
Then there were fauns and satyrs taking aim
At swelling apples with a frisky leap
And reaching fingers, 'mid a luscious heap
Of vine leaves. . . .
See, in another picture, nymphs are wiping
Cherishingly Diana's timorous limbs;—
A fold of lawny mantle dabbling swims
At the bath's edge, and keeps a gentle motion
With the subsiding crystal: as when ocean
Heaves calmly its broad swelling smoothness o'er
Its rocky marge, and balances once more
The patient weed, that now unshent by foam
Feel all about their undulating home. . . .

UNKNOWN ARTIST
46 *Hampstead Heath, 1816*
Pencil and wash, 19.4 x 16.7 cms
Guildhall Library, City of London

JOHN CONSTABLE (1776-1837)
47 *Hampstead Heath, from near Well Walk*
1834
Watercolour, 11.1 x 18 cms
*By Courtesy of the Board of Trustees
of the Victoria & Albert Museum*

Keats and his brothers moved into No. 1 Well Walk, near Hampstead Heath, in the spring of 1817. The heath, where most of their days were spent, offered some of the healthiest air and best scenery that could be found so close to London. It was a welcome change from the noise of Cheapside – 'We lounge on the Walk opposite as you might on the Den' Keats wrote to Marian and Sarah Jeffrey in June, and from Scotland he wrote wistfully to Tom: 'I assure you I often long for a seat and a Cup o' tea at well Walk, especially now that mountains, castles and Lakes are becoming common to me'.

But it was also at Well Walk that the close-knit relationship of Keats and his brothers was broken. In June 1818 George married Georgiana Wylie and emigrated to America. Then on 1 December Tom died of consumption. Keats had nursed him throughout the final stages of his illness, and the strain of being continually by his bedside in the house was evident. Leigh Hunt remembered: 'It was . . . sitting on the bench in Well Walk, at Hampstead, nearest the heath, that he told me, with unaccustomed tears in his eyes, that "his heart was breaking"'. It must have been with relief that he moved to nearby Wentworth Place after Tom's death.

Constable himself, incidentally, a few years later, came to live in Well Walk, only a few doors away from the house, now absorbed into *The Wells Tavern* pub, which Keats had shared with his brothers.

Drawn by Tho.H.Shepherd.

Engraved by W. Wallis

30

CHEAPSIDE, POULTRY, & BUCCLERSBURY.

T.M. BAYNES AFTER W. DURYER

48   *A View of Cheapside in the City of London*
Published London: 11 December 1823
Lithograph, 46.5 x 33 cms
Guildhall Library, City of London

Before moving to Hampstead with his brothers in
March 1817 Keats lived at No. 76 Cheapside. Never
comfortable in the city, his discomfort steadily turned
to active dislike. Writing in January 1820 to
Georgiana Keats, his sister-in-law rather bored in
Kentucky, he commented:

> To me it is all as dull here as Louisville could be
> . . . All I can say is that standing at Charing Cross
> and looking east west north and south I can see
> nothing but dullness—I hope while I am young to
> live retired in the Country, when I grow in years
> and have a right to be idle I shall enjoy cities more
> . . . Look at our Cheapside Tradesmans sons and

daughters—only fit to be taken off by a plague—I
hope now soon to come to the time when I shall
never be forc'd to walk through the City and hate
as I walk.

The need to 'live retired in the Country' in order to
write became an increasing preoccupation: for many
months Hampstead was his preferred solution.

W. WALLIS AFTER THOMAS SHEPHERD

49   *Cheapside, Poultry and Bucclersbury*
Stipple engraving, 13.5 x 18 cms
Guildhall Library, City of London

A view of Cheapside, taken from roughly the same
vantage as the print above, but looking in the opposite direction to where Cheapside is joined by
Bucclersbury, and runs into Poultry.

Drawn by W. Havell.   F. C. Stacey fec.   T. M. Baynes.   London, Pub.d Dec. 1.st 1823 by John Hodson 35 Cheapside

A VIEW OF CHEAPSIDE IN THE CITY OF LONDON.

Cat. 48

JOSEPH SEVERN
50 *John Hamilton Reynolds (1796-1852)*
Signed and dated, 1818
Miniature on ivory, 9.9 x 7.3 cms
National Portrait Gallery, London

John Hamilton Reynolds, one of Hunt's three promising young poets, was introduced to Keats by their promoter in or around October 1816. In turn, Reynolds introduced Keats to Charles Brown, the publishers John Taylor and James Hessey, James Rice, Benjamin Bailey and Charles Wentworth Dilke. Meanwhile their own friendship developed: 'your Brother John' Keats wrote to Reynolds's sisters Jane and Marianne on 14 September 1817, 'whom henceforth I shall consider as mine'; and in July 1818 to Reynolds himself: 'I have been getting more and more close to you every day, ever since I knew you'. Himself a published poet, Reynolds was a sensitive audience and a tireless campaigner for Keats's work, and his intelligence is shown by the evident sensitivity with which he acted for Taylor and Hessey in their dispute with Keats over the preface to *Endymion*. To Keats he was 'the playfullest' of his friends, 'Ginger beer', 'slovenly' in dress, 'inspired . . . by Mercury' (letter to George and Georgiana Keats, 17 January 1820) and to John Clare, who knew him from *London Magazine* dinners, he was 'the three in one of fun, wit and punning personified'.

After publishing *The Garden of Florence* (see below) in 1821 Reynolds gave up the ambition to be a serious poet, and began a law practice with James Rice. His literary activity was confined mainly to journalism, notably in Taylor and Hessey's *London Magazine* and the *Edinburgh Review*.

Ending his life in obscurity and disappointment, he looked back on his friendship with Keats (though later strained by his dislike of Fanny Brawne and arguments with Haydon and Hunt) as the high-point of his life. He was enthusiastic about Monckton Milnes's Life, not least because it brought him back into the public's notice. His tombstone bears the inscription: 'Friend of Keats'.

JOHN HAMILTON REYNOLDS
51 *The Eden of the Imagination*
London: James Cawthorn; John Martin, 1814
The Wordsworth Trust

JOHN HAMILTON REYNOLDS
52 *Letter to William Wordsworth*
12 November 1814
The Wordsworth Trust

Reynolds' inscription, 'To Wm Wordsworth Esq With the Author's respects', and his letter (see opposite) illustrate that his parody of Wordsworth in *Peter Bell. A Lyrical Ballad* (see below), was born out of an early admiration. Perhaps Wordsworth's cautious response to Reynolds' work may have fired the mischievous rejoinder of *Peter Bell*:

> your Poem would have told more upon me, if it had been shorter. How unceremoniously not to say ungraciously do I strike home! But I am justified to my own mind from a persuasion that it was better to put the objection in this abrupt way, than to introduce it by an accompanying compliment which, however well merited, would have stood in the way of the effect which I aim at—your Reformation. Your Fancy is too luxuriant, and riots too much upon its own creations . . . The Basis is too narrow for the superstructure; and to me it would have been more striking barely to have hinted at the deserted Fair One and to have left it to the Imagination of the Reader to dispose of her as he liked . . . I may be wrong but I speak as I felt, and the most profitable criticism is the record of sensations, provided the person affected be under no partial influence.

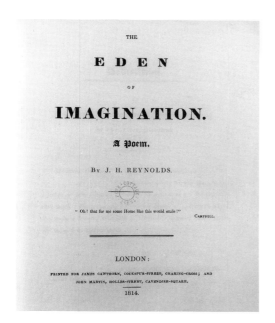

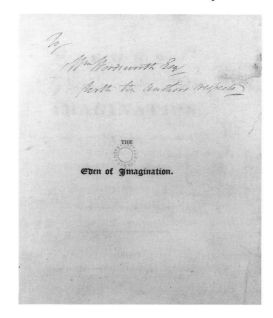

J. H. Reynolds to William Wordsworth, 12 Nov 1814

Sir,

Will you accept of the accompanying little Sketch of Aural Scenery?—Written not from the objects themselves before my eyes, but from the images of them on my mind. It may appear presumptuous in me to send the offspring of but an ill-stored memory to One who lives in a very friendship with nature and thinks daily over the wandering streams & in the silent fields:—But I have long wished to thank you for the deep pleasure your Poems have given me—and Time has strengthened my wish—Inclination would fain persuade me that an opportunity now occurs, and I would fain believe her.

To say that I fully enter into your feelings in reading your Poems, would be wrong—For I should imagine no one can feel so intensely as you do. But I believe I am right in saying that I enter pretty largely into them, and your thoughts always lead me to contemplation and leave me calm. The little blank verse pieces in Lyrical Ballads are my favourites—They are full of exquisite feeling and natural description & are clothed in the sweetest and simplest dress:—You show in them how nearly Simplicity & Feeling are related, & prove the importance of flowers & Rocks & Brooks to the Mind. For these most particularly and for all I thank you, and from the heart.

It is very much to be regretted that the world in general is so ill-calculated to prize the Treasures of Thought which you have discovered to them, or to comprehend even their value. Your poetry is too full of kind-heartedness and philosophical reflection for the present age—If it was placed more out of the reach of simplicity and had less Thought and feeling, it would be more popular.

Living as I do now in the bustle of London—oppotunities occur but seldom of feeding my mind in the fresh, clear, & calm Country:—When they do, I lose no time in improving my stock of reflections and preparing for retirement—I look at beautiful scenery in the boldness of Sunshine and in the delicacy of Moonlight with great mental pleasure—Though where you would find a harvest, I can but glean. The little poem I send you was completed from the remembrance of scenes in various counties—and the the piece at the end of the pamphlet was written from "the recollection" of a view I had from a Mountain on the border of North Wales . . .

In the hope that you will excuse the liberty I have taken in thus writing to you, I beg leave to subscribe myself—

Your grateful admirer,
J.H. Reynolds

JOHN HAMILTON REYNOLDS
53 *Peter Bell. A Lyrical Ballad*
London: Taylor & Hessey, 1819
Professor Michael Jaye

Reynolds' parody on Wordsworth was published by Taylor and Hessey in April 1819. 'I was told not to tell', Keats wrote to George and Georgiana on the fifteenth, 'but to you it will not be tellings—Reynolds hearing that said Peter Bell was coming out, took it into his head to write a skit upon it call'd Peter Bell.' The poem (which quickly reached a third edition) parodies Wordsworth's dwelling on the lowly. In its footnotes, which Coleridge thought 'very droll and clever', it exaggerates to absurdity what it sees as the pomposity and egotism of Wordsworth's prose: Shakespeare is 'a poet, scarcely inferior to myself'; 'See my story of the Leech-gatherer,' reads another, 'the finest poem in the world,—except this.'

Reynolds asked Keats to review the poem, and he did so in *The Examiner* in April. Keats wrote that the author was a great admirer of Wordsworth, and only parodied what diminished his genius:

> It may be seen from one or two passages in this little skit, that the writer of it has felt the finer parts of Mr Wordsworth, and perhaps expatiated with his more remote and sublimer muse. This as far as it relates to Peter Bell is unlucky. The more he may love the sad embroidery of the Excursion; the more he will hate the coarse samples of Betty Foy and Alice Fell; and as they come from the same hand, the better will be able to imitate that which can be imitated.

JOHN HAMILTON REYNOLDS
54 *Verses*
The British Library Board

These four short poems show Reynolds' early attempts at verse before he embarked upon the longer *Eden of the Imagination*. They include an 'Imitation of Martial' (Reynolds was a fine classicist), and a conventional love lyric, 'To Selina', which begins:

Peace to thy bosom, Selina my dove!
Rest to thy heart! and roses to thy cheek
In absence and in mirth, Oblivion seek,
Of all thy fondness, and of all my Love!

UNKNOWN ARTIST
55 *Jane Hood, née Reynolds*
c 1832-4
Millboard, 30.5 x 22.9 cms
National Portrait Gallery, London

Jane was one of the four Reynolds sisters whom Keats briefly befriended and corresponded with in 1817-18. His first letters are friendly and garrulous, but they soon tail off. It seems that the young sisters were a tight group, quick to pronounce judgment on their friends' behaviour – 'not a very enticing row' Keats described their joint appearance at a dance in January 1820. Their attitude towards his friend Jane Cox angered him, as he wrote to George and Georgiana in October 1818:

> The Miss Reynoldses are very kind to me—but they have lately displeased me much and in this way . . . the young ladies were warm in their praises down stairs calling her genteel, interesting and a thousand other pretty things to which I gave no heed, not being partial to 9 days wonders—Now all is completely changed—they hate her . . . there are the Miss Reynoldses on the look out—They think I dont admire her because I did not stare at her—They call her a flirt to me—What a want of knowledge? she walks across a room in such a manner that a Man is drawn

towards her with a magnetic Power. This they call flirting! they do not know things. They do not know what a woman is.

'The Miss Reynoldses' took a similar dislike to Fanny Brawne, who wrote bitterly to Fanny Keats after Keats's death: 'If you live [to] the age of Methusalem and I die tomorrow never be intimate with the Reynolds. . . . Every day I live I find out more of their malice against me.' Later, however, Jane (now married to the poet Thomas Hood) and Fanny became good friends, the latter staying with Jane with her husband on her first visit to Germany.

Jane is the subject of two poems by Keats, namely 'O Sorrow!' and 'On a Leander Gem Which Miss Reynolds, My Kind Friend, Gave Me'.

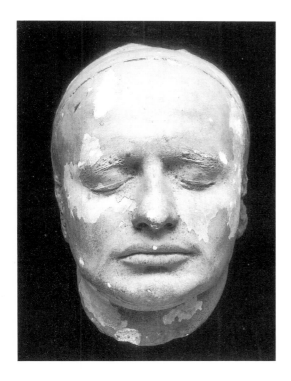

UNKNOWN ARTIST
56 *Lifemask of Benjamin Robert Haydon (1786-1846)*
c 1820
Plaster cast, 17.1 x 14 cms
National Portrait Gallery, London

DAVID WILKIE
57 *Portrait of Benjamin Robert Haydon*
Inscribed and dated, 1815
Black and white chalk, 12.7 x 19.7 cms
National Portrait Gallery, London

Illustrated on p. 10

Keats met the historical painter Benjamin Robert Haydon in October 1816, and first visited his studio on 3 November. Again, it seems to have been Cowden Clarke who made the introductions – 'I will be punctual as the Bee to the Clover', Keats wrote to him on 31 October, 'Very glad am I at the thought of meeting this glorious Haydon and all his creation.' The two were immediately united by the intensity and seriousness of their ambition, the exalted position in which they held their art, and their belief in the other's genius. 'I am convinced that there are three things to rejoice at in this Age' Keats wrote to Haydon on 10 January 1818, 'The Excursion Your Pictures, and Hazlitt's depth of Taste'; 'I feel greatly delighted by your high opinion,' Haydon replied, 'allow me to add sincerely a fourth to be proud of—*John Keats' genius!*—this I speak from my heart—You & Bewick are the only men I ever liked with all my heart'.

The main difference seems to have been that whereas Haydon was fully convinced of and confident in his own genius, Keats was not. So for a time Keats practically worshipped him, while Haydon, standing before his vast historic canvasses, saw it as his duty to nurture and advise the young poet. 'Last evening wrought me up', Keats wrote to Haydon on 20 November 1816, 'and I cannot forbear sending you the following:

Great Spirits now on Earth are sojourning
   He of the Cloud, the Cataract the Lake
   Who on Helvellyn's summit wide awake
Catches his freshness from Archangel's wing,
He of the Rose, the Violet, the Spring
   The social Smile, the Chain for freedom's sake:
   And lo!—whose stedfastness would never take
A Meaner Sound than Raphael's Whispering.
And other Spirits are there standing apart
   Upon the Forehead of the Age to come;
These, these will give the World another heart
   And other pulses—hear ye not the hum
Of mighty Workings in a distant Mart?
   Listen awhile ye Nations, and be dumb!'

Haydon immediately sent this poem to Wordsworth, reporting that Keats promised a great deal, and quoting Keats's words: 'the very idea of your sending this to Wordsworth puts me out of breath: you know with what reverence I would send my well-wishes to him' (*ms. Wordsworth Trust*). Having written out the sonnet, Haydon then adds: 'What recommends him to me is that he has a very fine head'. Undoubtedly Keats and Wordsworth were two subjects who brought out the very best of his skill as an artist.

As Keats's confidence and individualism grew, however, and Haydon's vanity increased, the painter's 'mighty Workings' came to seem like interference, and Haydon's report of their final meeting records his disappointment that Keats was not conforming to his own ideal.

It was in his position as a practising, deeply serious artist, however, that Haydon's chief benefit for Keats lay, and most particularly in his belief in the permanent worth of classical and renaissance art. It was to Haydon that Keats's owed his first informed acquaintance with painting, engraving and sculpture.

The friendship was later marred by quarrels between Haydon, Hunt and Reynolds, and ended somewhat tamely when Haydon refused to repay a loan (not due) of £30. 'I shall perhaps still be acquainted with him,' Keats wrote angrily, 'but for friendship that is at an end.'

Wilkie shows Haydon asleep, and wearing spectacles. Plagued by defective eyesight, his self-belief is illustrated by his remark to his parents while still in his native Plymouth, that, if an attack of measles was to make him blind, then he 'would be the first blind painter'.

JAMES TASSIE (1735-1799)
58 *A Collection of 'Tassie's Gems'*
    By Courtesy of the Board of Trustees
    of the Victoria & Albert Museum

a) Leander Swimming (3.7 x 3.2 cms)
b) Leander Swimming (2.6 x 3.1 cms)
c) Endymion Resting (2.6 x 2.4 cms)
d) Diana and Endymion (4.0 x 4.25 cms)
e) William Shakespeare (3.0 x 2.5 cms)
f) William Shakespeare (2.7 x 2.2 cms)

Keats, and members of his circle, collected 'Tassie's Gems', a series of small, inexpensive paste reproductions of classical, renaissance and contemporary works of art by James Tassie. So much in vogue were they, that by the time of Tassie's nephew William's death in 1860 there were some 20,000 gems in circulation. Hunt, in *The Indicator* for November 1819, has the following note:

> Impressions from the ancient gems are now also to be had with singular cheapness, in consequence of an invention of Mr. Tassie's, of Leicester-square. He has found out a composition, which enables him to procure in a few days, for three-and-six-pence, an impression exactly resembling that of any gem you may select. This you may either have set for your watch-chain, or keep in your desk or pocket . . . Mr. Tassie's collection of antiques appears to be very extensive. You may have your choice among all the gods and graces of the ancient world,—Jupiters, Apollos, Venuses, the Graces, the Muses, Lyres, Loves, Festivals, Pastorals, Patriots, Poets and Philosophers.

The vitreous paste that Tassie used exclusively on the gems was a form of glass based on lead potash; it was not only easily fusible, allowing fine details to be reproduced with the greatest accuracy, but was extremely hard, allowing a gem to be used 'for your watch-chain, or [to] keep in your desk or pocket'.

The gems showed here would have been among those available to Keats. A head of Shakespeare he used to seal his letters; those of Endymion remind us that the theme was fairly commonplace, and a gem on Leander directly inspired the sonnet, 'On a Leander Gem which Miss Reynolds, my kind Friend, gave me'. The sonnet ends:

> Tis young Leander toiling to his death.
> Nigh swooning, he doth purse his weary lips
> For Hero's cheek, and smiles against her smile.
> O horrid dream! see how his body dips
> Dead-heavy; arms and shoulders gleam awhile:
> He's gone: up bubbles all his amorous breath!

59 *Letter from John Keats to Fanny Keats*
13 March 1819
The British Library Board

Shelley wrote to Peacock from Italy asking him to
send a collection, of his own choice, of Tassie's Gems.
Here, Keats writes to Fanny similarly revealing them
as common, fashionable accessories, collectable in
large numbers:

> On looking at your seal I cannot tell whether it is
> done or not with a Tassi—it seems to me to be
> paste but not knowing but you might have some I
> would not run the chance of buying duplicates—
> Tell me if you have any or if you would like any—
> and whether you would rather have motto ones
> like that with which I seal this letter; or heads of
> great Men such as Shakespeare, Milton &c—or
> fancy pieces of Art; such as Fame, Adonis &c—
> those gentry you read of at the end of the English
> Dictionary.

60 *Self-portrait of William Hilton (1786-1839)*
Oil on canvas, 76 x 63.5 cms
Lincolnshire County Council:
Usher Gallery, Lincoln

Though known for his portraits of Keats, Hilton is
entered as an 'historical painter' in the *Annals of the
Fine Arts*. A member of the Royal Academy and a
close friend of John Taylor, Hilton was also the brother-in-law of Peter De Wint; both artists were two of
the five subscribers who agreed to contribute £10 each
to Keats's expenses in Italy. Keats records seeing Sir
John Fleming Leicester's exhibition of his collection
of British art in April 1819 – 'there I saw Northcote—
Hilton—Bewick and many more of great and little
note.' Hilton exhibited his painting *The Rape of
Europa*, and the *Annals of the Fine Arts* in its review
of the exhibition comments:

> the Rape of Europa, by Hilton, perhaps his best
> picture, treated in a splendid way, after the man-
> ner of Sebastian Ricci, and presenting an harmo-
> nious glow of colouring, and a pleasing arrange-
> ment of figures, with delicate expression, an easy
> flow of drapery, and feeble drawing. The bull is à
> l'antique, and unnatural.

Writing to Taylor, Keats would often send his

remembrances to 'Percy Street' where Hilton and De
Wint lived. He wrote to him on 21 June 1818:

> prythee Remember me to Percy Street—Tell
> Hilton that one gratification on my return will
> be to find him engaged in a History Piece to his
> content—and Tell De Wint I shall become a dis-
> putant on the Landscape.

A near contemporary of Keats, Hilton was, like the
poet, championed by Leigh Hunt. The latter's quarterly, *The Reflector*, singles him and Haydon out as
'the two most promising of our young students', and
he and De Wint are mentioned in the same number
of *The Examiner* that printed Keats's first poem, 'O
Solitude' on 5 May 1816. De Wint is praised for 'his
rich and natural and novel display of our island
scenery', while Hilton 'has been working with intense
and sufficiently prolonged application to produce
what will bear the warm praises of criticism, and to
show that our damp and chill atmosphere, if not so
congenial to Art, is not preventive of its lofty efforts.'

Although Hilton and Severn were both friends of
Keats, they were not friends of each other, Hilton and
probably De Wint having a poor opinion of Severn's
work. Keats here is reported by Severn (in Sharpe's
Life and Letters of Joseph Severn, 1892) to be the latter's
defender:

> He recounted his being at a dinner with Hilton
> and some other artists at the house of Hilton's
> brother-in-law, and the subject of conversation
> was the Royal Academy's having given me the long

unawarded gold medal. Some one scornfully explained that the picture was very inferior, but as that the artist was an old fellow, and had made frequent attempts for the prize, the Council had given the medal out of pity and not for any merit. Keats, after a few moments, expressed his disgust at such a mean lie, having first awaited a flat contradicition from one of the three artists present besides Hilton, who knew it to be a lie; and he declared that he would not any longer sit at the same table with such traducers and snobs . . .

Benjamin Robert Haydon

61 *Lifemask of John Keats*
Electrotype copy
The Wordsworth Trust

Illustrated on p. 14

'You may now look at Minerva's Ægis with impunity' Keats wrote to Cowden Clarke on 17 December 1816, shortly after this lifemask was made, 'seeing that my awful Visage did not turn you into a John Doree you may have accordingly a legitimate title to a Copy—I will use my interest to procure it for you.' Haydon, who had decided to introduce Keats into his crowded *Christ's Entry into Jerusalem* (placing his head immediately behind Wordsworth's, and yet, because of the high viewpoint, entirely visible) tended to make casts of his subjects; he also cast Wordsworth. Haydon describes in his journals his attempt to make a cast of Francis Jeffrey's face, and his account (dated 4 May 1821) gives some idea of the discomfort and hilarity the process caused:

> By this time Jeffrey's coat was off, his chin towelled, the plaster ready, and the ladies watching everything with the most intense interest. Mrs. Jeffrey began to look anxious, the preparations for casting a face being something like those for cutting off a man's head. Not liking to seem too fond before others, she fidgeted in her seat, and at last settled on the sofa with her smelling-bottle, barely visible, grasped tightly in her hand. The plaster was now brought, a spoonful taken up, Jeffrey ordered to keep his mouth closed, his nerve firm, and the visitors be quiet. Sydney Smith was dying with laughter, and kept trying to make Jeffrey laugh, but it would not do. When Jeffrey's face was completely covered, up jumped Sydney, mock

heroically, exclaiming: "There's immortality! but God keep me from such a mode of obtaining it." Unfortunately Jeffrey's nostrils were nearly blocked up, breathing became difficult, his nerve gave way and the mould was obliged to be jerked off and broken.

T. Sampson, after Benjamin Robert Haydon

62 *Portrait of John Keats*
Signed, inscribed and dated, 1888
Oil on canvas, 29.2 x 24.1 cms
National Portrait Gallery, London

The portrait is based upon the Haydon lifemask.

John Keats

63 *Manuscript fragment of 'I stood tip-toe upon a little hill'*
Lines 87-106 and 123-50
The British Library Board

64 *Manuscript fragment of 'I stood tip-toe upon a little hill'*
Lines 157-173, 181-192, (193-5 cancelled)
Private Collection

Two fragments of the original manuscript of 'I stood tip-toe upon a little hill', originally of ten leaves, which after Keats's death was cut up by Charles Cowden Clarke and given away piecemeal as souvenirs of the poet. The other surviving fragments are in five different libraries in three different countries.

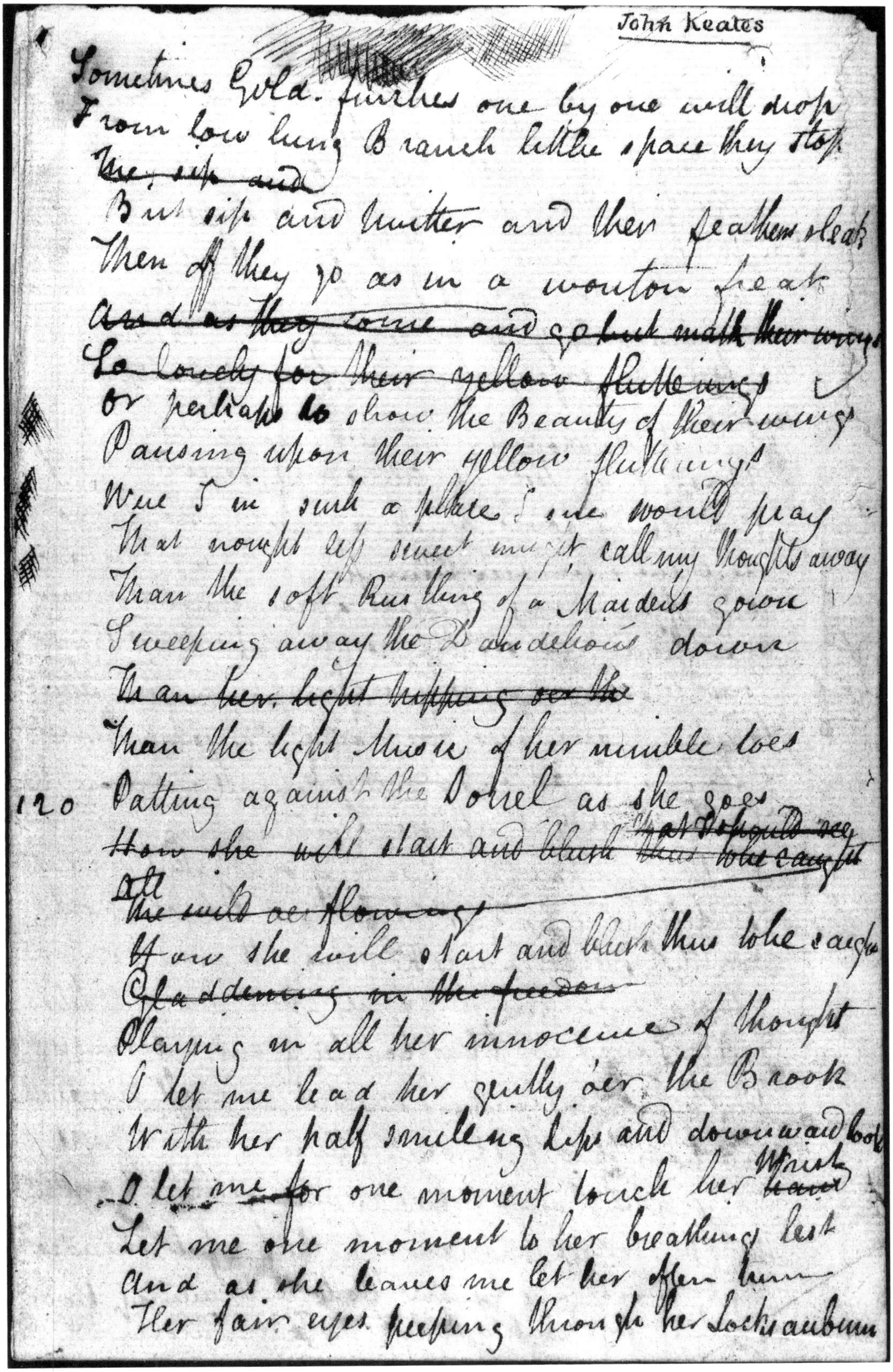

John Keates

Sometimes Gold. further one by one will drop
From low hung Branch little space they stop
~~But sip and~~
But sip and twitter and their feathers sleak
Then off they go as in a wanton heat
~~And as they come and go but mark their ways~~
~~So lovely for their yellow flutterings~~
Or ~~perhaps~~ to show the Beauty of their wings
Pausing upon their yellow flutterings
Were I in such a place I one would pray
That nought less sweet might call my thoughts away
Than the soft Rustling of a Maidens gown
Sweeping away the Dandelions down
~~Than her light tripping oer the~~
Than the light Music of her nimble toes

120 Patting against the Sorrel as she goes
~~How she will start and blush ~~that I should see~~ but caught~~
~~at~~
~~the wild oer flowers~~
How she will start and blush ~~thus~~ to be ~~caught~~
~~Gladdening in the freedom~~
Playing in all her innocence of thought
O let me lead her gently oer the Brook
With her half smiling lips and downward boo(k)
—O let me ~~for~~ one moment touch her Wrist
Let me one moment to her breathing list
And as she leaves me let her often turn
Her fair eyes peeping through her Locks auburn

Cat. 63

The poem, Keats's first attempt at a lengthy composition and the opening poem of the 1817 volume, was begun in the summer of 1816 on Hampstead Heath, and completed by December. It is a direct response to this new landscape, and also a reminiscence of the fields between Edmonton and Enfield. Leigh Hunt later wrote that it 'was suggested to him by a delightful summer-day, as he stood beside the gate that leads from the Battery on Hampstead Heath into a field by Caen Wood'. As the personal opening shows, it is one of his first attempts towards Hazlitt's 'gusto', capturing the spirit, or what he called the 'idea' of a place, through felicity of language and imaginative projection:

A bush of May flowers with the bees about them;
Ah, sure no tasteful nook would be without them;
And let a lush laburnum oversweep them,
And let long grass grow round the roots to keep them
Moist, cool and green; and shade the violets,
That they may bind the moss in leafy nets.

The poem also contains the story of Endymion, and for some time Keats spoke of it by that name:

He was a Poet, sure a lover too,
Who stood on Latmus' top, what time there blew
Soft breezes from the myrtle vale below;
And brought in faintness solemn, sweet and slow
A hymn from Dian's temple; while upswelling,
The incense went to her own starry dwelling.
But though her face was clear as infant's eyes,
Though she stood smiling o'er the sacrifice,
The Poet wept at her so piteous fate,
Wept that such beauty should be desolate:
So in fine wrath some golden sounds he won,
And gave meek Cynthia her Endymion.

THOMAS GIRTIN (1775-1802)

65 *Lane at Hampstead*
Watercolour, 31.7 x 28.2 cms
*By Courtesy of the Board of Trustees
of the Victoria & Albert Museum*

In his memoir of Keats Hunt recalls the occasion when Keats, meeting him on Millfield Lane, presented him with a copy of the recently-published *Poems*:

It was in the beautiful lane, running from the road between Hampstead and Highgate to the foot of Highgate Hill that, meeting me one day, he first

gave me the volume. If the admirer of Mr. Keats's poetry does not know the lane in question, he ought to become acquainted with it, both on his author's account and its own. It has been also paced by Mr. Lamb and Mr. Hazlitt, and frequented, like the rest of the beautiful neighbourhood, by Mr. Coleridge; so that instead of Millfield Lane, which is the name it is known by "on earth," it has sometimes been called Poet's Lane, which is an appellation it richly deserves.

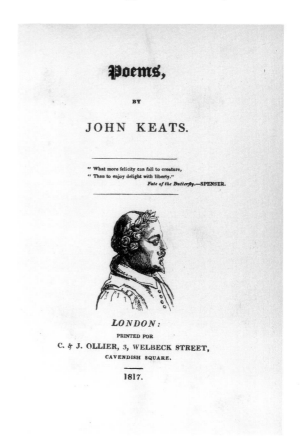

JOHN KEATS

66 *Poems*
London: C. & J. Ollier, 1817
a) Private Collection
*b) The London Borough of Camden from the
Collections at Keats House, Hampstead*

On 3 March 1817, against Shelley's advice, Keats published his first volume of poetry. It contained one great sonnet, 'On first looking into Chapman's Homer', a host of minor sonnets and verse epistles, his first known poem, 'Imitation of Spenser', and the

Cat. 65

two long poems, 'I stood tip-toe on a little hill' and 'Sleep and Poetry'.

Among his immediate circle, the book was received with celebration. Among the world at large, it made little, if any impact. Charles Cowden Clarke recalled:

> The first volume of Keats's minor muse was launched amid the cheers and fond anticipations of all his circle. Every one of us expected (and not unreasonably) that it would create a sensation in the literary world; for such a first production (and

a considerable portion of it from a minor) has rarely occurred . . . Alas! the book might have emerged in Timbuctoo with far stronger chance of fame and approbation.

The volume was scarcely reviewed outside Keats's circle (although the sonnet and particularly the dedication to Leigh Hunt were fuel for the hostile reviews of the later *Endymion*) and the first edition remained unsold for many years. As Keats himself wrote in his original, rejected preface to *Endymion*:

About a twelvemonth since, I published a little
book of verses; it was read by some dozen of my
friends, who lik'd it; and some dozen who I was
unacquainted with, who did not. Now when a
dozen human beings are at words with another
dozen, it becomes a matter of anxiety to side with
one's friends;—more especially when excited thereto by a great love of Poetry.

In the final phrase, 'excited by a great love of poetry', Keats gives his justification against Shelley's cau-
tion not to publish. His own sternest critic, he saw
that *Poems* (1817) was an immature volume, but the
enthusiasm, the excitement and honesty of intent had
its own value, and would not be fettered by the inex-
perience of youth. As he writes in 'Sleep and Poetry':

What though I am not wealthy in the dower
Of spanning wisdom; though I do not know
The shiftings of the mighty winds that blow
Hither and thither all the changing thoughts
Of man: though no great minist'ring reason sorts
Out the dark mysteries of human souls
To clear conceiving: yet there ever rolls
A vast idea before me, and I glean
Therefrom my liberty; thence too I've seen
The end and aim of Poesy.

(l. 284-93)

4. 'ENDYMION', 1817-18

'My brothers are anxious that I shod go by myself into the country', Keats wrote to Reynolds on 17 March 1817, 'and . . . Haydon has pointed out how necessary it is that I shod be alone to improve myself'. A month later he departed for the Isle of Wight, his intention, to 'make 4000 Lines of one bare circumstance and fill them with poetry.' *Endymion* was to be 'a test, a trial of my Powers of Imagination and chiefly of my invention'. So, in narrating the quest of Endymion, the shepherd king of Greek legend who was loved by the moon goddess Cynthia, Keats was himself searching for his own poetic voice.

What immediately struck him on the Isle of Wight was the wide gap that had grown up between the 'vast idea' he had proclaimed in 'Sleep and Poetry', and his present inability to realise it, between the vision of what his poetry would be, and the inadequacy of his past achievements; 'the idea has grown so monstrously beyond my seeming power of attainment' he wrote to Hunt (punning on 'Phaeton', meaning carriage as well as the over-ambitious youth who drove the chariot of the sun with such disastrous results), 'that the other day I nearly consented to drop into a Phaeton'. By his own admission, therefore, he read over his lines and hated them. Increasingly, he came to see *Endymion* as a necessary experience, rather than as a finished work of art. It was 'a huge attempt', guiding him towards future maturity: 'all the good I expect from my employment this summer is the fruit of Experience which I hope to gather in my next Poem', he wrote to Haydon.

For this reason, though he knew as well as anyone that it was a flawed poem, he never apologised for *Endymion*. On 8 October 1818 he wrote to its publisher, James Hessey:

> The Genius of Poetry must work out its own salvation in a man: It cannot be matured by law & precept, but by sensation & watchfulness in itself—That which is creative must create itself—In Endymion, I leaped headlong into the Sea, and thereby have become better acquainted with the Soundings, the quicksands, & the rocks, than if I had stayed upon the green shore, and piped a silly pipe, and took tea & comfortable advice.—I was never afraid of failure; for I would sooner fail than not be among the greatest . . .

It also helps to explain why he was able to accept the ruthlessly unfavourable reviews of *Endymion* with such apparent equanimity. 'Praise or blame has but a momentary effect on the man whose love of beauty in the abstract makes him a severe critic on his own Works', as he explained to Hessey, 'My own domestic criticism has given me pain without comparison beyond what Blackwood or the Quarterly could possibly inflict.' He had seen *Endymion* through the press, and was now better acquainted with his strengths and weaknesses; his mind was already looking forward to his next poems.

WILLIAM TURNER OF OXFORD (1789-1862)

67 *Shanklin, Isle of Wight*
Watercolour, 62.5 x 76.5 cms
By Courtesy of the Board of Trustees
of the Victoria & Albert Museum

Keats visited Shanklin en route for Carisbrooke on 16 April 1817, and the following day wrote to Reynolds:

> Yesterday I went to Shanklin, which occasioned a great debate in my mind whether I should live there or at Carisbrooke. Shanklin is a most beautiful place—sloping wood and meadow ground reaches round the Chine, which is a cleft between the Cliffs of the depth of nearly 300 feet at least. This cleft is filled with trees & bushes in the narrow part; and as it widens becomes bare, if it were not for primroses on one side, which spread to the very verge of the Sea, and some fishermen's huts on the other, perched midway in the Ballustrades of beautiful green Hedges along their steps down to the sands.—But the sea, Jack, the sea—the little waterfall—then the white cliff—then St Catherine's Hill—"the little sheep in the meadows, the

cows in the corn."

On the Isle of Wight images of cliffs and the sea became increasingly vivid presences in his imagination. 'From want of regular rest, I have been rather *narvus*', he noted to Reynolds, 'and the passage in Lear—"Do you not hear the Sea?"—has haunted me intensely'. Surrounded by the 'eternal whisperings' of the sea, and with 'the Cliff of Poesy' towering above him, he became aware of the weight of his unaccustomed solitude and the spectre of his ambition.

A further visit was made to Shanklin in June and July 1819, this time in the company of James Rice and Charles Brown, and the first act of *Otho the Great* and the first part of 'Lamia' were completed there.

JOSEPH CHARLES BARROW (C.1789-1802)

68 *Carisbrooke Castle*
Signed and dated 1796
Watercolour, 4.4 cms
By Courtesy of the Board of Trustees
of the Victoria & Albert Museum

As he explained to Reynolds on 17 April, it was this castle that finally swayed the balance between Shanklin and Carisbrooke as suitable for his lodgings:

I see Carisbrooke Castle from my window, and have found several delightful wood-alleys, and copses, and quick freshes—As for Primroses—the Island ought to be called Primrose Island; that is, if the nation of Cowslips agree thereto, of which there are diverse Clans just beginning to lift up their heads and if and how the Rain holds whereby that is Birds eye abate . . . I have not seen many specimens of Ruins—I dont think however I shall ever see one to surpass Carisbrooke Castle. The trench is o'ergrown with the smoothest turf, and the walls with ivy—The Keep within side is one Bower of ivy—a colony of Jackdaws have been there many years—I dare say I have seen many a descendant of some old cawer who peeped through the Bars at Charles the first, when he was there in Confinement.

In Barrow's deft watercolour, some soldiers can be seen in the foreground, and there was indeed a barracks (for some three thousand soldiers, built during the Napoleonic Wars) stationed near Carisbrooke when Keats was there, an addition which he noted, with displeasure, in the same letter to Reynolds:

On the road from Cowes to Newport I saw some extensive Barracks which disgusted me extremely with Government for placing such a Nest of Debauchery in so beautiful a place—I asked a man on the Coach about this—and he said that the people had been spoiled—In the room where I slept at Newport I found this on the Window "O Isle spoilt by the Milatary"

JOHN COLLINS (fl. c. 1811)
69 *Entrance to Carisbrooke Castle, with a Youth and a Lamb standing near a Gate*
Watercolour, 22.5 x 30.1 cms
By Courtesy of the Board of Trustees of the Victoria & Albert Museum

This view of Carisbrooke seems to be taken from the other side of the castle.

WILLIAM SHAKESPEARE (1564-1616)
70 *The Dramatic Works of William Shakespeare*
Chiswick: C. Whittingham, London, 1814
The British Library Board

While he was on the Isle of Wight Keats was especially conscious of, even comforted by, thoughts of Shakespeare. He first opened his copy (the 1814 edition) at Southampton: 'I felt rather lonely this Morning at breakfast', he wrote to his brothers on 17 April, 'so I went and unbox'd a Shakespeare—"There's my Comfort"'. More than a comfort, though; Shakespeare stood before him as the embodiment of 'the vast idea' of poetry. Indeed, so challenging was his example that Keats said he felt like the tiny gatherer of samphire, hanging halfway up the cliff in *King Lear*. It was, he felt, a good omen that his lodgings had an engraving of Shakespeare, particularly when his landlady first let him hang it above his books (usurping a 'french Ambassador'), and then pressed him to have it; on 10 May he wrote to Haydon:

I remember your saying that you had notions of a good Genius presiding over you—I have of late had the same thought . . . Is it too daring to Fancy

Shakspeare this Presider? When in the Isle of Wight I met with a Shakspeare in the Passage of the House at which I lodged—it comes nearer to my idea of him than any I have seen—I was but there a Week yet the old Woman made me take it with me though I went off in a hurry—Do you not think this is ominous of good?

DANIEL ORME (1766-POST 1832)

71 *The New Pier, Margate*
Signed and dated 1799
Watercolour, 12 x 18.9 cms
*By Courtesy of the Board of Trustees
of the Victoria & Albert Museum*

Oppressed by his solitude and his sense that he ought to be producing poetry, Keats decided to cut short his stay on the Isle of Wight and joined his brother Tom at Margate, then a popular pleasure resort for Londoners, at the end of April. He had first visited Margate the previous August, again with Tom, and just after he had passed his examination at Apothecaries' Hall and decided not to pursue a career in medicine. His relaxed mood on that occasion, as he looked over the cliffs and sea, is shown by the verse epistle he wrote there to his brother George:

E'en now I am pillow'd on a bed of Flowers
That crowns a lofty cliff, which proudly towers
Above the Ocean-Waves. The Stalks, and Blades,
Checquer my Tablet with their quivering shades.
On one side is a field of drooping Oats,
Through which the Poppies show their scarlet coats;
So pert and useless, that they bring to Mind
The scarlet Coats that pester human-kind.
And on the other side, outspread, is seen

Ocean's blue mantel, streak'd with purple, and green.
Now 'tis I see a Canvass'd ship, and now
Mark the bright silver curling round her prow.
I see the Lark down-dropping to her nest . . .

But now, in 1817, exhausted by his recent exertions and by the task ahead of him, his mood was despondent. Before he left he wrote to his publishers in an effort to explain:

I went day by day at my Poem for a Month at the end of which time the other day I found my brain so overwrought that I had neither Rhyme nor reason in it . . . instead of Poetry I have a swimming in my head—And feel all the effects of a Mental Debauch—lowness of Spirits—anxiety to go on without the Power to do so which does not at all tend to my ultimate Progression—However tomorrow I will begin my next Month—This Evening I go to Canterbury—having got tired of Margate—I was not right in my head when I came.

72 *Letter from John Keats to Leigh Hunt*
10 May 1817
The British Library Board

Keats's letter to Leigh Hunt from Margate gives a long explanation for his departure from Carisbrooke. By now, however, he was withdrawing from Hunt's influence. The next day he confessed to Haydon: 'I wrote to Hunt yesterday—scarcely know what I said in it—I could not talk about Poetry in the way I should have liked for I was not in humor with either his or mine'.

I went to the Isle of Wight, thought so much about Poetry so long together that I could not sleep at night. . . . I became not over capable in my upper Stories, and set off pell mell for Margate, at least 150 miles—because forsooth I fancied that I should like my old lodging here, and could contrive to do without Trees. Another thing I was too much in solitude, and consequently was obliged to be in continual burning of thought as an only resource. However Tom is with me at present and we are very comfortable. . . . I vow that I have been down in the Mouth lately at this Work. These last two days however I have felt more confident—I have asked myself so often why I should be a Poet more than other Men,—seeing how great a thing it is,—how great things are to be gained by it—What a thing to be in the Mouth of Fame—that at last the Idea has grown so monstrously beyond my seeming Power of attainment that the other day I nearly consented with myself to drop into a Phæton —yet 'tis a disgrace to fail even in a huge attempt, and at this moment I drive the thought from me. I began my Poem about a Fortnight since and have done some every day except travelling ones—Perhaps I may have done a good deal for the time but it appears such a Pin's Point to me that I will not coppy any out—When I consider that so many of these Pin points go to form a Bodkin point (God send I end not my Life with a bare Bodkin, in its modern sense) and that it requ[i]res a thousand bodkins to make a Spear bright enough to throw any light to posterity—I see that nothing but continual uphill Journeying? Now is there any thing more unpleasant (it may come among the thousand and one) than to be so journeying and miss the Goal at last—But I intend to whistle all these cogitations into the Sea where I hope they will breed Storms violent enough to block up all exit from Russia.

Keats ends the letter in a jocular fashion, making reference to Shelley's peculiar habit of reciting lines from Shakespeare's *Richard II* at any given moment, and signing himself 'John Keats alias Junkets', perhaps a nickname among his circle referring to the way he pronounced his name.

James Roberts (fl. 1766-c.1809)
73   *The Back of the Fellows' Quadrangle, Merton College, Oxford; and the Tower of Magdalen, seen from Merton Field*
Signed and dated 1793
Watercolour, 18.5 x 23.6 cms
By Courtesy of the Board of Trustees of the Victoria & Albert Museum

Keats stayed with Benjamin Bailey at Magdalen Hall, Oxford, for a month in September 1817. 'This Oxford I have no doubt is the finest City in the world', he wrote to his sister Fanny on 17 September (see below), 'it is full of old Gothic buildings—Spires—

towers—Quadrangles—Cloisters Groves &c and is surrounded with more Clear streams than ever I saw together.' His love of gothic architecture was further stimulated by later visits to Chichester and Winchester, influencing his two poems, 'The Eve of St. Agnes' and 'The Eve of St. Mark'.

In the company of the sympathetic, scholarly and philosophical Bailey, Keats boated regularly on the Isis, and on one occasion visited Stratford-on-Avon. He rushed through the third book of *Endymion*, which was now becoming a burden. Even so, while pressing on at speed with the poem, the remarkable sense of resurrection showing Keats's fundamental optimism was forcibly present. On 28 September he explains his progress to Haydon:

> You will be glad to hear that within these last three weeks I have written 1000 lines—which are the third Book of my Poem. My Ideas with respect to it I assure you are very low—and I would write the subject thoroughly again. But I am tired of it and think the time would be better spent in writing a new Romance which I have in my eye for next summer—Rome was not built in a Day.

74   *Letter from John Keats to Fanny Keats*
10 September 1817
The British Library Board

'Let us now begin a regular question and answer' Keats writes to his younger sister (then fourteen years old), 'a little pro and con; letting it interfere as a pleasant method of my coming at your favorite little

Cat. 76

wants and enjoyments, that I may meet them in a way befitting a brother'. From then on, his frequent letters (some fifty have survived) are notable for their lively information, interest in Fanny's reading and hobbies, their emotional candour, and a brotherly, sometimes parental concern for her well-being – 'I feel myself the only protector you have' he wrote to her on 11 February 1819 For most of Keats's life she was under the guardianship of Richard Abbey, who, with his wife, was both possessive and unsympathetic - on 5 January 1818 Keats reported to his brothers: 'Mrs Abbey was saying that the Keatses were ever indolent—that they would ever be so and that it was born in them—Well whispered Fanny to me 'If it is born with us how can we help it'. For her part, Fanny kept to Keats's request to 'preserve all my letters'; in old age she said that only once, and then only for a few days, were they out of her possession.

Here Keats gives her the story of Endymion, offering to tell her 'of others quite as delightful', speaks of his preference for the Italian over the French language, and offers his impressions of Oxford.

75 *Letter from Leigh Hunt to Charles Cowden Clarke*
1 July 1817
Leeds University Library, Brotherton Collection

Perhaps sensing Keats's new sympathies, Hunt writes rather critically to Cowden Clarke:

What has become of Junkets, I know not. I suppose Queen Mab has eaten him. If not, I have no doubt that he will appear before us all again very penitent, & poetical, & really sorry. He wants a little more adversity perhaps to make him attend to others as much in reality, as he wishes to do in theory; & all that we can hope at present is, that a youth of his ardour may not bring too much upon him too soon.

J.M.W. TURNER (1775-1851)
76 *Teignmouth from Babbercombe Bay*
?1811
Watercolour, 15.4 x 22.2 cms
Thomas Agnew & Sons Ltd

Keats was at Teignmouth with his brother Tom from March to May 1818. His visit was constrained by the wet weather ('—it cannot be' he wrote to Reynolds, 'Rain! Rain! Rain!'), which prevented him from seeing as much as he would have liked, though he did go to this part of the coast. On 9 April he wrote to Reynolds:

> Devonshire continues rainy. As the drops beat against the window, they give me the same sensation as a quart of cold water offered to revive a half-drowned devil—No feel of the clouds dropping fatness; but as if the roots of the Earth were rotten cold and drench'd—I have not been able to go to Kents' Ca[ve] at Babbicun—however on one very beautiful day I had a fine Clamber over the rocks all along as far as that place

He must have got there eventually however, for a year later, on 21 September 1819, he recommended it to Reynolds: 'If you can get a peep at Babbicomb before you leave the country do.—I think it is the finest place I have seen, or—is to be seen in the South. There is a Cottage there I took warm water at, that made up for the tea.'

'I think I Did very wrong to leave you to all the trouble of Endymion' he wrote from Teignmouth on 24 April to John Taylor, but he was anxious to put the poem behind him, and disputed with Taylor over the preface. He wrote to Reynolds (who was acting as go-between):

> I have not the slightest feeling of humility towards the Public—or to any thing in existence,—but the eternal Being, the Principle of Beauty,—and the Memory of great Men . . . a Preface is written to the Public; a thing I cannot help looking upon as an Enemy, and which I cannot address without feelings of hostility . . . I never wrote one single Line of Poetry with the least Shadow of Public thought.

'I want to forget it and make my mind free for something new' he wrote to Taylor, 'I was purposing to travel north this summer'. The resulting tour of the Lake District and Scotland was the prelude to his greatest period as a poet.

UNKNOWN ARTIST
77 *John Taylor (1781-1864)*
Wax medallion, D 9.2 cms
National Portrait Gallery, London

On 15 April 1817 John Taylor wrote to his father: 'We have agreed for the next Edit. of Keats's Poems, and are to have the Refusal of his future Works. I cannot think he will fail to become a great Poet'. As a publisher committed to promoting and encouraging new literature, he saw Keats as a valued addition to the list of Taylor and Hessey. Henceforth he would struggle to find a balance between his continual belief in Keats's greatness (or potential greatness), and his need to recover the financial losses caused by publishing a poet who not only sold badly, but who expressed a complete indifference towards 'mawkish popularity' and 'public thought'.

Endymion was published by Taylor and Hessey in 1818. Taylor had advanced Keats money during its composition, and had taken it through the press with especial care. When the hostile reviews appeared he was active in his defence – 'it has been thought necessary,' he wrote to John Clare, 'in the leading Review, the Quarterly, to damn his [poetry] for imputed political Opinions – Damn them who could act in so cruel a way to a young man of undoubted Genius.' To William Blackwood, the editor of *Blackwoods*, he said angrily: 'It was done in the Spirit of the Devil,

Mr Blackwood . . . No man would insult Mr Keats in this Manner in his Company, and what is the difference between writing and speaking of a person except that the written Attack is the more base from being made anonymously & therefore at no personal Risk.'

After *Endymion*, Taylor and Keats, who had argued over the preface to that work, then argued over the sexual consummation of Madeline's and Porphyro's love in 'The Eve of St. Agnes'. 'It will render the poem unfit for ladies', Richard Woodhouse had declared to Taylor, and as these ladies made up nearly half the reading public, Taylor, out of pocket after *Endymion*, was necessarily concerned about sales. It was a clear illustration of the tension Taylor lived with between his belief in a writer's imaginative independence (which he described as 'Absorbent of all other Considerations'), and his responsibility, as a bookseller, to consider the complex pressures of finance, sales, public attitudes, and critical opinion.

When, however, Taylor received the completed manuscripts for Keats's new volume, disagreement was replaced by a re-affirmation of Keats's genius. At the end of June 1820 he wrote to his father:

> Next week Keats's new Volume of Poems will be published, & if it does not sell well, I think nothing will ever sell again. I am sure of this that for poetic Genius there is not his equal living & I would compare him against any one with either Milton or Shakespeare for beauties.

And when Keats, now in wretched health, prepared to go to Italy, it was Taylor who organised a fund to finance the trip. Although the *Lamia* volume was also selling badly, he wrote to Keats on 11 September 1820 with characteristic generosity:

> if it does not answer, the Loss is ours: whatever succeeds we deem the Profit wholly yours . . You will do well to publish again as soon as you have the power to produce anything, and the Success you may rely upon it will in every Instance increase. I hope yet to see you as rich and renowned as you deserve to be.

E. SCRIVEN AFTER WILLIAM HILTON
78 John Clare (1793-1864)
Stipple engraving
National Portrait Gallery Archive

There is no evidence that Keats and Clare met, but the two poets shared a sympathetic publisher in Taylor, and he brought their poetry to each other's notice. Before leaving for Italy, Keats commented on Clare's poetry, arguing that the 'description' of his first volume prevailed too much over the 'sentiment' or 'prevailing Idea' of the verse. Taylor wrote to Clare on 27 September 1820:

> I think he wishes to say to you that your Images from Nature are too much introduced without being called for by a particular Sentiment. . . . His Remark is only applicable now & then when he feels as if the Description overlaid and stifled that which ought to be the prevailing Idea.

For his part, the rural Clare saw Keats's mythologising and fancifying of nature as spoiling the purity of the description; he wrote in a fragment (1825-37):

> He keeps up a constant alusion or illusion to the grecian mythology & there I cannot follow—yet when he speaks of woods Dryads & Fawns are sure to follow & the brook looks alone without her naiads to his mind yet the frequency of such classical accompaniment make it wearisome to the reader where behind every rose bush he looks for a Venus & under every laurel a thrumming Apollo —In spite of all this his descriptions of scenery are often very fine but as it is the case with other

inhabitants of great cities he often described nature as she appeared to his fancies & not as he would have described her had he witnessed the things he describes—Thus it is he has often undergone the stigma of Cockneyism & what appears as beautys in the eyes of a pent-up citizen are looked upon as consciets by those who live in the country . . .

Clare was however an astute reader and admirer of Keats's third volume, which he saw as 'not so warm' as *Endymion*, yet wrote to Hessey that 'I like Keats last poem the best *Hyp:*—'. His comments on the 1820 volume are strikingly similar to Keats's own comments on *Endymion*; he wrote, again to Hessey, on 4 July 1820:

I began on our friend Keats new Vol—find the same fine flowers spread if I can express myself in the wilderness of poetry—for he launches on the sea without compass—& mounts pegassus without saddle or bridle as usual . . . but he is a child of nature warm and wild.

79 *The London Magazine*
   1820-22
   Private Collection

'We have long entertained the wish of establishing a 'Quarterly Magazine' of genuine original Writers' wrote Taylor to his father in 1817. Some three years later Taylor and Hessey bought the name and good-will of *The London Magazine*, a brilliant periodical that had brought before the public Hazlitt's *Table Talk* and Charles Lamb's *Elia*. It was their desire to conduct the magazine 'on principles of fairness, without any bias from party spirit.' Turning to a magazine, the firm continued its policy of supporting 'genuine original writers', with personal faith and at financial risk, only this time with an added communal spirit. Lamb wrote to Taylor that 'The Lond. Mag. is chiefly pleasant to me, because some of my friends write in it.' Other contributers were Hazlitt, John Clare, John Hamilton Reynolds, Thomas Hood, Henry Cary and Thomas De Quincey. It was the *London Magazine* that, in September and October 1821, first published the *Confessions of an English Opium Eater*.

The magazine was polymathic in its subject-matter, embracing literature, history, fine art, architecture,

and music. Nor did it, quite deliberately, ally itself to any particular political or intellectual stance – the January 1820 issue, with its new and brilliant editor John Scott in charge, had outlined its policy: 'The spirit of things generally, and, above all, of the present time, it will be our business, or at least our endeavour, to catch, condense, and delineate.' In many ways, it embodied in print the literary and artistic spirit of Keats and his circle between 1816 and 1820.

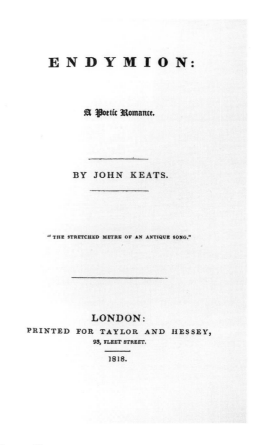

ENDYMION:

A Poetic Romance.

BY JOHN KEATS.

" THE STRETCHED METRE OF AN ANTIQUE SONG."

LONDON:
PRINTED FOR TAYLOR AND HESSEY,
93, FLEET STREET.
1818.

JOHN KEATS

80 *Endymion*
   London: Taylor & Hessey, 1818
   a) *The London Borough of Camden from the Collections at Keats House, Hampstead*
   b) *Private Collection*
   c) *Professor Michael Jaye*

Taylor supervised the process of the publication of *Endymion* during February and March of 1818, with Keats's last minute revisions (sometimes in response to Taylor's own suggestions) forcing many of the pages to be reset. When it was finally published in

April, Keats wrote to Taylor: 'the book pleased me much—it is very free from faults; and although there are one or two words I should wish replaced, I see in many places an improvement greatly to the purpose'. But by December, it was becoming clear that the book was not selling. Over three years later Taylor and Hessey were still £110 out of pocket by the book, and by 1820 it had to be remaindered. Edward Stibbs, a bookseller, brought it for 1½*d.* a copy, paid 2½*d.* for the binding, and sold it slowly at 1/6*d.* a copy (compared to the original price of nine shillings).

H. WINSTANLEY AFTER SALVATOR ROSA

81 *Glaucus and Scylla*
Engraving, 39 x 31.2 cms
Courtauld Institute Galleries

For his description of Glaucus in the third book of *Endymion* (lines 192-9), Keats had various visual sources to draw upon, particularly this image by Salvator Rosa, which was well-known at the time:

Upon a weeded rock this old man sat,
And his white hair was awful, and a mat
Of weeds were cold beneath his cold thin feet;
And, ample as the largest winding-sheet,
A cloak of blue wrapp'd up his aged bones,
O'erwrought with symbols by the deepest groans
Of ambitious magic . . .

JOHN HOPPNER (1758-1810)

82 *William Gifford (1756-1826)*
Oil on canvas, 76.2 x 63.5 cms
National Portrait Gallery, London

Gifford was the editor of the *Quarterly*, where a savaging review of *Endymion* (by John Wilson Croker), appeared in September 1818. He was the subject of some of Hazlitt's finest and most sustained invective; in *The Spirit of the Age* he is condemned for his prejudiced, unintellectual, class-conscious approach to modern literature:

His standard of ideal perfection is what he himself now is, a person of mediocre literary attainments: his utmost contempt is shewn by reducing any one to what he himself once was, a person without the ordinary advantages of education and learning. It is accordingly assumed, with much complacency in his critical pages, that Tory Writers are classical

and courtly as a matter of course; as it is a standing jest and evident truism, that Whigs and Reformers must be persons of low birth and breeding—imputations from one of which he has narrowly escaped, and both of which he holds in suitable abhorrence. He stands over a contemporary performance with all the self-conceit and self-importance of a country schoolmaster, tries it by technical rules, affects not to understand its meaning, examines the hand-writing, the spelling, shrugs his shoulders and chuckles over a slip of the pen, and keeps a sharp look-out for a false concord and—a flogging. There is nothing liberal, nothing humane in his style of judging: it is altogether petty, captious, and literal. . . . His slow, snail-paced, bed-rid habits of reasoning cannot keep up with the whirling, eccentric motion, the rapid, perhaps extravagant combinations of modern literature. He has long been stationary himself, and is determined that others shall remain so. . . . He inclines, by a natural and deliberate bias, to the traditional in laws and government; to the orthodox in religion; to the safe in opinion; to the trite in imagination; to the technical in style; to whatever implies a surrender of individual judgement into the hands of authority, and a subjection of individual feeling to mechanic rules. . . .

Hazlitt recognises (as did Keats himself) that the real crime in Gifford's eyes was not so much *Endymion* itself, but its author's association with Leigh Hunt and the radical *Examiner*.

Mr Keats's ostensible crime was that he had been praised in the Examiner Newspaper: a greater and more unpardonable offence probably was, that he was a true poet, with all the errors and beauties of youthful genius to answer for. Mr Gifford was insensible to the one as he was inexorable to the other.

JOHN WILSON CROKER (1780-1857)
83 *Review of 'Endymion' in the 'Quarterly Review'*
April 1818
The British Library Board

Croker begins with the cheerful admission that he has failed to read more of *Endymion* than the first book: 'Not that we have been wanting in our duty' he writes, 'far from it—indeed, we have made efforts almost as superhuman as the story itself appears to be, to get through it; but with the fullest stretch of our perseverance, we are forced to confess that we have not been able to struggle beyond the first of the four books of which this Poetic Romance consists.'

He admits that Keats has 'real powers of language, rays of fancy, and gleams of genius' but, again, he is 'unhappily a disciple of the new school of what has been somewhere called the Cockney poetry; which may be defined to consist of the most incongruous ideas in the most uncouth language.' Hunt is the 'hierophant' of the Cockney School, and Keats is merely 'a copyist of Mr. Hunt; but he is more unintelligible, almost as rugged, twice as diffuse, and ten times more tiresome and absurd than his prototype . . . he writes it for his own sake, and, being bitten by Mr. Leigh Hunt's insane criticism, more than rivals the insanity of his poetry.'

UNKNOWN AUTHOR
84 *Review of 'Endymion' in the 'British Critic'*
June 1818
The British Library Board

Another guardian of established morality, the *British Critic* also had to voice disapproval of Keats. The reviewer (whose identity is not known) reserves most of his scorn for Leigh Hunt and the 'Cockney school', and the subversive 'Jacobinism' that they represent:

Mr Keats is not contented with a half-initiation into the school he has chosen. And he can strike from unmeaning absurdity into the gross slang of voluptuousness with as much skill as the worthy prototype whom he has selected. We will assure him, however, that not all the flimsy veil of words in which he would involve immoral images, can atone for their impurity; and we will not disgust our readers by retailing to them the artifices of vicious refinement, by which under the semblance of "slippery blisses, twinkling eyes, soft complexion of faces, and smooth excess of hands," he would palm upon the unsuspicious and the innocent imaginations better adapted to the stews. . . The third book begins in character, with a jacobinical apostrophe to "crowns, turbans, and tiptop nothings"; we wonder how mitres escaped from their usual place.

'z' / JOHN GIBSON LOCKHART (1794-1854)
85 *Review of 'Endymion' in 'Blackwood's Edinburgh Magazine'*
August 1818
The British Library Board

Writing over the infamous signature of 'Z', John Gibson Lockhart had been running a periodic column on the 'Cockney School of Poetry' for some time before *Endymion* appeared, and Keats knew that his turn would eventually come, as it did in part four. 'There has been but one Number published,' he wrote to Bailey on 3 November 1817, 'that on Hunt to which they have prefixed a Motto from one Cornelius Webb Poetaster . . . In the Motto they have put Hunt and Keats in large Letters—I have no doubt that the second Number was intended for me.' Unwittingly, Bailey was to provide Lockhart (they had met by chance at dinner in Scotland) with the knowledge that Keats was once an apprentice apothecary, a detail which Lockhart used to the full:

His friends, we understand, destined him to the career of medicine, and he was bound apprentice some years ago to a worthy apothecary in town. But all has been undone by a sudden attack of the malady to which we have alluded. . . . It is a better and a wiser thing to be a starved apothecary than a starved poet; so back to the shop Mr John, back to "plasters, pills, and ointment boxes," &c. But,

for Heaven's sake, young Sangrado, be a little
more sparing of extenuatives and soporifics in
your practice than you have been in your poetry.'

(Sangrado is the quack doctor in *Gils Blas*, who treat-
ed his patients by bleeding them or by giving them
hot water). Here Hunt is 'the most worthless and
affected of all the versifiers of our time', the author of
'the odious and incestuous "Story of Rimini."'

As well as of their politics, *Blackwoods* was always
particularly scornful of the 'cockneys' use of classical
material: 'There they are,' it wrote in October 1822, 'a
pack of poor illiterate creatures, (not one of whom
could tell, within fifty miles, what is the meaning of a
Middle Voice,) all piping about Pan, and Apollo, and
Endymion, and the Muses, and the Graces . . .'
Lockhart laments that Keats has this same tendency:

> From his prototype Hunt, John Keats has acquired
> a sort of vague idea, that the Greeks were a most
> tasteful people, and that no mythology can be so
> finely adapted for the purposes of poetry as theirs.
> It is amusing to see what a hand the two Cock-
> neys make of this mythology; the one confesses
> that he never read the Greek Tragedians, and the
> other knows Homer only from Chapman; and
> both of them write about Apollo, Pan, Nymphs,
> Muses, and Mysteries, as might be expected from
> persons of their education.

'This is a mere matter of the moment' Keats commented on the reviews to his brother and sister in
law, 'I think I shall be among the English Poets after
my death.'

86 Letter From John Gibson Lockhart to John Aitken
15 September 1820
*The London Borough of Camden from the
Collections at Keats House, Hampstead*

Lockhart's letter to Aitken, a Scottish bank clerk and
future editor, of the same age as Keats (1795-1833),
makes clear that his chief motive in attacking Keats
was his being a part of the so called 'Cockney
School':

> I have already been tempted to say something
> kind of Mr Keats in Blackwood's Magazine but
> have been thwarted I know not well how. In truth
> I do utterly despise the Cockney School – &

almost hate it seeing (as I do see) that whoever
joins it – be he possessed of what genius he will –
must by the connection simply be damned. Ecce
Keats – a fine lad full of feeling but cocknified
into (half) a mere laughing stock. Writing Modern
Greek & guilty of all other abominations.
    I trust his health will mend . . .

COMMON SENSE.

I HAVE no genius. Though I make no doubt,
Sage reader, thou would'st soon have found this out:
I tell thee, lest thou waste thy precious time
In seeking here for aught but sense and rhyme—
Plain common sense, but no ecstatic feats,
And rhymes at least as good as Mister Keates' *.

   Time was when bards were few: then might you see
In Button's room the whole fraternity;
But now, like Egypt's frogs, on every hand
They spread and croak and darken all the land:

* Mr. John Keates, the muse's child of promise, is a rising poet of the
Cockney School; who, if he had but an ear for rhyme, a little knowledge of
grammar, and sufficient intellect to distinguish sense from nonsense, might perhaps do very well.

B

Charles H. Terrot (1790-1872)
87 Common Sense: A Poem
Edinburgh: David Brown, 1819
Professor Michael Jaye

Terrot, a young Edinburgh cleric, recently from
Trinity College, Cambridge, was a future Bishop of
Edinburgh. His first performance, critical of poets
and politicians of the day, draws upon Lockhart's
contemptuous review of Keats as a cockney poet:

> Plain common sense, but no ecstatic feats,
> And rhymes at least as good as Mister Keates

In his footnote to these lines, calling Keats 'the muses'
child of promise', Terrot, arguably, attempts to soften
Lockhart's 'back to the shop Mr John, back to "plaster, pills, and ointment boxes"':

> "*Mr, John Keates, the muse's child of promise, is
> a rising poet of the Cockney School, who, if he
> had but an ear for rhyme, a little knowledge of
> grammar, and sufficient intellect to distinguish
> sense from nonsense, might perhaps do very well."

ANDREW GEDDES (1783-1844)
88 *Francis Jeffrey (1773-1850)*
Signed with initials and dated, 1820/26?
Oil on canvas, 144.1 x 112.1 cms
National Portrait Gallery, London

Jeffrey, the editor of *The Edinburgh Review*, kept silent about Keats until the publication of the *Lamia* volume in 1820. Taylor had tried to recruit the *Edinburgh Review* to counter the blasts against *Endymion*, and Keats saw their silence as the same cowardice and duplicity that he found in the *Quarterly Review*. He wrote to his brother and sister-in-law on 20 September 1819:

> The Edinburgh review are affraid to touch upon my Poem—They do not know what to make of it—they do not like to condemn it and they will not praise it for fear—They are as shy of it as I should be of wearing a Quaker's hat—The fact is they have no real taste—they dare not compromise their Judgements on so puzzling a Question—If on my next Publication they should praise me and so lug in Endymion—I will address [them] in a manner thay will not at all relish—The Cowardliness of the Edinburgh is worse than the abuse of the Quarterly.

Unlike Gifford, however, Jeffrey sought to free literary criticism from undue political bias, he wrote in December 1808:

> no party politics, and nothing but exemplary moderation and impartiality on all politics. I have allowed too much mischief to be done from my mere indifference and love of sport; but it would be inexcusable to spoil the powerful instrument we have got hold of, for the sake of teazing and playing tricks. . . .

William Hazlitt sent his 'Reply to 'Z'' (see below) to the *Edinburgh Review*, and retained Jeffrey as counsel in his lawsuit against the *Quarterly*, and is far more charitable to Jeffrey and the *Edinburgh* in *The Spirit of the Age*:

> It was not the principles of the Edinburgh Review, but the spirit that was looked at with jealousy and alarm. The principles were by no means decidedly hostile to existing institutions: but the spirit was that of fair and free discussion; a field was open to argument and wit; every question was tried upon its own ostensible merits, and there was no foul play.

It is particularly noticeable that Jeffrey understood Keats's quite original use of myth:

> Instead of presenting its imaginary persons under the trite and vulgar traits that belong to them in the ordinary systems, little more is borrowed from these than the original character and distinct individuality is bestowed upon them, which has all the merit of invention, and all the grace and attraction of the fictions on which it is engrafted.

WILLIAM BEWICK (1795-1866)
89 *William Hazlitt*
1825
Chalk, 57.5 x 37.5 cms
The Wordsworth Trust

When Keats numbered Hazlitt's 'depth of taste as one of 'the three things to rejoice at in this age', he was paying tribute to an essayist, lecturer and friend who exerted an almost unparalleled influence on his ideas. Many parallels can be drawn. In his *Round Table* essay on 'Mr. Wordsworth's Excursion', Hazlitt talked of the poet's 'intense intellectual egotism'; Keats would later translate this into his conception of 'the egotistical or Wordsworthian sublime'. Again, Hazlitt's insistence that a poet should go beyond his own senses

through an identification with people and objects is echoed by Keats's account of himself to Woodhouse on 27 October 1818: 'it is not itself—it has no self—it is everything and nothing—It has no character—it enjoys light and shade; it lives in gusto, be it foul or fair, high or low, rich or poor, mean or elevated . . . When I am in a room with People if I ever am free from speculating on creations of my own brain, then not myself goes home to myself: but the identity of every one in the room begins to press upon me so that I am in a very little time annihilated'. (Hazlitt's word 'gusto' is defined by him in the *Annals of the Fine Arts* as 'power or passion defining any object'.)

Hazlitt's energy and gift for verbal self-defence was particularly admired by Keats: 'Hazlitt has damned the bigotted and the blue-stockined', he wrote to Haydon, 'how durst the Man?! he is your only good damner and if ever I am damn'd—I should'nt like him to damn me.'

At least during his lifetime, Keats's admiration was not reciprocated; 'When Keats was living,' remarked Haydon, 'I could not get Hazlitt to admit Keats had common talents!' To Hazlitt, Keats was a poet of youth: 'the reading of Mr Keats's "Eve of St. Agnes" lately made me regret that I was not young again', he wrote in *The London Magazine* in February 1821. What is more, his poetry had the 'effeminacy' that

was the principal charge levelled against Hunt; 'I cannot help thinking that the fault of Mr. Keats's poems was a deficiency in masculine energy of style', he wrote in his essay 'On Effeminacy of Character', 'He had beauty, tenderness, delicacy, in an uncommon degree, but there was a want of strength and substance'. This charge of 'unmanliness' was to haunt Keats's reputation for years after his death.

William Hazlitt (1788-1830)
90   A Reply to 'Z'
Autograph manuscript
The British Library Board

Hazlitt and the Tory reviewers were long-time enemies. The situation came to a head in January 1818 when the *Quarterly* reviewed Hazlitt's *Shakespeare's Plays*. Extremely hostile, referring to his 'sedition' and 'senseless and wicked sophistry', it was soon followed by the August number of *Blackwood's* which contained a sustained personal attack upon 'pimpled Hazlitt' next to the hostile review of Keats's *Endymion*. In contrast to the apparent equanimity of Keats's response, Hazlitt responded with fury in 'A Reply to 'Z', which was sent to the *Edinburgh Review*, though never published. At the same time he instituted a claim for libel against *Blackwood's*, retained Francis Jeffrey as counsel, and demanded damages of £2,000. finally, in March the following year, he published the *Letter to William Gifford*, which treats Gifford to a sustained fury that stretches to some forty pages. The 'Reply' begins forcefully:

> Sir,—Before I answer your questions, give me leave to tell you my opinion of the person who asks them. I think then that you are a person of little understanding, with great impudence, a total want of principle, an utter disregard to truth or even to the character of common veracity, and a very strong ambition to be picked up and played as a cat's-paw. If I were in the habit of using the words, Liar, Fool, Coxcomb, Hypocrite, Scoundrel, Blackguard, &c., I should apply them to you, but this would be degrading them still lower unnecessarily, for it is quite as easy to prove you the things as to call you the names.

91   *Admission Ticket to a Lecture given by*
      Hazlitt at the Surrey Institution
      The British Library Board

Hazlitt ran his lecture series *Lectures on the English Poets* from 13 January to 3 March 1818. They were held at the Surrey institution near Blackfriars Bridge. Keats missed only one, on Chaucer and Spenser, when he arrived too late, but their general popularity can be attested by those he met on their way out; on 23 January he wrote to his brothers: 'I went last Tuesday, an hour too late, to Hazlitt's Lecture on poetry, got there just as they were coming out, when all these pounced on me. Hazlitt, John Hunt & son, Wells, Bewick, all the Landseers, Bob Harris, Rox of the Burrough Aye & more'. On 21 February he wrote, again to his brothers, 'I hear Hazlitt's Lectures regularly—his last was on Grey Collins, Young &c and he gave a very fine piece of discriminating criticism on Swift, Voltaire And Rabelais—I was very disappointed in his treatment of Chatterton—I generally meet with many I know there.'

SAMUEL PALMER (1805-1881)
92   *The Sleeping Shepherd*
      Pen and wash, 15.7 x 18.8 cms
      Whitworth Art Gallery

Palmer's images of sleeping shepherds (with their apparent echoes of *Endymion*) are often used for modern editions of Keats's poetry. This drawing dates from the artist's visionary years at Shoreham (1825-32), when, as he put it, he looked at landscape with 'the eye of the imagination and not the eye of sense', and saw his inner vision as having a greater reality than outward appearances. Keats expresses a similar approach when he wrote to Bailey in November 1817:

> I am certain of nothing but the holiness of the Heart's affections and the truth of the Imagination—What the Imagination seizes as beauty must be truth—whether it existed before or not . . . The Imagination may be compared to Adam's dream—he awoke and found it truth . . .

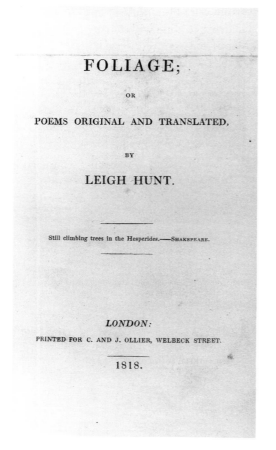

LEIGH HUNT

93 *Foliage: or Poems Original or Translated*
London: C. and J. Ollier, 1818
Professor Michael Jaye

Hunt addresses poems to almost everyone in this volume except Wordsworth and Coleridge, including two to Shelley, three to Keats, to Byron, Hazlitt, Lamb, Haydon and Reynolds. Published just before *Endymion*, *Foliage* contained all that the reviewers objected to in the 'Cockney School', and served to draw further scornful attention upon Keats. Woodhouse wrote to Keats on the *Quarterly Review* article:

> I take it the precious article in question once formed a portion of the critique in the former Nᵒ upon L. Hunts foliage.—That the reviewer, in a moment of compunction, changed his plan, & reviewed Hunts work by itself, intending to leave you alone; tho' the scissors which this sentence of divorce was carried into effect, left in the earlier article a few traces of the orig¹ union.—But that the Editor, finding himself at a loss for a few

pages of matter to eke out his presᵗ Nᵒ, bethought himself of the fragments of his former review, which he has cooked up afresh, as a side dish for his reviewers.

Keats's own opinion of *Foliage* was that 'It is a great Pity that People should by associating themselves with the finest things, spoil them. Hunt has damned Hampstead and Masks and Sonnets and Italian tales . . .'

JOHN HAMILTON REYNOLDS

94 *The Garden of Florence*
London: John Warren 1821
Private Collection

Writing to Richard Monckton Milnes, who was working on his Life of Keats, on 17 April 1848, Reynolds described the original purpose of this volume:

> Two of the Poems in the little Book are from Boccacio—& were to have been published with one or two more,—& Keats was to have joined me—but he only wrote "Isabella & the Pot of Basil."—His illness & death put an end to the work—and I referred to the circumstance in my preface.

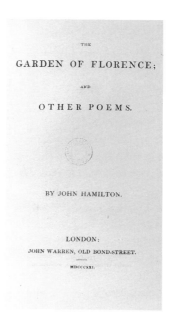

In the preface he writes:

> He, who is gone, was one of the very kindest friends I possessed, and yet he was not kinder perhaps to me, than to others. His intense mind and powerful feelings would, I truly believe, have done the world some service, had his life been spared—but he was of too sensitive a nature—and thus he was destroyed! One story ['Isabella'] he completed, and that is to me now the most pathetic poem in existence!

The volume is published under the name 'John Hamilton'. This may have been to avoid the anti-Cockney attacks of the Tory critics; as a professional journalist himself, and as the reviews of Keats's *Endymion* had proved, Reynolds would have known that a work could be damned merely because of the author's associations. Yet he had published anonymously before, and the choice of name may have been through an older instinct (or sense of mischief). John Clare, for instance, was fooled: 'There is a good deal of Reynolds manner of expression about the poetry as I think,' he wrote, '& some things are as good as his.'

94a *Letter from Benjamin Robert Haydon to Thomas Monkhouse*
c. December 1817
Private Collection

Haydon writes to Thomas Monkhouse, Mary Wordsworth's cousin with whom she and the poet were staying, to arrange the first meeting between Keats and Wordsworth. He asks if Wordsworth will be at home the following morning 'as Keats is down and very anxious to see him'.

On 23 January 1818, Keats told Bailey: 'I have seen a great deal of Wordsworth'. There were at least five, possibly six, meetings between Wordsworth and Keats. They met on 28 December 1817 at Haydon's famous dinner party. Earlier, Keats, at Thomas Monkhouse's, had recited his 'Hymn to Pan' to which, according to Haydon, 'Wordsworth drily said "a Very pretty piece of Paganism—"'. Haydon's comment in 1845 that Keats 'never forgave' Wordsworth seems untrue. The two men met on 31 December 1817 on Hampstead Heath; on 3 January 1818, Keats called at Wordsworth's lodging, and to Keat's surprise, after he had been kept waiting, Wordsworth (with his wife and, probably, Sara Hutchinson) appeared in a stiff collar, departing to dine with Mr Kingston, the comptroller of the Stamp Office. Keats himself had declined Kingston's invitation – 'not liking that place' – but he arranged to dine with Wordsworth on Monday, 5 January. Perhaps it was on this occasion that Mary Wordsworth prevented Keats from disagreeing on a point with Wordsworth by putting her hand on his arm: 'Mr. Wordsworth is never interrupted.' Wordsworth left London on 20 January; on 21 February, Keats wrote to his brothers: 'I am sorry that Wordsworth has left a bad impression wherever he visited in Town—by his egotism, Vanity and bigotry —yet he is a great Poet if not a Philosopher.'

Cat. 122 Joshua Cristall, *Highland Drovers near Inverary*

5. The Lake District and Scotland, 1818

'I purpose within a Month to put my knapsack at my back and make a pedestrian tour through the North of England, and part of Scotland', Keats wrote to Haydon on 8 April 1818, 'to make a sort of Prologue to the Life I intend to pursue.' On 24 June he and Brown left Lancaster for the Lake District. Their route took them through Bowness, Ambleside, Rydal (where they called on Wordsworth, who was not at home), Grasmere, Thirlmere and Keswick (where they walked around Derwentwater and climbed Skiddaw). As they travelled north, they left the luxuriant scenery of Hampstead and the Isle of Wight behind them, and moved through a grander, more epic landscape. Keats, with his mind on a projected poem of epic magnitude, 'Hyperion', for once felt his imagination surpassed by the 'space, the magnitude of mountains and waterfalls'. Where he had, as Leigh Hunt wrote in his *Autobiography*, 'luxuriated on the Isle of Wight', 'the lakes and mountains of the north . . . he beheld with an epic eye'.

Walking through Scotland, Keats turned his eye away for a moment from the landscape, and towards the people; 'Scenery is fine', he had written to Bailey that March, 'but human nature is finer', and to Fanny Brawne he wrote the following August, 'I am getting a great dislike of the picturesque.' The landscape, he saw, was inseparable from the life within it, and its austerity was mirrored in the poverty and squalor of its inhabitants. Description of external appearances, therefore, was less important to the poet than the patterns of mood and ideas that are evoked. The subterranean solemnity of Fingal's Cave, for example, which, he admitted in trying to describe it to Tom, 'can only be represented by a first-rate drawing', became the home of the fallen Titans in 'Hyperion':

> It was a den where no insulting light
> Could glimmer on their tears . . .
> Crag jutting forth to crag, and rocks that seem'd
> Ever as if just rising from a sleep,
> Forehead to forehead held their monstrous horns;
> And thus in thousand hugest phantasies
> Made a fit roofing to this nest of woe.'

The tour exhausted Keats physically, and he was forced to return alone to England upon their reaching Inverness on 7 August. But it had, he felt, been a success; 'I should not have consented to myself these four Months tramping in the highlands', he wrote to Bailey from Inverary, 'but that I thought it would give me more experience, rub off more Prejudice, use [me] to more hardship, identify finer scenes load me with grander Mountains, and strengthen more my reach in Poetry, than would stopping at home among Books even though I should reach Homer.'

JOHN DOWNMAN (1750-1824)

95 *A Series of sketches on the spot made by J.
Downman when he took a Tour to the Lakes
in Westmoreland and Cumberland. 1812'*
1812
*By Courtesy of the Board of Trustees
of the Victoria & Albert Museum*

Downman earned his living as a portrait painter, but
as a young man he had painted landscapes in Rome
(with Joseph Wright of Derby). One of his closest
friends was Francis Towne. The album recalls his
journey through the Lakes to Keswick, where he was
to paint the portrait of Robert Southey. The views
include Penrith, Ullswater, Windermere, Thirlmere,
Derwentwater, Buttermere and Crummockwater, and
conclude with a pencil sketch of Greta Hall, Keswick
where Southey lived. These thirty-three sketches were
mounted and bound, probably by Downman himself,
for his friend, John Parry of Wrexham.

JOHN GLOVER (1767-1849)

96 *Lancaster – After Sunset*
Watercolour, 27.3 x 40 cms
R.E Alton, MC

Keats and Brown began their walking tour at
Lancaster, where they arrived by coach on Thursday,
25 June 1818. From there they travelled to the Lake
District by way of Bolton-le-Sands, Burton, Endmoor
and Kendal. 'imagine me setting out from Lancaster,'
Brown wrote in his account of the trip (published in
1840), 'accompanied by a dear and lamented friend,
each with his knapsack on his back, to enjoy the
scenery of Cumberland and Westmoreland, in our
way to the Highlands of Scotland'. Lancaster, the

County Town, a busy market dominated by the
castle with its courts and prison, was in the midst of
a national election, and full of the prospects ahead of
them, they did not linger. Brown wrote of their leaving: 'we rejoiced to be out of that city, at the time of a
general election, where "the aspiring blood of Lancaster" deprived us of all comfort. There we had to
wait two hours for our promised dinner; and were
then told—"Not a bed in the house, gentlemen!"'
Coming out of the city they came across the first of
several local comments, from a labourer: '"There go
a couple of gentlemen!—having nothing to do, they
are finding out hard work for themselves!"'

JAMES BOURNE (1773-1854)

97 *Windermere*
Watercolour, 26 x 37 cms
The Wordsworth Trust

Keats's first view of Windermere impressed him
deeply; 'there is no such things as time and space' he
wrote to Tom on 25 June, 'which by the way came
forcibly upon me on seeing for the first hour the Lake
and Mountains of Winander—I cannot describe
them—they surpass my expectation—beautiful
water—shores and islands green to the marge—
mountains all round up to the clouds . . . the two
views we had of it are of the most noble tenderness—
they can never fade away—they make one forget the
divisions of life; age, youth, poverty and riches; and
refine one's sensual vision into a sort of north star
which can never cease to be open lidded and stedfast
over the wonders of the great Power.' The sublimity
was, however, spoiled by 'disfigurements': 'the miasma
of London', the fashionable visitors and the contami-
nated 'borderers' that surrounded the lake itself.

Thomas Sunderland (1744-1828)
98 *View over Windermere from Ecclerigg*
Pencil, pen and watercolour, 32.7 x 45.4 cms
Whitworth Art Gallery

Keats and Brown would have seen this view, from
Ecclerigg, on their way to Ambleside, along the eastern shore of the lake: 'We walked to Ambleside yesterday along the border of Winandermere' he wrote
to Tom on the 27th, 'all beautiful with wooded shores
and Islands—our road was a winding lane, wooded
on each side, and green overhead, full of floxgloves—
every now and then a glimpse of the Lake, and all the
while Kirkstone and other large hills nestled together
in a sort of grey black mist.'

John Bernard Gilpin (1701-1776)
99 *The Falls at Ambleside*
Pencil and wash, 27.2 x 36 cms
The Wordsworth Trust

Keats's response to Stock Ghyll, the falls at Ambleside
was a deep conception of the power of nature over
the mind. He wrote to Tom:

> First we stood a little below the head about half
> way down the first fall, buried deep in trees, and
> saw it streaming down two more descents to the
> depth of near fifty feet—then we went on a jut of
> rock nearly level with the fall-head, where the first
> fall was above us, and the third below our feet
> still—at the same time we saw that the water was
> divided by a sort of cataract island on whose other
> side burst a glorious stream—then the thunder
> and the freshness. At the same time the different
> falls have as different characters; the first darting
> down the slate-rock like an arrow; the second

> spreading out like a fan—the third dashed into a
> mist—and the one on either side of the rock a sort
> of mixture of all of these. We afterwards moved
> away a space, and saw nearly the whole more
> mild, streaming silverly through the trees. What
> astonishes me more than any thing is the tone, the
> coloring, the slate, the stone, the moss, the rock-
> weed; or, if I may so say, the intellect, the counte-
> nance of such places. The space, the magnitude of
> mountains and waterfalls are well imagined before
> one sees them; but this countenance or intellectual
> tone must surpass every imagination and defy any
> remembrance. I shall learn poetry here and shall
> henceforth write more than ever, for the abstract
> endeavour of being able to add a mite to that mass
> of beauty which is harvested from these grand
> materials, by the finest spirits, and put into ether-
> ial existence for the relish of one's fellows. I cannot
> think with Hazlitt that these scenes make man
> appear little. I never forgot my stature so com-
> pletely—I live in the eye; and my imagination,
> surpassed, is at rest.

Cat. 100

Cat. 101

FRANCIS TOWNE (C. 1740-1816)
100 Ambleside
1786
Pen and watercolour, 15.9 x 35.2 cms
Whitworth Art Gallery

Having seen the falls before breakfast, Keats and
Brown, full of the desire to catch Wordsworth, did
not stay in Ambleside, but pressed on for Rydal.
Between Towne's visit and that of Keats, the significant change was the increase in large gentlemen's
homes: Brathay Hall, Calgarth Hall, Croft Lodge,
Iveing Cottage and Green Bank.

FRANCIS TOWNE
101 Rydal Water
Signed and dated 1789
Watercolour, 15.7 x 23.7 cms
*By Courtesy of the Board of Trustees
of the Victoria & Albert Museum*

Towne's drawing shows Loughrigg across Rydal
Water. 'It [Rydal] did not greatly please us', wrote
Brown, 'it is small; besides, there is not enough wood
about it. A little onward, as we looked from a height,
it came admirably into view; and the number of
reeds, which I disliked while passing, gave a shadowing in of the banks which had a good effect.'

BENJMAMIN ROBERT HAYDON
102 William Wordsworth (1770-1850)
Pencil, 44.5 x 31.1 cms
Study for *Christ's Entry into Jerusalem*
The Wordsworth Trust

Illustrated in colour on p. 7

This brilliant life-size portrait, hidden until 1993 for
over one hundred years in a private collection, is
arguably Haydon's finest work. Hazlitt, who would
know it since it hung in Haydon's studio, praised it in
his essay *On my First Acquaintance with Poets* (1825):

> The next day Wordsworth arrived from Bristol at
> Coleridge's cottage. I think I see him now. He
> answered in some degree to his friend's description
> of him, but was more gaunt and Don Quixote-
> like. He was quaintly dressed (according to the

costume of that unconstrained period) in a brown
fustian jacket and striped pantaloons. There was
something of a roll, a lounge in his gait, not
unlike his own Peter Bell. There was a severe,
worn pressure of thought about his temples, a fire
in his eye (as if he saw something in objects more
than the outward appearance), an intense high
narrow forehead, a Roman nose, cheeks furrowed
by strong purpose and feeling, and a convulsive
inclination to laughter about the mouth, a good
deal at variance with the solemn, stately expression
of the rest of his face. Chantry's bust wants the
marking traits; but he was teazed into making it
regular and heavy: Haydon's head of him, introduced into the Entrance of Christ into Jerusalem
is the most like his drooping weight of thought
and expression.

Above the 'drooping weight' of Wordsworth's head
Haydon introduced the 'very fine head' of Keats, as
part of the crowd watching Christ enter Jerusalem.

103 Letter from Wordsworth to B.R. Haydon
16 January 1820
*The London Borough of Camden from the
Collections at Keats House, Hampstead*

Wordsworth is congratulating Haydon on the completion of *Christ's Entry into Jerusalem*: '[I] congratulate you with all my heart on the completion of your
Picture; of which I hear from our common Friends
the Beaumonts the most excellent accounts. Indeed
they speak of it in the highest terms'. His own admiration of Haydon's powers of portraiture (which
Haydon tended to scorn as a minor occupation next
to historical painting) is evidenced by his approval of
the chalk drawing of him that Haydon had done:
'Your drawing is much admired as a work of art;
some think it a stodgy likeness; but in general it is
not deemed so—for my own part I am proud to pos-
sess it as a mark of your regard, and for its own mer-
its.' With his mind perhaps on their group portrait in
Christ's Entry, Wordsworth then enquires after Keats –
like Byron and Shelley, he had·a high opinion of
Keats's talents, but he had a distaste for his circle:
'How is Keates, he is a youth of promise too great
for the sorry company he keeps.'

WILLIAM WESTALL (1781-1850)
104   The Garden at Rydal Mount
1831
Watercolour, 11.5 x 13.1 cms
The Wordsworth Trust

'We slept at Ambleside not above two Miles from Rydal the Residence of Wordsworth', Keats wrote to George and Georgiana Keats on 27 June 1818. 'We ate a Monstrous Breakfast . . . (which by the way we do every morning) and after it proceeded to the Wordsworths. He was not at home nor was any Member of his family—I was much disappointed. I wrote a note for him and stuck it up over what I knew must be Miss Wordsworth's Portrait and set forth again . . .'

Keats had already expressed to Tom his disappointment at Wordsworth's apparent separation from the landscape when, at Bowness, he enquired after him: 'I enquired of the waiter Wordsworth—he said he knew him, and that he had been here a few days ago, canvassing for the Lowthers. What think you of that—Wordsworth versus Brougham!! Sad—sad—sad—and yet the family has been his friend always. What can we say? . . . Lord Wordsworth, instead of being in retirement, has himself and his house full in the thick of fashionable visitors quite convenient to be pointed at all the summer long.' However, in a later letter to his brothers Keats made it clear that any personal differences between him and Wordsworth took second place to the latter's power as a poet: he wrote to them on 21 February: 'I am sorry that Wordsworth has left a bad impression wherever he visited in Town—by his egotism, Vanity and bigotry—yet he is a great Poet if not a Philosopher.'

DAVID LYONS
105   Rydal Falls
June, 1984
Photograph
The Wordsworth Trust

Guided by an unnamed old man, Keats and Brown visited the falls at Rydal after leaving Rydal Mount. Brown recalled the first as 'not so grand as that at Ambleside', but perhaps 'it was better for a picture'. Guided to a second waterfall, Brown was again dismissive: 'Our old man then led us to another, which he called—"the beauty of the world!" It had nothing sublime about it, however beautiful it deserves to be called. The fall itself is a trifle. Its effect depends on being viewed through the window of a summer-house, and having a little bridge thrown over it. The date on the summer-house is 1617.'

The date 1617 is on the wainscotting of the building, which was taken from an earlier construction; the hut was in fact built by Sir Daniel Fleming at the close of 1668. Its purpose was to establish a grotto for contemplation. Its change into a painters' hut takes place during the Eighteenth Century. It is no surprise that the shelter it afforded stimulated many artists to paint or draw these falls – Joseph Farington, Copleston Warre Bampfylde, Francis Towne, John Constable and Joseph Wright of Derby.

John White Abbott (1763-1851)
106   Grasmere, Helm Crag
Watercolour, 18.7 x 29.4 cms
The Wordsworth Trust

The 'beautiful Vale' of Grasmere, as Keats described it, made a better impression than Rydal. 'Grasmere lake . . . is far preferable', writes Brown, 'The opposite shore is beautiful. Mr Wordsworth formerly had a house there.' Helm Crag made a particular impression: 'Some whimsically, though naturally disposed stones on the summit of the mountain', observed Brown, 'certainly suggest the idea of a gigantic old woman sitting there'. 'I have seen Kirkstone, Loughrigg and Silver How', wrote Keats to George and Georgiana on 27 June, 'and discovered without a hint "that ancient woman seated on Helm Craig"'. He is quoting from Wordsworth's poem, 'To Joanna':

> The Rock, like something starting from a sleep,
> Took up the Lady's voice, and laughed again;
> That ancient Woman seated on Helm-Crag
> Was ready with her cavern.

William Green (1761-1823)
107   Grasmere looking towards Loughrigg
Watercolour, 13.9 x 20.2 cms
The Wordsworth Trust

Turning from Helm Crag, Keats and Brown then took the opportunity to view Grasmere from the north, looking towards Loughrigg. 'The finest landscape we enjoyed in this stage was then looking back on Grasmere' Brown writes. Perhaps they were particularly pleased by the surrounding woods (sadly lacking at Rydal); shown clearly in Green's picture, they were shortly to be felled, to the dismay of the Wordsworths, for they had been favourite walking places.

William Green
108   Thirlmere
Watercolour, 13.9 x 20.2 cms
The Wordsworth Trust

Climbing up Dunmail Raise out of Grasmere, and so entering Cumberland, Keats and Brown headed for Keswick via Thirlmere. Keats describes it as 'a defile in the Mountains', Brown as 'a pretty place, just within Cumberland, we had to walk through a defile of treeless mountains, probably the pass which in former times, served as a protection to either county.'

Cat. 107

Cat. 108

JOHN CONSTABLE (1776-1837)

109 Helvellyn
21 September [1806]
Watercolour, 19.7 x 36.5 cms
The Wordsworth Trust

On 27 June 1818 Keats wrote a letter to his brother and sister-in-law from the foot of Helvellyn, 'whose summit is out of sight four Miles off rise above rise'. The next day, after sleeping at the Nag's Head Inn at Wythburn, his and Brown's intention to climb it was frustrated by mist. However their disappointment was allieviated by the prospect of Skiddaw ahead of them.

During his one and only visit to the Lakes, in late August, September and early October 1806, Constable produced over eighty drawings. From this outburst of amazing independent creativity, it is disappointing that no known finished oils survive, though four were exhibited at the British Institution in 1808 and 1809.

JOHN BAVERSTOCK KNIGHT (1785-1859)

110 Derwentwater, Cumberland
Watercolour, 28 x 47 cms
By Courtesy of the Board of Trustees of the Victoria & Albert Museum

JAMES BOURNE

111 Bassenthwaite
Watercolour, 12.8 x 20.1 cms
The Wordsworth Trust

On 28 June Keats and Brown walked around Derwentwater, taking in the falls of Lodore on the way. The approach to Derwentwater, and the subsequent view of Bassenthwaite, seems to have surpassed the one to Windermere, perhaps because of the added pleasure of trees and a shady road. Keats wrote to Tom: 'The approach to Derwent Water surpassed Winandermere—it is richly wooded & shut in with rich-toned mountains'. To George and Georgiana he wrote: 'The Approach to derwent water is rich and magnificent beyond any means of conception—the Mountains all round sublime and graceful and rich in colour—Woods and wooded Islands here and there— and at the same time in the distance among Mountains of another aspect we see Bassenthwaite.'

JOHN BAVERSTOCK KNIGHT

112 Lodore, Derwentwater
Watercolour, 27.6 x 47 cms
By Courtesy of the Board of Trustees of the Victoria & Albert Museum

The falls at Lodore were the third major falls in the Lake District that Keats visited, – first Ambleside and then Rydal: none perhaps equalled his excitement at seeing the falls at Ambleside. Of Lodore he wrote:

> I had an easy climb among the streams, about the fragments of Rocks & should have got I think to the summit, but unfortunately I was damped by slipping one leg into a squashy hole. There is no great body of water, but the accompaniment is delightful; for it ooses out from a cleft in perpendicular Rocks, all fledged with Ash & other beautiful trees.

JOSHUA CRISTALL (C. 1767-1847)

113 *Borrowdale, Cumberland*
Signed and dated 1814
Watercolour, 34.9 x 40.3 cms
*By Courtesy of the Board of Trustees
of the Victoria & Albert Museum*

Illustrated in colour on p. 13

JOSHUA CRISTALL

114 *Borrowdale, Cumberland*
Signed and dated 1824
Watercolour, 19.3 x 27.5 cms
*By Courtesy of the Board of Trustees
of the Victoria & Albert Museum*

Cristall made his tour of the Lake District in 1805. Here he has chosen to depict not mountains and lakes, but the more intimate scenery of shores and woods. Similarly, the Grecian figures are not dwarfed by the landscape but have an equal prominence. Indeed, they are central to the serene, arcadian atmosphere of both drawings.

EDWARD DAYES (1763-1804)

115 *Derwentwater and Skiddaw*
Watercolour, 28.1 x 39.8 cms
The Wordsworth Trust

On 29 June, rising at four in the morning, Keats and Brown, accompanied by a guide, ascended Skiddaw. Keats gave his account of the climb to Tom:

> It promised all along to be fair, & we had fagged & tugged nearly to the top, when at halfpast six there came a mist upon us & shut out the view; we did not however lose anything by it, we were high enough without mist, to see the coast of Scotland; the Irish sea; the hills beyond Lancaster; & nearly to the large ones of Cumberland & Westmoreland, particularly Helvellyn & Scawfell. It grew colder & colder as we ascended, & we were glad at about three parts of the way to taste a little rum which the Guide brought with him, mixed, mind ye with mountain water, I took two glasses going & one returning . . . We went up with two others, very good sort of fellows. All felt on arising into the cold air, that same elevation, which a cold bath gives one—I felt as if I were going to a Tournament.

Daye's view of Derwentwater and Skiddaw is taken from Barrow Common. The rough vigorous foreground contrasts with the more exquisite distant view, which gains formality through his shadowing Skiddaw in the lake. He has a characteristic manner of catching the play of light on the landscape, giving a notion of its clarity by a brilliant definition of detail on the background hills.

JOSEPH FARINGTON (1747-1821)

116 Carlisle from across the River Eden
?1788
Pencil, pen and wash, 32 x 46.2 cms
Whitworth Art Gallery

Keats wrote from Carlisle to Tom:

> July 1st—We are this morning at Carlisle . . . The Cathedral does not appear very fine. The Castle is very Ancient, & of Brick. The City is very various, old whitewashed narrow streets; broad red brick ones more modern—I will tell you anon, whether the inside of the Cathedral is worth looking at. It is built of a sandy red stone or Brick. We have now walked 114 miles & are merely a little tired in the thighs & a little blistered.

117 Letter from John Keats to Thomas Keats
10-14 July 1818
The British Library Board

Keats writes to his brother Tom in brown iron-based ink on the large, coarse paper that he used for his travel letters. Beginning to write at Ballantrae on 10 July he traces the journey from Stranraer, through Ayshire to Glasgow, where they arrived on the 13th. He begins by stressing the importance of travel as a personal experience, rather than as a thing read – 'I shall endeavour that you may follow our steps in this walk—it would be uninteresting in a Book of Travels—it can not be interesting but by my having gone though.' For what is important is not merely the landscape itself, but the observer's imaginative response to it, giving oneself an 'idea' of what is seen with the eye. Keats describes his own reaction on seeing Ailsa Rock:

> I descried in the Sea Ailsa Rock 940 feet high—it was 15 Miles distant and seemed close upon us— The effect of Ailsa with the peculiar perspective of the Sea in connection with the ground we stood on, and the misty rain then falling gave me a complete Idea of a deluge—Ailsa struck me very suddenly—really I was a little alarmed . . .

After a lengthy discourse on the differences of Scotsmen and Irishmen, they approach Burns's cottage, Keats wondering why the grand scenery 'did not Beckon Burns to some grand attempt at Epic':

> We drank some Toddy to Burns's Memory with an old Man who knew Burns—damn him—and damn his Anecdotes—he was a great bore—it was impossible for a Southren to understand above 5 words in a hundred—There was something good in his description of Burns's melancholy the last time he saw him.

After meeting a drunken admirer of Edmund Kean ('He said he had seen him at Glasgow "in Othello in the Jew, I me an er, er, er, the Jew in Shylock"'), they arrived in the city Glasgow ('a very fine one') and, as at Lancaster, attracted the attention of the local populace:

> We entered Glasgow last Evening under the most oppressive Stare a body could feel—When we had crossed the Bridge Brown look'd back and said its whole population had turned to wonder at us— we came on till a drunken Man came up to me— I put him off with my Arm—he returned all up in Arms saying aloud that 'he had seen all foreigners bu-u-u-t he never saw the like o' me—I was obliged to mention the word Officer and Police before he would desist.

Ah! ken ye what I met the day
Out oure the Mountains
A coming down by craggies grey
An mossie fountains
A goud hair'd Marie yeve I pray
Ane minute's guessing
For that I met upon the way
To past expressing.

As I stood where a rocky brig
A torrent crosses
I spied upon a misty rig
A troup o' Horses—
And as they trotted down the glen
I sped to meet them
To see if I might know the Men
To stop and greet them.

First Willie on his sleek mare came
At canting gallop
His long hair rustled like a flame
On board a shallop.
Then came his brother Rab and then
Young Peggy's Mither
And Peggy too—down the glen
They went togither.

I saw her wrappit in her hood
Fra wind and raining—
~~There was a blush upon~~
Her cheek was flush wi timi'd blood
Gi' mirth and warming—
She turn'd her dazed head full oft
For there her Brothers
Came riding with her Bridegroom soft
An' gaiety others.

Young Tam came up an' eyed me quick
With reddened cheek
Braw Tam was daffed like a chick
He coud na speak—
Ah Marie they are all gaun hame
Through blustering weather
An' every heart is full on flame
An' light as feather
Ah! Marie they are all gane hame
Fra happy wedding
Whilst I ... is it not a shame?
Sad tears am shedding—

The Rain we feared held up bravely
And it has been fu fine this day...

My dear Tom,   Ballantrae July

The reason for my writing these lines was that Brown wanted to impose a Galloway song upon Dilke—but it wont do. The subject I got from meeting a wedding just as we came down into this place—where I am afraid we shall be emprisoned awhile by the weather—Yesterday we came 27 Miles from Stranraer—entered Ayrshire a little beyond Cairn, and had our path through a delightful country. I shall endeavour that you may follow our steps in this walk—it would be uninteresting in a Book of Travels—it can not be interesting but by my having gone through it. When we left Cairn our Road lay half way up the sides of a green mountainous shore, full of Clefts of verdure and eternally varying—sometimes up sometimes down, and over little Bridges going across green chasms of moss rock and trees—winding about every where. After two or three Miles of this we turned suddenly into a magnificent glen finely wooded in Parts—seven Miles long with a Mountain Stream winding down the Midst—full of cottages in the most happy Situations—the sides of the Hills covered with sheep—the effect of cattle lowing I never had so finely—At the end we had a great deal ascent and got among the tops of the Mountains whence In a little time I descried in the Sea Ailsa Rock 940 feet high—it was 15 Miles distant and seemed close upon us— The effect of ailsa with the peculiar perspective of the Sea in connection with the ground we stood on, and the misty rain then falling gave me a complete Idea of a deluge—Ailsa struck me very suddenly—really I was a little alarmed—Thus far had I written before we set out this morning—Now we are at Girvan 13 Miles north of Ballantrae Our Walk has been along a more grand shore to day than yesterday—Ailsa beside us all the way—From the heights we could see quite at home Cantire and the large Mountains of ~~Arran~~ Annan one of the Hebrides—We are in comfortable Quarters...

Cat. 117

THE
VISION ;
OR,
HELL, PURGATORY,
AND
PARADISE,
OF
DANTE ALIGHIERI.

TRANSLATED BY
THE REV. H. F. CARY, A.M.

IN THREE VOLUMES.
VOL. I.

London :
PRINTED FOR THE AUTHOR,
BY J. BARFIELD,
Printer to his Royal Highness the Prince Regent.
1814.

tion to the larger edition, Cary wrote that this minis-cule set of volumes 'was printed in so small a charac-ter as to deter a numerous class of readers from perus-ing it', but clearly the small size was convenient to Keats's needs on the walking tour.

J.M.W. TURNER (1775-1851)
119 *Inverary Pier, Loch Fyne, Morning*
Published 1 June 1811
Engraver's proof
*By Courtesy of the Board of Trustees
of the Victoria & Albert Museum*

DANTE ALIGHIERI (1265-1321)
118 *The Vision; or, Hell, Purgatory, and Paradise*
London: Taylor and Hessey, 1814
The British Library Board

This miniature (32mo) edition of Dante's *Divine Comedy*, was Keats's reading material during the walk-ing tour. He had evidently been advised to read Dante by Benjamin Bailey, for in a letter to him of 10 July 1818 Keats writes: 'if I take any book with me it shall be those minute volumes of carey for they will go into the aptest corner'. Again, on 18,22 July 1818 he writes to Bailey from Inverary: 'You say I must study Dante—well the only Books I have with me are those three little Volumes. I read that fine passage you men-tioned a few days ago . . .'

On his return Keats began to write his projected epic, 'Hyperion'. This, and more especially its revised version, 'The Fall of Hyperion: A Dream', show the influence of both Dante and Milton (whom Keats was quoting in his travel letters).

Cary's translation was published, as was Keats's later work, by John Taylor and James Hessey, at the recom-mendation of Samuel Taylor Coleridge. Cary had published this tiny edition at his own expense in 1814, and it soon fell into obscurity. As part of the agree-ment with Taylor & Hessey, the remaining unsold copies were reissued by the publishers under their own imprint. They then published a more sumptuous edition, with a lengthened introduction, footnotes and an index, and type twice the size. In an introduc-

CHARLES TURNER (1773-1857)
AFTER J.M.W. TURNER
120 *Inverary Castle and Town, Scotland*
Published 1 January 1816
Engraving (1st published state)
*By Courtesy of the Board of Trustees
of the Victoria & Albert Museum*

Charles Turner, one of the most eminent of English engravers, was particularly successful as an interpreter of J.M.W. Turner, for whom he engraved twenty-three numbers of the *Liber Studiorum*.

JOSHUA CRISTALL
121 *Fishing Boats with Nets Drying, Loch Fyne*
1833
Pencil and watercolour, 31.7 x 47.1 cms
Whitworth Art Gallery

Keats's formative tour of Scotland in 1818 was preceded by those made by Joshua Cristall in the same year, and by J.M.W. Turner in 1801. Each would record their immediate observations – Keats in his travel letters and occasional poems, Cristall and Turner in their sketches, and just as many of the clear images found in Keats's letters would find their way into his mature poetry, so Cristall and Turner, years later, would work their sketches up into finished works: watercolours, oil paintings and engravings.

Keats recorded his visit in a letter to his brother Tom of 18 July 1818:

> Last Evening we came round to the end of Loch Fine to Inverary—the Duke of Argyle's Castle is very modern magnificent and more so from the

place it is in—the woods seem old enough to remember two or three changes in the Crags about them—the Lake was beautiful and there was a Band at a distance by the Castle.

The site was a favourite with all types of travellers in the early part of the Nineteenth century; 'hardly any place can vie with Inverary' maintains *The Traveller's Guide to Scotland* (third edition, 1806), going on to note that 'it has become so much a resort of travellers, of late, that any description is almost unnecessary.'

JOSHUA CRISTALL
122 *Highland Drovers, near Inverary*
Watercolour, 54.6 x 43.2 cms
By Courtesy of the Board of Trustees of the Victoria & Albert Museum

Illustrated in colour on p. 100

Cristall has placed a group of colourful, statuesque figures in the foreground, their size and composure in balance with the waterfall and mountains behind them.

JOSHUA CRISTALL

123 *Landscape with Cattle and Mountains*
Signed and dated 1836
Watercolour, 17.8 x 28 cms
*By Courtesy of the Board of Trustees
of the Victoria & Albert Museum*

Unusually, Cristall has made a landscape without the balancing accompaniment of figures.

JOHN WHITE ABBOT

124 *Fall at Cladish*
Signed and dated 1791
Watercolour, 19.1 x 24.2 cms
*By Courtesy of the Board of Trustees
of the Victoria & Albert Museum*

Keats wrote to Tom from Cladich on 18 July, but makes no special mention of the falls there. Since his first experience of waterfalls and mountainous scenery, he found himself becoming more used to large-scale landscapes. He wrote to Benjamin Bailey on the same day:

> 'By this time I am comparatively a mountaineer—I have been among wilds and Mountains too much to break out much about their Grandeur. I have fed upon Oat cake—not long enough to be very much attached to it—The first Mountains I saw, though not so large as some I have since seen, weighed very solemnly upon me. The effect is wearing away—yet I like them mainely'.

WILLIAM DANIELL (1769-1837)

125 *In Fingal's Cave, Staffa*
London: Longmans and Co., 1 July 1817
Acquatint
The Wordsworth Trust

Keats and Brown came to Staffa on 24 July. Keats wrote to Tom:

> I am puzzled how to give you an Idea of Staffa. It can only be represented by a first rate drawing—One may compare the surface of the Island to a roof—this roof is supported by grand pillars of basalt standing together as thick as honey combs. The finest thing is Fingal's Cave—it is entirely a hollowing out of Basalt Pillars. Suppose now the giants who rebelled against Jove had taken a whole Mass of black Columns and bound them together like bunches of matches—and then with immense Axes had made a cavern in the body of these columns—of course the roof and floor must be composed of the broken ends of the Columns—such is Fingal's Cave except that the Sea has done the work of excavations and is continually dashing

there—so that we walk along the sides of the cave on the pillars which are left as if for convenient Stairs—the roof is arched somewhat gothic wise and the length of some of the entire pillars is 50 feet—About the island you might seat an army of Men each on a pillar—The length of the Cave is 120 feet and from its extremity the view into the sea through the large Arch at the entrance—the colour of the columns is a sort of black with a lurking gloom of purple therin—For solemnity and grandeur it far surpasses the finest Cathedrall—At the extremity of the Cave there is a small perforation into another cave, at which the waters meeting and buffetting each other there is sometimes produced a report as of a canon heard as far as Iona which must be 12 Miles—As we approached in the boat there was such a fine swell of the sea that the pillars appeared rising immediately out of the crystal—But it is impossible to describe it.

WILLIAM HENRY FISK (1827-84)
126 *Ben Nevis from above Navin*
Signed and dated 1868
Watercolour, 29.9 x 59.7 cms
*By Courtesy of the Board of Trustees
of the Victoria & Albert Museum*

Though Keats and Brown continued to Inverness after Ben Nevis, their reaching its summit on 2 August, in heavy mist, was in many ways the climax of the tour. Increasingly, Keats's thoughts had been turning towards the south, and his impressions of the mountainous scenery were every day becoming more thoughtful and judged. On the summit, depressed by the mist around him, he wrote the following dark sonnet:

> Read me a lesson, Muse, and speak it loud
>   Upon the top of Nevis, blind in mist!
> I look into the chasms, and a shroud
>   Vaporous doth hide them; just so much I wist
> Mankind do know of hell: I look o'erhead,
>   And there is sullen mist; even so much
> Mankind can tell of heaven: mist is spread
>   Before the earth beneath me; even such,
> Even so vague is man's sight of himself.
>   Here are the craggy stones beneath my feet;
> Thus much I know, that, a poor witless elf,
>   I tread on them; that all my eye doth meet
> Is mist and crag—not only on this height,
> But in the world of thought and mental might.

Cat. 127 John Keats by Joseph Severn, 1819

6. Hampstead, 1818-20

Returning from Scotland, Keats was faced with a new family tragedy. Tom, now in the last stages of tuberculosis, died on 1 December 1818. On top of this, the harsh reviews of *Endymion* had appeared, and his peace of mind was threatened by his growing love for Fanny Brawne. Yet as his outward circumstances grew more complicated, his poetry matured. For with his increasing technical mastery he was able to translate these circumstances into verse: 'I live under an everlasting restraint', he wrote in his first letter George and Georgiana Keats since Tom's death, 'Never relieved except when I am composing—so I will write away'.

'Hyperion' showed a new concentration and immediacy in Keats's writing after the 'sober-sadness' of 'Isabella'. The series of 'gothic' poems he wrote after a visit to Chichester in January 1819 - 'The Eve of St. Agnes', 'The Eve of St. Mark' and 'La Belle Dame sans Merci' - recreate the world of sensual imagery and young love, but this time it is held by a tight narrative line, and shown against the backdrop of a darker vision. Pre-eminent are the great Odes that he wrote whilst at Wentworth Place in the spring of 1819 - 'To Psyche', 'To a Nightingale', 'On a Grecian Urn', 'On Melancholy' - , and then later at Winchester - 'To Autumn'. Here the concentration of thought and density of expression, set against the formality of tone and construction, created a perfect vehicle for his meditations upon impermanence and the co-existence of pain, sorrow and delight. Finally, 'Lamia' and the revised 'Hyperion' ('The Fall of Hyperion. A Dream'), are largely successful attempts to sustain these elements within a longer narrative.

When these poems were published by Taylor and Hessey in 1820, under the title *Lamia, Isabella, The Eve of St. Agnes and other Poems*, Keats was too ill with consumption to give much attention to the book's fortunes. 'Nothing could have in all its circumstances fallen out worse for me than the last year has done,' wrote Keats to his brother and sister-in-law on 12 November 1819, 'or could be more damping to my poetical talent.' But his talent had, on the contrary, thrived amidst the tragedy, and created poetry of a quality that belies his bitter verdict.

JOSEPH SEVERN

127 *John Keats*
1819
Oil on ivory, 10.8 x 7.9 cms
National Portrait Gallery, London

Illustrated in colour on p. 116

Severn's miniature was made in 1819, and exhibited that year. Though Keats tried to dissuade Severn from exhibiting it at the Royal Academy, he evidently became fond of it, writing to his sister Fanny that it was 'too dear' to him to let it go, and sending a 'very capital profile' by Charles Brown instead.

CHARLES WASS AFTER WILLIAM HILTON

128 *John Keats*
Stipple engraving
National Portrait Gallery, London

Illustrated on p. 17

This engraving is made from a chalk drawing done by William Hilton in 1819-20 in the home or office of John Taylor; the drawing is now lost and survives only in this version. Severn disliked it, claiming that it made Keats look like 'a sneaking fellow', but it does bear closer resemblance to Haydon's lifemask than anything by Severn himself. Hilton later made a much better-known portrait of Keats after Severn's miniature, keeping the portrait plain, unweakened by those romantic nuances of which Severn became so fond.

CHARLES ARMITAGE BROWN

129 *John Keats*
1819
Pencil, 22.9 x 41.9 cms
National Portrait Gallery, London

Illustrated in colour on back cover

Charles Brown, Keats's companion on the walking tour, was an amateur artist, and subsequent to the tour made this sketch of Keats after a sketching trip with the poet to Shanklin Church. Brown's granddaughter, to whom the portrait passed, gave the following account of its origin to Sidney Colvin in 1871:

Keats and my grandfather were sketching together; when they came in Keats was a little tired, and he half reclined in a couch or easy chair. My grandfather opened his portfolio and made this pencil copy. He was pleased with the result and kept it. Then it passed on to my father; after his death my mother gave it to me.

The circumstances of its making, as well as the character of the artist, make this one of the most lifelike portraits of the poet. Where Severn and Hilton (particularly in their later, posthumous portraits) were aiming to produce not just Keats, but their idea of what a great poet should look like for posterity, the unromantic Brown, tired after a day's sketching, was seeking to make a portrait of his friend at a particular moment. That the head is tipped back is documentary, and not, as in symbolic portraits, a suggestion that the writer sought inspiration from above. The hand and upper body are roughly done, but the head is completed with some care. The eyes, showing fatigue, nevertheless lack the rather hazy, 'inspired' look of Severn's miniature and Hilton's posthumous portrait. The hair falls untidily over the forehead, and the lips are fuller than is usual.

Brown also made two, possibly three silhouettes of Keats in 1819, one of which is illustrated below.

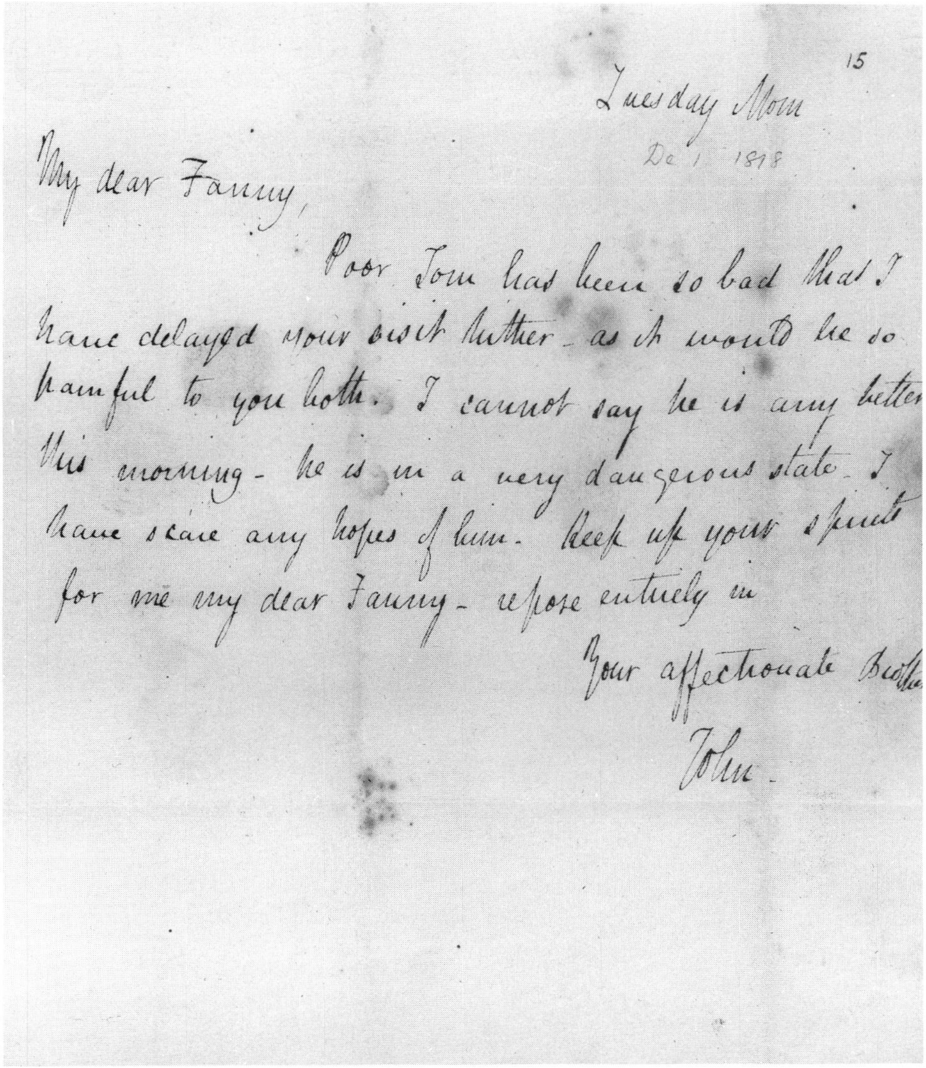

Tuesday Morn
Dec 1. 1818

My dear Fanny,

Poor Tom has been so bad that I have delayed your visit hither - as it would be so painful to you both. I cannot say he is any better this morning - he is in a very dangerous state. I have scarce any hopes of him. Keep up your spirits for me my dear Fanny - repose entirely in

Your affectionate Brother

John.

130 *Letter from John Keats to Fanny Keats*
30 November 1818
The British Library Board

'Poor Tom has been so bad that I have delayed your visit hither' writes Keats, 'as it would be so painful to you both. I cannot say he is any better this morning—he is in a very dangerous state—I have scarce any hopes of him—Keep up your spirits for me my dear Fanny'. Tom, who had been ill with consumption for months, finally died at 8 am the following morning. Keats then posted this letter to prepare her for the news.

Tom, whom George Keats claimed understood the poet better than anyone else, haunted Keats's imagination. The words 'Poor Tom' (Edgar's cry of helplessness in his assumed madness in *King Lear*) echo through his letters, and the 'Ode to a Nightingale' has the line 'Where youth grows pale, and spectre-thin, and dies'. Clearly Fanny always served as a reminder of his youngest brother – at the close of his very last letter (to Charles Brown, exactly two years later), Keats describes how Fanny 'walks about my imagination like a ghost—she is so like Tom'.

UNKNOWN ARTIST

131 *Portrait of Fanny Brawne*
Miniature (replica)
The London Borough of Camden from the
Collections at Keats House, Hampstead

UNKNOWN ARTIST

132 *Portrait of Fanny Brawne*
Silhouette
The British Library Board

In April 1819, Fanny Brawne and her mother moved
into the half of Wentworth Place owned by Charles
Dilke. Keats was thus Fanny's next-door neighbour
from October of that year to May 1820. He first refers
to her lightly in a letter to George and Georgiana
Keats that December:

> Shall I give you Miss Brawn? . . . she is not seven-
> teen—but she is ignorant—monstrous in her
> behaviour flying out in all directions, calling peo-
> ple such names—that I was forced lately to make
> use of the term *Minx*—this is I think not from
> any innate vice but from a penchant she has for
> acting stylishly. I am however tired of such style
> and shall decline any more of it.

Yet Keats, who had always maintained his need to be
unmarried for the sake of poetry, later wrote to her:
'from the very first week I knew you I wrote myself
your vassal'. His happiness would now be tied perma-
nently and painfully to earthly circumstance; a 'sweet
unrest' would be its highest state, and this, as his
yearning for it suggests in the 'Bright Star' sonnet
of April 1819, has no possibilities of lasting.

Keats and Fanny were formally engaged in October
1819. Between August and September the following
year, desperately ill, he stayed with the Brawnes. He
last saw Fanny on 13 September, and henceforth neither wrote to her nor read her letters. As he explained
to Charles Brown from Naples on 1 November, when
'my imagination is horridly vivid about her—I see
her—I hear her', 'I am afraid to write to her—to
receive a letter from her—to see her hand writing
would break my heart—even to hear of her any how,
to see her name written would be more than I could
bear.'

Many of Keats's friends seem to have disapproved of
Fanny Brawne, who twelve years later married Louis
Lindo, and early biographers tended to see her as
somehow unworthy of the great poet. Keats's private
love-letters are often possessive, jealous and demanding, but always strong (sometimes vehement, as he

himself admitted) in their expression of love. What is clear is that the love-affair contributed towards Keats's ever-maturing poetic vision of light and shade held in tense, sometimes painful balance.

133 A Lock of Keats's Hair
The British Library Board

Most contemporary accounts of Keats's appearance contain a description of his hair. Leigh Hunt describes it as 'of a brown colour, was fine, and hung in natural ringlets'; 'His hair was beautiful' Benjamin Bailey wrote to Richard Monckton Milnes in 1849, 'a fine brown, rather than auburn, I think; & if you placed your hand upon his head, the silken curls felt like the rich plumage of a bird.' Cowden Clarke also corrected Milnes's description of Keats's hair as 'auburn', marking in his copy, 'Light brown, not auburn at all.'

UNKNOWN ARTIST
134 Wentworth Place
1890
Photograph
The London Borough of Camden from the Collections at Keats House, Hampstead

Wentworth Place (named after its creator, Charles Wentworth Dilke) was originally built as two adjoining, but separate dwellings. Dilke and Charles Brown moved into their respective halves in 1816, with Brown taking the smaller, eastern side of the house, and Dilke taking the larger western side. Keats shared Brown's part of the house from the middle of October 1819 until May 1820, and while living there he wrote

his great odes.

Dilke had moved out in April 1819, and his part of the house was rented by the Brawnes.

This is the earliest known photograph of Wentworth Place (now Keats House). It shows the house as it was; the fanlight above the door was blown out in the Second World War. Dimly, at the left-hand side, is the house that was the next house to Wentworth Place in Keats's time. The land was later built on.

GUIDO RENI (1575-1642)
135 Adoration of the Virgin by the patron saints of Bologna
Engraving
Courtauld Institute

Keats found the 'naked and grecian manner' of 'Hyperion' in Raphael, an insight that he came to through looking at a print of this image by Reni. He wrote to George and Georgiana Keats on 31 December 1818:

A year ago I could not understand in the slightest degree Raphael's cartoons—now I begin to see them a little—and how did I learn to do so? By seeing something done in quite an opposite spirit—I mean a picture of Guido's in which all the saints, instead of that heroic simplicity and unaffected grandeur which they inherit from Raphael, had each of them both in countenance and gesture all the canting, solemn, melodramatic mawkishness of Mackenzie's father Nicholas.

Keats reading at Wentworth Place, a posthumous portrait by Joseph Severn
(National Portrait Gallery, London)

IL TRIONFO DELLA MORTE   LE TRIOMPHE DE LA MORT

LASINIO AFTER UNKNOWN ARTIST

136   *The Triumph of Death*
1812
Stipple engraving
The British Library

Keats went on to describe to George and Georgiana a
book of prints, *Pitture al Fresco del Campo Santo di
Pisa intagliate da Carlo Lasionio*, he had recently seen
at Haydon's, one of which was *The Triumph of Death*:

> I looked over a Book of Prints taken from the fres-
> co of the Church at Milan the name of which I
> forget—in it are comprised Specimens of the first
> and second age of art in Italy—I do not think I
> ever had a greater treat out of Shakespeare—Full
> of Romance and the most tender feelings—
> magnificence of draperies beyond any I ever saw
> not excepting Raphael's—But Grotesque to a curi-
> ous pitch—yet still making up a fine whole—even
> finer to me than more accomplish'd works—as
> there was left so much room for Imagination.

The engraving places various aspects of life against a
general background of death and decay. To the left, a
hunting party look upon three open coffins, their
corpses in various states of decay. To the right of that,
angels and devils snatch at a pile of corpses, while a
grim reaper figure turns his attention threateningly to
a courtly group on the far right. Top left is a small
group of religious figures in a rural landscape, surrounded by trees and animals. Above the whole a
crowd of angels and devils compete for the departed
souls. The entire composition draws back the perspective to illustrate life and death as simultaneous aspects
of a single state - in a corner a praying man sits right
beside a devil who throws a corpse into the furnace;
in another, a corpse is held at the feet by a devil, at
the arms by an angel.

This concept of life and death inextricably together
was becoming central to Keats's maturing vision.
Poems such as 'La Belle Dame sans Merci', 'The Eve
of St. Agnes', 'Hyperion', and indeed the Odes, play
out their action against this sober, unsentimental
background.

JOHN KEATS

137 Original manuscript of 'Hyperion'
   The British Library Board

   Illustrated in colour on p. 25

'Hyperion' was probably begun around November
1818, after Keats returned from Scotland and while he
nursed his dying brother Tom. It was, as he described
it to Fanny Brawne on 25 July 1819, 'a very abstract
Poem', much pre-occupied with the processes of
change, decay and progress. The legend of Hyperion
recounts the overthrow of the majestic, changeless
deities, the Titans, at the hands of the younger gods,
led by Jove. The poem, which remained a fragment,
was to concentrate on the one Titan still remaining,
Hyperion, and the newly-created god, Apollo who
was to replace him. Keats, moving on from where he
left off at the end of *Endymion* was himself changing
in his conception of poetry: his new god of poetry,
Apollo, would know pain - 'agonies' as well as 'sovran
voices'; 'destroyings' as well as 'creations'.

After prefacing it with some new lines while at
Winchester, Keats eventually gave up the poem, no
doubt finding that the 'naked grecian manner' and
austere tone was restricting his notions of experience
and feelings. He wrote to Reynolds from Winchester
on 21 September 1819: 'I have given up Hyperion—
there were too many Miltonic inversions in it—
Miltonic verse cannot be written but in an artful or
rather artist's humour. I wish to give myself up to
other sensations. English ought to be kept up.'

138 Letter from John Keats to B.R. Haydon
   23 January 1818
   The British Library Board

It was John Taylor's original intention that *Endymion*
be published with a frontispiece by Haydon. Here
Keats, perhaps influenced by the classical images he
had seen at Haydon's and Hunt's writes that his current poem, 'Hyperion', would be better suited to
illustration:

> when that poem is done there will be a wide range
> for you—in Endymion I think you may have
> many bits of the deep and sentimental cast—the
> nature of *Hyperion* will lead me to treat it in a
> more naked and grecian Manner—and the march
> of passion and endeavour will be undeviating—

and one great contrast between them will be—that
the Hero of the written tale being mortal is led
on, like Buonaparte, by circumstance; whereas the
Apollo in Hyperion being a fore-seeing God will
shape his actions like one.

Haydon was certainly keen to illustrate *Endymion*,
taking the idea seriously enough to promise to do a
painting beforehand. Keats, writing to Taylor on the
same day as he wrote to Haydon, quotes Haydon's
saying to him:

> "When I do anything for your poem, it must be
> effectual—an honor to both of us—to hurry up a
> sketch for the season won't do. I think an engrav-
> ing from your head, from a Chalk drawing of
> mine—done with all my might—to which I
> would put my name, would answer Taylor's Idea
> more than the other indeed I am sure of it—this I
> will do & this will be effectual and as I have not
> done for it for any other human being—it will
> have an effect".

In the event, the book appeared without the proposed illustration.

JOHN CONSTABLE (1776-1837)

139 Chichester Cathedral
   Watercolour, 14 x 23.5 cms
   *By Courtesy of the Board of Trustees
   of the Victoria & Albert Museum*

Keats stayed at Chichester in the second part of
February 1819, there writing 'The Eve of St. Agnes'
and 'The Eve of St. Mark', both poems strongly
influenced by the Gothic richness of the town. As he
was to be at Winchester, Keats was delighted by the
Cathedral, also visiting the nearby Stansted Chapel.

33

The Eve of Saint Mark. 1816

~~It~~ ~~in a twice holy day~~

~~Twice holy was the sabbath day bell~~

Upon a sabbath day it fell

Twice holy was the sabbath bell,

That call'd the folk to evening prayer.

The City streets were clean and fair

From wholesome drench of April rains

And on the western window panes

The chilly sunset ~~blaz'd~~ faintly told

Of unmatured green vallies cold

Of the green thorny bloomless hedge

Of rivers new with springtide sedge

Of Primroses by sheltered rills

And daisies on the aguish hills.

Twice holy was the sabbath bell:

The silent streets were crowded well

With staid and pious companies

Warm from their fire-side oratries

And moving with demurest air

To even song and vesper prayer

John Keats, original manuscript of 'The Eve of St. Mark', contained in George Keats's notebook (Cat. 147)

140   The Indicator, 10 May 1820
The British Library Board

Containing the first publication of 'La Belle Dame sans Merci'. The poem first appears in a letter to George and Georgiana Keats of 21 April 1819, where Keats has, albeit humorously, drawn their attention to its deliberate spareness after the richness of *Endymion*:

> Why four kisses—you will say—why four because I wish to restrain the headlong impetuosity of my Muse—she would have fain said 'score' without hurting the rhyme—but we must temper the Imagination as the Critics say with Judgement. I was obliged to choose an even number that both eyes might have fair play; and to speak truly I think two a piece quite sufficient—Suppose I had said seven; there would have been three and half a piece—a very awkward affair—and well got out of on my side—

THE
ANATOMY
OF
MELANCHOLY,
WHAT IT IS, WITH ALL THE
KINDS, CAUSES, SYMPTOMES, PROGNOSTICS,
AND
SEVERAL CURES OF IT.
IN THREE PARTITIONS.
WITH THEIR SEVERAL
SECTIONS, MEMBERS, AND SUBSECTIONS,
Philosophically, Medicinally, Historically opened and cut up.
BY
DEMOCRITUS JUNIOR.
WITH
A SATYRICALL PREFACE CONDUCING TO THE FOLLOWING DISCOURSE.
The Eleventh Edition corrected.
To which is now first prefixed
AN ACCOUNT OF THE AUTHOR.
Omne tulit punctum, qui miscuit utile dulci.
VOL. I.
LONDON:
PRINTED FOR J. WALKER; R. LEA; J. CUTHELL; J. NUNN; LONGMAN AND
CO., LACKINGTON, ALLEN, AND CO., OTRIDGE AND SON; S. BAGSTER;
J. BLACK; T. HAMILTON; CRADOCK AND JOY; AND R. SAUNDERS.
1813.

ROBERT BURTON (1577-1640)

141   The Anatomy of Melancholy
London: J. Walker; R. Lea; J. Cuthell; J. Nunn; Longman and co . . . and R. Saunders, 1813
The British Library Board

Burton's *Anatomy of Melancholy* was Keats's almost constant reading during this period. From it he derived the story of Lamia, and for the nightmarish world of 'La Belle Dame sans Merci' he drew upon

Burton's account of bewildered men, melancholy abandoned lovers:

> That wandered in the woods sad all alone,
> Forsaking mens society, making great moan

they delight in floods and waters, desert places, to walk alone in orchards, gardens, private walks back-lanes. . . . He foresook the city, and lived in groves and hollow trees, upon a green bank by a brook side, by confluence of waters, all day long, and all night. . . . They are much given to weeping, and delight in waters, ponds, pools, rivers, fishing, fowling . . . they are pale of colour, slothful, apt to sleep, much troubled with the head-ach.

JOHN KEATS

142   Original Manuscript of 'Ode to a Nightingale'
Autograph manuscript
Lent by the Syndics of the Fitzwilliam Museum, Cambridge

Illustrated in colour on p. 28

The composition of this poem was described by Charles Brown:

> In the spring of 1819 a nightingale had built her nest near my house. Keats felt a tranquil and continual joy in her song; and one morning he took his chair from the breakfast-table to the grass plot under a plum-tree, where he sat for two or three hours. When he came into the house, I perceived he had some scraps of paper in his hand, and these he was quietly thrusting behind the books. On inquiry, I found these scraps, four or five in number, contained his poetic feeling on the song of our nightingale. The writing was not well legible; and it was difficult to arrange the stanzas on so many scraps. With his assistance I succeeded, and this was his *Ode to a Nightingale*, a poem which has been the delight of everyone.

Charles Wentworth Dilke later dismissed this as 'pure delusion', annotating his copy of Monckton Milnes's account in his 1848 biography with the words, 'We do not usually thrust waste paper behind books.' It is, of course, on two sheets of paper, not 'four or five', and the arrangement of the stanzas is relatively clear. The manuscript does, however, show signs of being a first draft, not only in the heavy corrections, but also in the rather haphazard way in which the paper has been used; after the false start on sheet two, Keats wrote two and a half stanzas on sheet two, turning it upside down to avoid the false start. He then, realising that the poem was becoming longer than he expected, wrote stanzas six and seven on the verso of sheet one, returning to the verso of sheet two for stanza eight ('Fearing to break the continuity of what seemed more and more a fluent process of creation, he did not return to the house, but started the next stanzas on the back of his first sheet' – Robert Gittings, *The Odes of Keats and their Earliest Known Manuscripts* (London, 1970)).

CLAUDE LORRAIN (1604/5-1682)

143 Landscape with Psyche outside the Palace of Cupid ('The Enchanted Castle')
1664
Oil on canvas, 87 x 151 cms
National Gallery, London

Illustrated in colour on p. 29

Exhibited at the British Library only

'You know, I am sure, Claude's *Enchanted Castle* and I wish you may be pleased with my remembrance of it', Keats wrote to Reynolds on 25 March 1818:

You know the Enchanted Castle it doth stand
Upon a Rock on the Border of a Lake
Nested in Trees, which all do seem to shake
From some old Magic like Uganda's sword.
O Phoebus that I had thy sacred word
To shew this castle in fair dreaming wise
Unto my friend, while sick and ill he lies.

Keats's wonderfully Gothic and imaginative commentary stretches for 40 lines. The picture was not before him; his recollection was probably based on the 1782 engraving by William Woollett and François Vivarès. Keats of course, uses Claude's painting to his own purpose , just as later, he will create his own Grecian urn.

Claude's reputation stood high among Keats's immediate circle. Hazlitt, whose 'depth of taste' Keats believed to be one of the 'three things superior in the modern world', wrote:

Claude Lorrain pours the spirit of air over all objects, and new-creates them of light and sunshine. In several of his master-pieces which are shewn here, the vessels, the trees, the temples and middle distances glimmer between air and solid substance, and seem moulded of a new element in nature. No words can do justice to their softness, their precision, their sparkling effect.

Hazlitt was a painter himself, and a connoisseur of that art. If, as we believe, Keats would first meet *The Enchanted Castle* as a print, it was through Leigh Hunt and Benjamin Robert Haydon that he would make his discovery. Both Hunt and Haydon had a large collection of engravings; Claude's painting was to remain a haunting presence for Keats, namely in his composition of the penultimate stanza of *Ode to a Nightingale*. In his earliest reference to *The Enchanted Castle* (in his letter to Reynolds, 25 March 1818), Keats spoke of the solitary figure as:

. . . the poor herdsman who doth bring
His beasts to trouble the enchanted spring:
He tells of the sweet music and the spot

To all his friends, and they believe him not.

In the great *Ode*, there is no mention of the solitary figure or the huntsman, or Psyche (perhaps Keats did not know the present title of the painting with its reference to her); instead Keats introduced a new image, the Old Testament figure of Ruth, more dependent on Poussin (see no. 136b) than on Claude. He returns to Claude's painting in the last lines of the stanza, and needs no foreground figure to his castle to suggest a haunting, empty and strange desolation:

Perhaps the self-same song that found a path
Through the sad heart of Ruth, when, sick for home,
  She stood in tears amid the alien corn;
The same that oft-times hath
Charm'd magic casements, opening on the foam
Of perilous seas, in faery lands forlorn.

Michael Wilson, in his pamphlet, Acquisition in Focus - Claude 'The Enchanted Castle', 1982, notes that: 'at the very time Keats was composing his *Ode*, in the early summer of 1819, *The Enchanted Castle* was on show at the British Institution'.

It is perhaps unnecessary to cite other subtle discussions of the painting and Keats, though Michael Levey's essay, '"The Enchanted Castle" by Claude:

Woollett and Vivarés after Claude, *The Enchanted Castle* (1782)

Subject, Significance and Interpretation' in *The Burlington Magazine*, November 1988, is outstanding: it points out that 'fairyland' is first used by Sir Joshua Reynolds to describe Claude's work in his Thirteenth Discourse to the Royal Academy students; that Keats's archaic spelling clearly points to Spenser's *Faerie Queene*; Keats' 'fairyland', according to Levey, 'is less tranquil-seeming than Sir Joshua Reynolds had assumed in his *Discourse*, not unalien and perhaps evanescent'. Levey memorably concludes his essay:

> When Leigh Hunt came to comment on the phrase about 'magic casements', he enthusiastically noted, unaware apparently of what had inspired it, 'This beats Claude's "*Enchanted Castle*" . . . '. In fact, no competition between two arts is involved. Without Claude's painting, we would conceivably not have had Keats's lines. But without Keats's lines, there might have gone unexpressed the essence of the spell that lies at the heart of a painting that rightly goes on being known best as 'The Enchanted Castle'.

144   *The Townley Vase*
Resin copy
Trustees of the British Museum

The Townley Vase is possibly one of the several urns that suggested the subject of the 'Ode on a Grecian Urn'. It is one of the large marble neo-Attic urns made in Rome between *c*.50 BC and *c*.50 AD. Their size is an indication of their use as funerary caskets, though their function could also be purely decorative. The Townley Vase was acquired by the British Museum in 1805, and Keats would certainly have seen it during his regular visits there. Its bright figures are reminiscent of the lines in the first stanza:

> What men or Gods are these? What maidens loth?
>   What mad pursuit? What struggle to escape?
>   What pipes and timbrels? What wild ecstacy?

Henry Moses (1782?-1870)

144 A Collection of Antique Vases

(a) London: J. Taylor, 1814
    The British Library Board

Few remains of antiquity have aroused more interest than vases. The variety and the elegance of
their forms, the singularity of the designs, the
beauty of the compositions with which they are
adorned, and the important instruction which the
subject of these pictures convey, have conspired to
render them peculiarly attractive.

So Moses begins his treatise on Greek vases. He
recognises that the vases that have survived have
largely been recovered from tombs, and in some way
are connected with funeral rites; the 'urn' is used for
the vases dedicated to the burial of bones or ashes, or
of both together. Moses notes that the urn could be
rounded or square and his plates illustrate both
shapes. Though the themes on the reliefs are varied,
many deal with myths:

> When the sunjects are mythological they convey
> much important information relating to the histo-
> ry of the gods and to the rites and ceremonies
> used in the worship, particularly those observed in
> the sacred and solemn mysteries of the Greeks and
> in the frantic orgies of Bacchus . . . (p. 6)

FRAGMENT OF THE PARTHENON
(SOUTH FRIEZE, SLAB XL)

*145   Heifers led for sacrifice at the Great
Panathenaic Festival*
c. 440 BC
Plaster copy, 102 x 120 cms
Trustees of the British Museum

Between 1808 and 1816 Haydon led a tireless and
aggressive campaign that the Elgin Marbles be pur-
chased for the nation. Indeed, he claimed that the
final purchase was a direct result of his onslaught
against the British Institution in *The Examiner*. He
took Keats to see the great fragments on 2 March
1816, and Keats responded with a sonnet, 'On Seeing
the Elgin Marbles'. The part of the frieze shown here
is thought to be behind the fourth stanza of 'Ode on
a Grecian Urn'.

JOSHUA CRISTALL

146   Io Metamorphosed into a Heifer
Exh 1816
Watercolour, 45.7 x 60.9 cms
Dyer Collection

Cristall here illustrates the story from Ovid's *Meta-
morphoses* (Book One) of Io, priestess, beloved of
Jove. In his attempt to save her from Juno's jealousy
Io was turned into a heifer, but Juno, suspecting
Jove's lascivious intentions appointed Argus – reputed
to have a thousand eyes – to guard the heifer. Jove
then sent Hermes to kill Argus, which he did by first
lulling him with the music of the panpipes, and then
by stories. Cristall shows the naked figure of Hermes,
divested of his wings and helmet (as Ovid notes)
playing his pipes, and, behind him, the sitting figure
of Argus, his hands trying to keep his entranced and
baffled self awake. The heifer is surrounded by seven
female figures who appear to be concerned and

lamenting, and seem to represent her sisters (who according to Ovid were driven away by Argus. Interestingly the scenery, with cliffs, waterfalls and an arcadian river, resembles Cristall's evocations of Borrowdale.Like Keats, Cristall mingles classical subjects with English landscapes. Again, it is difficult not to think that Cristall's treatment of the heifer has been influenced by the lowing heifer in the Parthenon frieze.

Keats uses the image of Argus and Hermes at the beginning of his remarkable sonnet, written *c* 16 April 1819: 'A Dream, after reading Dante's Episode of Paulo and Francesca':

As Hermes once to his feathers light,
   When lulled Argus, baffled, swoon'd and slept,
So on a Delphic reed, my idle spright
   So play'd, so charm'd, so conquer'd, so bereft
The dragon-world of all its hundred eyes.

In his poem Keats arrives at the world of Paulo and Francesca not only seeing the lovers kiss, but kissing himself: 'Pale were the lips I kiss'd – a 'La Belle Dame sans Merci' episode.

JOHN KEATS
147 'Ode on a Grecian Urn'
Manuscript in the hand of George Keats
The British Library Board, Egerton 2780

Keats's original manuscript has been lost, so that the nearest to his first draft is probably this transcript, contained in a small notebook, made by his brother George in January 1820. George Keats was in England from America on business matters, and during his stay made copies of all the great odes, and other major poems such as 'The Eve of St. Agnes'; 'George is busy this morning making copies of my verses' wrote Keats to his sister-in-law Georgiana on 15 January, 'He is making now one of an Ode to the nightingale, which is like reading an account of the b[l]ack hole of Calcutta'. Keats gave him for this purpose a small leather-bound octavo notebook, which had formerly been his own working notebook, containing a fair draft in his own hand of 'Isabella' and 'Souls of poets dead and gone', and a first draft of 'The Eve of St. Mark'.

Cat. 148 (a)

RICHARD EARLOM (1734-1822)

148 Engravings after Claude Lorrain
London: Boydell & Co, 1777
Courtauld Institute Galleries

In 1777 Earlom brought out the *Liber Veritatis*, comprising two hundred plates, executed by him in the style of Claude Lorrain.

a)   *Landscape with Narcissus and Echo*
      20.4 x 25.7 cms

Claude's 'Landscape with Narcissus and Echo' was owned in Keats's day by Sir George Beaumont, and it is almost certain that Keats saw at least a print of it. It is a likely source for the lines in 'I stood tip-toe upon a little hill':

> What first inspires a bard of old to sing
> Narcissus pining o'er the untainted spring?
> In some delicious ramble, he had found
> A little space, with boughs all woven round;

And in the midst of all, a clearer pool
Than e'er reflected in its pleasant cool
The blue sky here, and there, serenely peeping
Through tendril wreaths fantastically creeping.

b)   *View of Delphi with Procession*
      20.8 x 26.1 cms
c)   *View of Delphi with Procession*
      20.8 x 25.7 cms
d)   *Landscape with Bacchus at the Palace of the
      dead Staphylus*
      20.7 x 26. cms
e)   *Landscape with Father of Psyche sacrificing
      at the Milesian Temple of Apollo*
      47.6 x 62.5 cms

These four prints, b, c, d and e, suggest themselves as possible influences upon the penultimate stanza of 'Ode to a Grecian Urn': the towns seem empty and the figures, sketchy as Earlom makes them, are about some mysterious business – a sacrifice, a funeral, a serene religious procession.

Cat. 148 (b)

Cat. 148 (c)

Cat. 148 (d)

Cat. 148 (e)

John Constable (1776-1837)

149 *Winchester Cathedral: West Front*
1821
Watercolour, 15.9 x 23.4 cms
By Courtesy of the Board of Trustees
of the Victoria & Albert Museum

Winchester, it seems, supplanted Oxford as 'the finest city in the world; 'It is the pleasantest Town I ever was in,' Keats writes to his sister Fanny on 28 August 1819 (see below), 'and has the most recommendations of any'. Again, as with Oxford, what most impresses him is the combination of trees, clear streams and gothic architecture:

> There is a fine Cathedrall which is to me always a source of amusement; part of it built 1400 years ago; and the more modern by a magnificent Man, you may have read of in our History, called William of Wickham. The whole town is beautifully wooded—From the Hill at the eastern extremity you see a prospect of Streets, and old Buildings mixed up with Trees—Then There are the most beautiful streams I ever saw—full of Trout.

In Winchester Keats, stimulated by the season and the English countryside, composed some of 'The Fall of Hyperion' and most notably the last great ode, 'To Autumn'.

150 *Letter to from John Keats to Fanny Keats*
28 August 1819
The British Library Board

Writing from Winchester, Keats describes to Fanny his relief at being away from London, and his love of the season and weather:

> The delightful Weather we have had for two Months is the highest gratification I could receive—no chill'd red noses—no shivering—but fair Atmosphere to think in . . . Still I enjoy the Weather I adore fine Weather as the greatest blessing I can have. Give me Books, fruit, french wine and fine weather and a little music out of doors, played by somebody I do not know . . . and I can pass a summer very quietly without caring much about fat Louis, fat Regent or the Duke of Wellington.

Keats also says he has 'completed a Tragedy', *Otho the Great*, but that its performance has been threatened by the absence of Edmund Kean:

> I had hoped to give Kean another opportunity to shine. What can we do now? There is not another actor of Tragedy in all London or Europe—The Covent Garden Company is execrable—Young is the best among them and he is a ranting, coxcombical tasteless Actor—A Disgust A Nausea—and yet the very best after Kean—What a set of barren asses are actors!

Peter De Wint (1784-1849)

151 *Harvesting in a Valley near Lowther*
Watercolour over pencil, 28.3 x 45.2 cms
R.E. Alton, MC

De Wint visited the Lakes on drawing excursions over a thirty year period – and was at Lowther in 1839 and 1840. His work has the Keatsian element of celebration for the natural world: 'I am never so happy as when looking at Nature. Mine is a beautiful profession'.

PETER DE WINT
152 *Gathering the Corn*
Watercolour, 29.4 x 65.7 cms
Whitworth Art Gallery

WILLIAM TURNER OF OXFORD (1789-1862)
153 *The Glebe Corn*
c.1810-12?
Oil on canvas, 33 x 48 cms
R.E. Alton, MC

The Glebe was land owned by the Rector of a parish
and represented part of his income. Here it would seem
the minister is checking the yield and quality of his evidently golden crops.

JOSHUA CRISTALL
154 *Country Girl in a Cornfield*
Signed and dated 1816
Watercolour, 38.7 x 26 cms
Dyer Collection

Cristall's depiction of this single figure carrying a sheaf
of corn reminds one of the theme of harvest that was
popular among artists who were Keats's contemporaries:
besides Cristall there was George Stubbs, De Wint and
William Turner of Oxford. Keats's image of Ruth in the
'Ode to a Nightingale' could be prompted by more
than the single image of Ruth and Boaz by Nicolas
Poussin.

Cat. 156 (a)

SEB. LE ROI, DE SAULX, BOVINET,
CHARTAIGNER, DAMBRUN, NIQUET

155   *Engravings after Nicolas Poussin*
Galerie du Musée Napoleon, 1807
Courtauld Institute Galleries

a)   *Autumn, or the Grapes of the Promised Land*
12.3 x 15.6 cms

b)   *Summer, or Ruth and Boaz*
12.3 x 15.6 cms

c)   *Echo and Narciss*
12.8 x 15.2 cms

d)   *Triumph of Flora*
12.6 x 17 cms

Keats would probably have seen prints from Poussin
of earlier date in larger format, emphasising line over
tone, in some contrast to these fine French etchings.

JOAN PESNE

156   *Engravings after Nicolas Poussin*
Coutauld Institute Galleries

a)   *Autumn, or the Grapes of the Promised Land*
b)   *Summer, or Ruth and Boaz*
48.1 x 62.3 cms

Poussin's harvest images were seminal not only for
Keats writing 'To Autumn', but for the English
painters of that season, De Wint, Cristall, William
Turner of Oxford.

Cat. 156 (b)

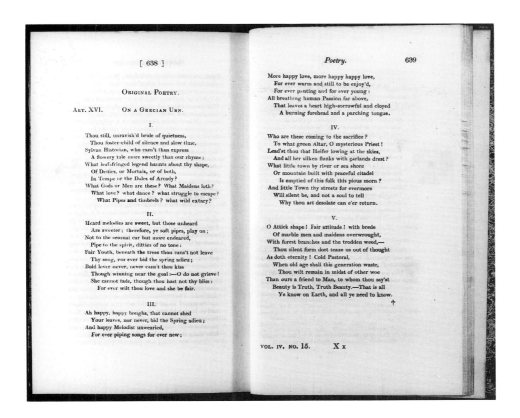

Running from 1816 to 1820, the *Annals of the Fine Arts* was the first quarterly in England to be devoted to the visual arts. Haydon who wrote almost exclusively there, embodied its principle aims: to raise the profile of renaissance and classical art, and to promote contemporary historical painting. The preface to the third volume (published in 1819, and dedicated to Lord Elgin 'in respect and admiration of his energy and perseverance in the splendid remains of Grecian genius from the hands of the barbarians), expressed it thus:

> We think then, the encouragement of historical painting, ought to be the first object in any great nation that wishes to encourage art . . . we conceive the Royal Academy to be a perverted institution, and that the members make use of the powers instructed to them, to the destruction, *instead* of the assistance, of that style of art, for which that power was created . . .

In first publishing the two great odes, 'To a Nightingale' and 'On a Grecian Urn' in the *Annals of the Fine Arts* Keats was in effect participating in a contemporary debate about the state of the visual arts in England, and their appreciation. The edition that contains the 'Ode on a Grecian Urn', for example, also has the essay, 'On Gusto' by Hazlitt, where he also contemplates the 'cold pastoral' of classical sculpture:

> Perhaps the Greek statues want Gusto . . . The sense of perfect form occupies the whole mind, and hardly suffers it to dwell on any other feeling.

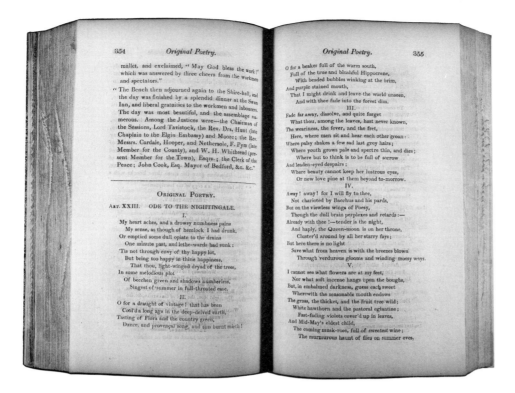

It seems enough for them *to be* without acting or suffering. Their forms are ideal, spiritual. Their beauty is power. "By their beauty they are raised above the frailties of pain or passion, by their beauty they are deified."

The two odes, unlike the two sonnets, are not signed by Keats's name, but by a dagger, presumably to avoid the political prejudice that marred the critical response to *Poems*, 1817, and *Endymion*. Keats's authorship could be discovered, with difficulty, from the index.

160 Letter from John Keats to James Elmes
12 June 1819
The British Library Board

Elmes endorsed this letter: 'From the late John Keats, the Poet, to Mr Elmes, about a Sonnet to Haydon. JE.'. It seems more likely, however, that 'the verses' Keats is promising to him are the 'Ode to a Nightingale', which was published by Elmes in the *Annals of the Fine Arts* a month later in July 1819 (James Elmes (1782-1862) was an architect and close friend of Haydon; he edited the *Annals* from 1816 to

1820). Keats was preparing himself for a further attempt at successful publication, and was perhaps publishing several of his latest poems as a prelude to this. In a letter to Haydon he regrets not being able to send him 'those lines' as he has given them to Elmes.

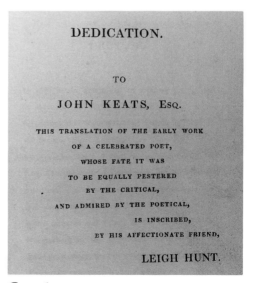

Cat. 161

LEIGH HUNT

161 *Amyntas, A Tale of the Woods*
London: T. and J. Allman, 1820
Professor Michael Jaye

Hunt's translation of Tasso's *Aminta* was published, as Hunt writes in his *Autobiography*, 'to enable me to meets some demands, occasioned by the falling off in the receipts of the *Examiner*, now declining under the two-fold vicissitude of triumphant ascendancy in the Tories, and the desertion of reform by the Whigs'. He dedicated it to John Keats in the following words: "To John Keats, Esq. This Translation of the Early Work of a Celebrated Poet, whose Fate it Was to Be Equally Pestered by the Critical, and Admired by the Poetical, is Inscribed, by his Affectionate Friend, Leigh Hunt."

HENRY HOPPNER MEYER

162 *Portrait of Charles Lamb (1775-1834)*
1826
Oil on canvas, 33 x 26.7 cms
National Portrait Gallery, London

Charles Lamb was of course one of the guests at the 'Immortal Dinner' at Benjamin Robert Haydon's on 28 December 1817. He and Keats seem to have met several times subsequent to this, but they were never close friends. Lamb did, however, in *The New Times*

of 19 July 1820, write a favourable review of the 1820 Lamia volume (praising especially 'Isabella' and 'The Eve of St. Agnes'), and apparently told Crabbe Robinson that he hated the treatment Keats had received from certain critics, and considered Keats's poetry as next to Wordsworth's.

JOHN KEATS

163 *'Lamia, Isabella, The Eve of St. Agnes and other Poems'*
London: Taylor & Hessey, 1820
a) Leeds University Library, Brotherton Collection
b) Private Collection
c) The London Borough of Camden from the Collections at Keats House, Hampstead

By April 1820, Taylor had the completed manuscripts for a new volume of Keats's poetry; 'Next week Keats's new Volume of Poems will be published', he wrote to his father on 26 June, '& if it does not sell well, I think nothing will ever sell again.' To Hessey he wrote three days later: 'The Book looks every thing that I could wish, & at 7/6 is cheap in my opinion'. Keats however was less confident: 'My book is coming out with very low hopes, though not spirits on my part', he had written to Charles Brown earlier that month, 'This will be my last trial; not succeeding, I shall try what I can do in the Apothecary line.'

Lamia, Isabella, The Eve of St. Agnes and other Poems was published at the beginning of July. The other poems included the Odes, 'Fancy', 'Lines on the Mermaid Tavern', 'Robin Hood' and the 'Hyperion' fragment. The inclusion of this last was explained in an advertisment which said that it was 'printed at the particular request' of the publishers. Seeing this, Keats, who had never wished it published, wrote angrily against it: 'I had no part in this; I was ill at the time'.

Like its two predecessors, the *Lamia* volume did not sell well; Taylor was still advertising the first edition eight years later.

Cat. 164 (a)

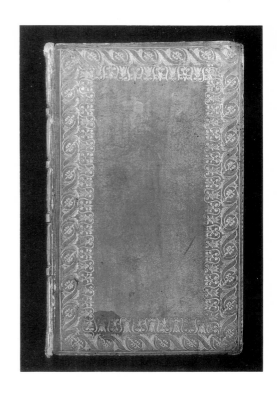

Cat. 164 (b)

Cat. 164 (a)

John Taylor by an unknown artist

164 *'Lamia, Isabella, The Eve of St. Agnes, and Other Poems'*
London: Taylor and Hessey, 1820
a) Professor Michael Jaye

b) The Wordsworth Trust

Two copies of the *Lamia* volume, the first in its original boards and label, the second in a fine leather binding by Taylor & Hessey. Until the mid-nineteenth century it was the practice for books to be sold in simple wrappers or boards, and then to be bound at the customer's expense. The bindery side of Taylor & Hessey's firm was one of the most prosperous aspects of their business. Hessey had published an advertisement in 1810 which put emphasis upon the fine appearance of their volumes: 'bound in the most beautiful and splendid manner in calf, russia leather, Morocco, vellum, &c &c . . . many of them ornamented and illustrated with *original Drawings*'.

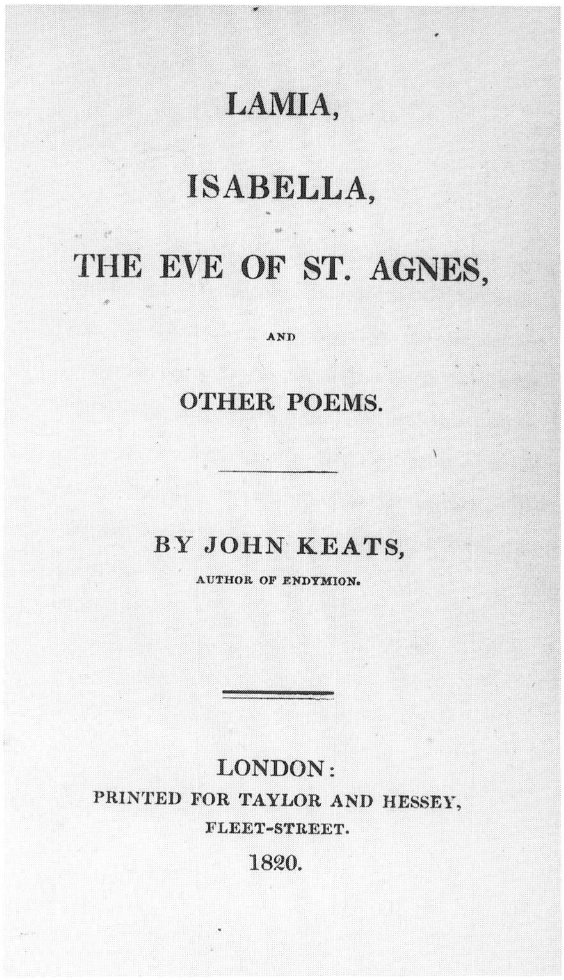

LAMIA,

ISABELLA,

THE EVE OF ST. AGNES,

AND

OTHER POEMS.

BY JOHN KEATS,
AUTHOR OF ENDYMION.

LONDON:
PRINTED FOR TAYLOR AND HESSEY,
FLEET-STREET.
1820.

7. The Stage, 1819-20

'I have . . . completed 4 Acts of a Tragedy', Keats wrote to Benjamin Bailey on 14 August 1819, 'It was the opinion of most of my friends that I should never be able to write a scene—I will endeavour to wipe away the Prejudice.' The tragedy was *Otho the Great*, written in collaboration with Charles Brown and, despite their efforts, never performed in Keats's lifetime.

Brown's initial suggestion that they write a play was prompted by a need for money. He proposed that he would supply the story and the dramatic interest, and Keats would write the verse. His comic opera, *Narensky*, had been produced at Drury Lane (without much success) in 1814, and with the lifetime admission he earned from this he regularly accompanied Keats to the theatre, and well understood Keats's delight in drama. In accepting his proposition that they write a play, Keats saw two opportunities. Firstly, it seemed the best chance for him to gain popularity as a writer: 'My hopes of success in the literary world are now better than ever' he wrote to Fanny Keats on 20 December 1819, after hearing that *Otho the Great* had been accepted at Drury Lane. Secondly, it was an opportunity for him to write for the leading actor of the day, whom he unreservedly admired: 'One of my Ambitions is to make as great a revolution in modern dramatic writing as Kean has done in acting', he wrote to Bailey.

Since his first triumphant appearance at Drury Lane, Edmund Kean had indeed revolutionised acting. It was characterised by its intensity and passion, and to theatre-goers more accustomed to the calm, ceremonial dignity of Kemble, the small figure and the ranging, sometimes piercing voice of Kean were a revelation; his passion was only matched by the excited, sometimes almost hysterical response of the audience. For the traditional measured cadences Kean substituted a broken, impetuous style of speech notable for its naturalness. Byron commented on his Richard III: 'By Jove, he is a soul! Life—Nature—truth, without exaggeration or diminution. Kemble's Hamlet is perfect, but Hamlet is not nature; Richard is a man, and Kean is Richard.' The hero of *Otho the Great*, who does noble deeds, is betrayed, and descends into madness, could have been, and indeed was, written for Kean to act.

In the event, however, the play did not receive its first performance until November 1950, at St. Martin's Theatre, London. From both a literary and a dramatic point of view, it is a failure. Keats himself admitted as much when he wrote to his sister-in-law: 'The only reliance I had on it was in Kean's acting'. But he began a new, and much more promising play, *King Stephen*, almost immediately (this time without the 'leading-strings' of Brown), and his initial desire remained: 'the writing of a few fine Plays—my greatest ambition'.

Cat. 171 Edmund Kean as Richard III by John James Halls, 1814

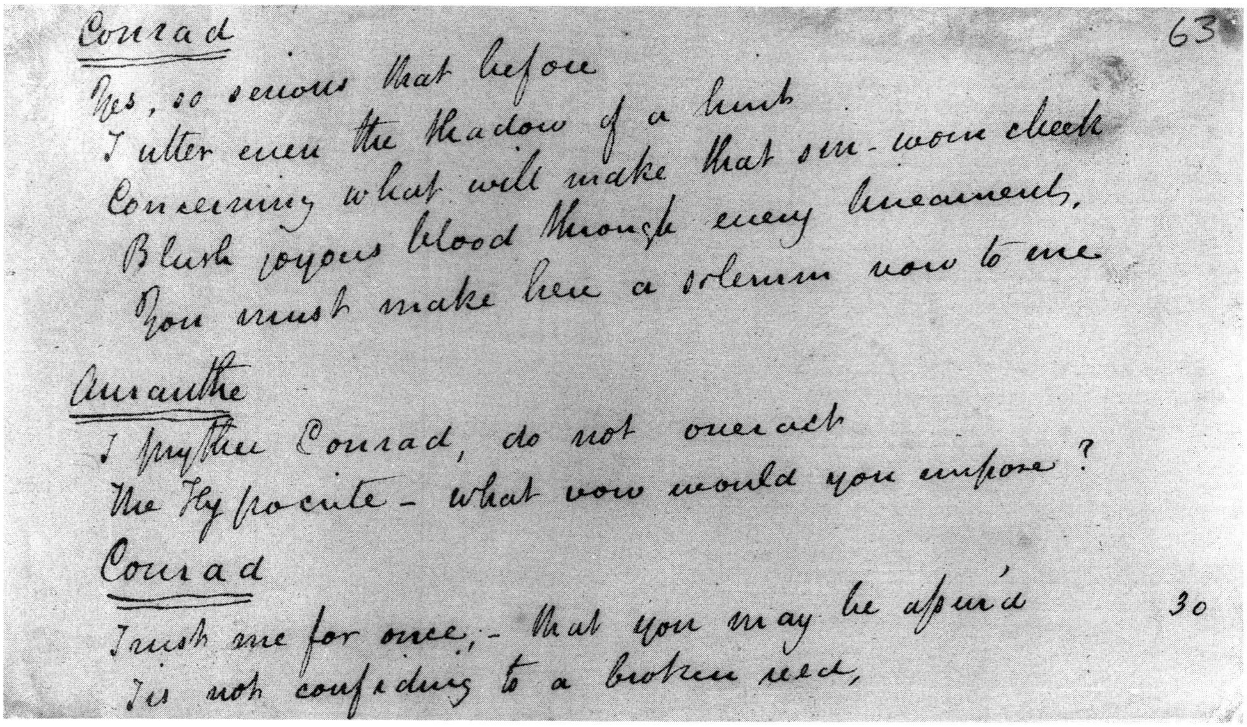

Conrad
Yes, so serious that before
I utter even the shadow of a hint
Concerning what will make that sun-worn cheek
Blush joyous blood through every lineament,
You must make here a solemn vow to me

Auranthe
I prythee Conrad, do not overact
The Hypocrite — what vow would you impose?

Conrad
Trust me for once;— that you may be assur'd
'Tis not confiding to a broken reed,

63

30

JOHN KEATS

165 Manuscript fragment of 'Otho the Great'
The British Library board

The fragment is of twelve lines from Act one, Scene one. The rough, energetic style of the verse owes much to Philip Massinger, whose plays Keats had been reading, and in one of which, *A New Way to Pay Old Debts*, he had seen Kean perform the comic role of Sir Giles Overrreach.

H. ROWLES AFTER BENJAMIN WYATT

166 Front View of the Theatre Royal, Drury Lane
London: 25 November 1812
Hand-coloured engraving, 27.2 x 43.5 cms
Guildhall Library, City of London

The original Theatre Royal, Drury Lane was set up under a charter granted by Charles II in 1662. The third theatre on the site, was built in 1793. It was on a suitably grand scale, costing £150,000 to build and seating 3,900, making it one of the largest theatres in Europe. When it burned down on the night of 24 February 1809, the by-then precarious financial position of the theatre company meant that there were no profits for rebuilding. A public subscription was therefore organised, under the leadership of the radical Whig and brewer Samuel Whitbread, and over £235,000 was raised. The new theatre by Henry Rowles and Benjamin Wyatt opened three years later, on 10 October 1812. At first the theatre struggled to recover from the interruption – the departure of Kemble and Mrs Siddons to Covent Garden had left the company without actors of great stature. When Edmund Kean made his debut there as Shylock in January 1814 however, he not only revived the company's fortunes, but instigated at Drury Lane a new style of acting.

An avid theatre-goer, Keats visited Drury Lane as often as he could. Entry was made easier by Charles Brown's 'silver ticket', that guaranteed free entry for life.

W. HOPWOOD AFTER N. HEIDELOFF

167 Interior of Drury Lane
1813
Engraving, 22.9 x 26.8 cms
By Courtesy of the Board of Trustees of the Victoria & Albert Museum from the Collections of the Theatre Museum

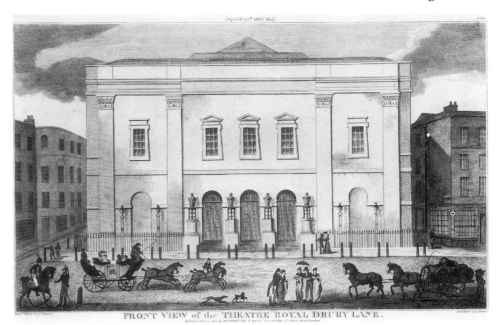

Cat. 166

FRONT VIEW of the THEATRE ROYAL DRURY LANE.

Cat. 167

The view is taken from one of the dress boxes, showing the scale of the auditorium. The social complications of regency life were an important factor in the design of the auditorium. Wyatt placed the entrances to the dress boxes, the most important seats, on a mezzanine level between the ground floor and first floor, segregating the respectable from the disreputable. Keats and his friends made use of the pit, where they were best placed to see Kean's subtlety of expression. Byron, after seeing Kean's Iago on 7 May 1814, commented: 'Was not Iago perfection? particularly the last look. I was *close* to him (in the orchestra), and never saw an English countenance half so expressive.'

Mindful of the dangers of fire, the auditorium was encased in a brick wall over three feet thick (rather than the usual timber frame), a primitive sprinkler system was installed, and the stairs were built entirely of stone.

The theatre still stands, with the statue of Kean in the well of the main staircase.

168   *Letter from John Keats to Fanny Keats*
20 December 1819
The British Library Board

Keats writes to Fanny about his hopes for *Otho the Great*: his sense of urgency to get it performed, and the play's dependence upon Kean for its success:

> Of the Tragedy I can give you news but semigood. It is accepted at Drury Lane with a promise of coming out next season: as that will be too long a delay we have determined to get Elliston to bring it out this Season or to transfer it to Covent Garden. This Elliston will not like, as we have every motive to believe that Kean has perceived how suitable the principal Character will be for him.

SAMUEL COUSINS
169   *Edmund Kean (1787-1833)*
1814
Pencil, oval 9.5 x 7 cms
National Portrait Gallery, London

From the outset, Edmund Kean was seen as essential to the success of *Otho the Great* – 'There is no actor who can do the principal character besides Kean',

Keats wrote to George and Georgiana on 17 September 1819. The early portrait of Keats by Severn, and Haydon's depiction of him in *Christ's Entry into Jerusalem*, show the intense stare, the open mouth and the avid energy that feature in many portraits of Kean. Cowden Clarke wrote in his *Recollections*:

> Not the less beloved was he [Keats] for having a highly pugnacious spirit, which, when roused, was one of the most picturesque exhibitions—off the stage—I ever saw. One of the transports of that marvellous actor, Edmund Kean—whom, by the way, he idolized—was its nearest resemblance; and the two were not very dissimilar in face and figure.

From a nearly destitute early life, Kean rose to become the foremost actor of the age. Abandoned on a doorstep at birth, he was successively a cabin-boy on a vessel bound for Madeira, a travelling singer and dancer, a tumbler in a circus and a strolling player around the provinces. While playing at Dorchester he was seen by Dr. Drury, and then, on Drury's recommendation, by Mr Arnold, the stage-manager of Drury Lane. His debut there, as Shylock, was made on 26 January 1814. 'This will never do, Mr. Kean,' the stage-manager was said to have told him on the opening night; 'it is an innovation, Sir, it is totally different from anything that has ever been done on these boards.' 'I wish it to be so,' was the response, and indeed the performance, and the triumphant first season at Drury Lane, not only improved Drury

Lane's ailing fortunes, but revolutionised acting. Between then and his final appearance at Drury Lane in 1833 Kean played a dozen or so tragic characters, including Richard III, Shylock, Othello, Hamlet, Lear and Sir Giles Overreach, all to both public and critical acclaim.

Seeing Kean as Richard III and as Luke in *Riches*, Keats reviewed the performances in *The Champion* on 21 December 1817. He thanks Kean for the 'heroic excitement' of his performances, as if 'just arrived from the camp of Charlemagne.' Praising 'the elegance, gracefulness, and music of elocution', he draws particular attention to his immediacy:

> There is an indescribable gusto in his voice, by which we feel that the utterer is thinking of the past and the future, while speaking of the instant . . . his exclamation of 'blood, blood, blood!' is direful and slaughterous to the deepest degree, the very words appear stained and gory. His nature hangs over them, making a prophetic repast . . . Surely this intense power of anatomizing the passion of every syllable – of taking to himself the wings of verse, is the means by which he becomes a storm with such fiery decision . . . Other actors are continually thinking of their sum-total effect throughout a play. Kean delivers himself up to the instant feeling, without a shadow of a thought about any thing else. He feels his being as deeply as Wordsworth, or any other of our intellectual monopolists.

To Bailey he had written on 22 November 1817: 'I scarcely remember counting upon any Happiness—I look not for it if it be not in the present hour—nothing startles me beyond the Moment. The setting sun will always set me to rights—or if a Sparrow come before my Window I take part in its existence and pick about the Gravel.' Similarly Keats was attracted by the spontaneous, unpredictable Kean, who avoided fashionable society. Having dinner with Horace Smith, he was angered by their fashionable wit: 'They talked of Kean and his low company,' he wrote to his brothers on 27 December 1817, 'Would I were with that company instead of yours I said to myself!'

Coleridge described Kean's Shakespearean acting: 'to see Kean act is like reading Shakespeare by flashes of lightning'.

ATTRIBUTED TO THOMAS WAGEMAN

170   *Edmund Kean*
Inscribed and dated, 1827
Pencil, 21 x 14.6 cms
National Portrait Gallery, London

The picture hanging behind Kean represents the portrait of the actor, as Richard III, by Halls (see below).

JOHN JAMES HALLS

171   *Edmund Kean as Richard III*
1814
Oil on canvas, 144 x 84 cms
By Courtesy of the Board of Trustees of the Victoria & Albert Museum

Illustrated in colour on p. 145

In this portrait by Halls, Kean is shown dressed for his most famous role, Richard III. The traditional style of costume for the part was a pastiche of sixteenth and early seventeenth century fashions. All leading actors of this period owned their own stage costumes and were rarely persuaded to wear costumes from the theatre wardrobe.

GEORGE CRUIKSHANK

172   Edmund Kean as Othello
Hand-coloured engraving
*By Courtesy of the Board of Trustees of the Victoria
& Albert Museum from the Collections of the
Theatre Museum*

Hazlitt commented on Kean's Othello in *The
Examiner*, 7 January 1816: 'Mr. Kean's Othello is his
best character, and his highest effort of genius on the
stage. We say this without any exception or reserve.'
On this occasion, however, he felt that Kean's passionate vigour was achieved at the expense of the
intellectual and emotional subtlety of the role, 'the
conflict of the soul' and 'the tug of war between love
and hatred', 'uniting sublimity of thought with the
anguish of the keenest woe':

> Mr Kean is in general all passion, all energy, all
> relentless will. He wants imagination, that faculty
> which contemplates events, and broods over feel-
> ings with a certain calmness and grandeur; his
> feelings almost always hurry on to action, and
> hardly ever repose upon themselves.

Keats, who must have read this review, was similarly
always on guard against a particular 'extravagance'
being achieved at the expense of a wider balance. He
wrote to George Keats (quoted in a letter to Bailey, 8
October 1817) that 'a long Poem is a test of Invention,
which I take to be the Polar Star of Poetry, as Fancy is
the Sails, and Imagination the Rudder'. Talking of 'La
Belle Dame Sans Merci' to George and Georgiana
Keats he had written: 'we must temper the Imagination as the Critics say with Judgement.'
  Cruikshank's print shows Kean's smallness of
stature, and he is crudely blacked-out for the role,
but as Hazlitt remarked: 'There are some technical
objections. Othello is tall; but that is nothing; he was
black, but that is nothing. But he was not fierce, and
that is every thing.'

GEORGE CLINT (1770-1854)

173   Edmund Kean as Sir Giles Overreach
Oil on canvas; 27.9 x 22.8 cms
*By Courtesy of the Board of Trustees
of the Victoria & Albert Museum*

Kean's Sir Giles Overreach in Massinger's comedy *A
New Way to Pay Old Debts* (published 1633) was one
of his most famous roles, and there are many instan-
ces of the profound effect it had on people. Hazlitt,
in no doubt, wrote in *The Examiner* a week after
reviewing Kean's Othello:

> We cannot conceive of any one's doing Mr. Kean's
> part of Sir Giles Overreach so well as himself. We
> have seen others in the part, superior in the look
> and costume, in hardened, clownish, rustic insen-
> sibility; but in the soul and spirit, no one is equal
> to him. He is a truly great actor. This is one of his
> very best parts. He was not at a single fault.

Often the audience would be quite carried away by
Kean's portrayal of madness. Thomas Moore reports
the response of Byron: 'Such effect had the passionate
energy of Kean's acting on his mind, that, once seeing
him play Sir Giles Overreach, he was so affected as to
be seized with a sort of convulsive fit . . .'

*174   Playbill advertising Edmund Kean in
'Richard III'*
15 December 1817
*By Courtesy of the Board of Trustees of the
Victoria & Albert Museum from the
Collections of the Theatre Museum*

175   Playbill advertising Edmund Kean in 'Riches'
18 December 1817
*By Courtesy of the Board of Trustees of the
Victoria & Albert Museum from the
Collections of the Theatre Museum*

After an absence due to ill-health, Kean made a triumphant return to Drury Lane as Richard III, and
then as Luke in Sir James Bland Burges's *Riches*
(adapted from Massinger's *City Madam*). Keats was at
both performances, on the second occasion as a
reviewer in place of Reynolds: 'I saw Kean return to
the public as Richard III', he wrote to his brothers a
week later, '& finely he did it, & at the request of
Reynolds I went to criticise his Luke in Riches—the
critique is in today's champion'. The playbills are
notable for the prominence they give to Kean.
Garrick had been the first to have his name featured
in larger type, and Kean is said never to have agreed
to play a second lead, and demanded (and got) star
billing for every performance.

Cat. 173

Cat. 184 John Robert Cozens, *The Bay of Naples*

8. ITALY, 1820-1

Marianne Hunt's silhouette of Keats propped on a chair and a stool, a book in his hands, illustrates the severely restricted nature of the poet's last months in England. Often unable to venture outside, he was also forbidden (and little inclined) to write poetry; the general opinion was that poetry, because of the nervous state in which it was written, had become his worst enemy. By July 1820, it had been decided that Keats would have to spend the winter in Italy if there was to be any chance of recovery. In September Joseph Severn offered to accompany him.

The month-long journey between 17 September and 21 October, often in heavy storms, probably ruined his health for good. The tiny cabin of the *Maria Crowther* was shared between Keats, Severn, the ship's captain and two other consumptives, the younger of whom, Severn noticed, closely resembled Fanny Brawne in both age and appearance. Arriving at Naples, they were forced to spend ten days in quarantine where Keats 'summoned up more puns, in a sort of desperation, in one week than in any year of my life'. Keats immediately saw the richness of Italy, but his health prevented him from taking anything more than cursory glances. 'I have an habitual feeling of my real life having past', he wrote from Rome to Charles Brown, 'and that I am leading a posthumous existence'.

In Rome, where he and Severn lodged beside the Spanish Steps, he was attended by Dr James Clarke - 'there is no bounds to attention' wrote Severn to Brown. But like all medical men of the day, his understanding of tuberculosis was extremely limited, even though he had become a specialist of the disease (Phthisis as it was called). Keats died on 23 February at 11 pm.

Silhouette of Keats by Marianne Hunt

176 Letter from John Keats to Fanny Keats
8 February 1820
The British Library Board

With his illness growing, Keats was less able to venture outside. Here he describes his new arrangements, reclined on a 'sofa-bed' at Wentworth Place – 'How much more comfortable than a dull room upstairs, where one gets tired of the pattern of the bed curtains' – and gives a description of the passers-by:

> On sunday between the hours of twelve and one I descried a Pot boy. I conjectured it might be the one o'Clock beer—Old women with bobbins and red cloaks and unpresuming bonnets I see creeping about the heath. Gipseys after hare skins and silver spoons. Then goes by a fellow with a wooden clock under his arm that strikes a hundred and more. Then comes the old french emigrant (who has been very well to do in france) with his hands joined behind on his hips, and his face full of political schemes. Then passes Mr David Lewis a very goodnatured, goodlooking old gentleman who has been very kind to Tom and George and me. As for those fellows the Brickmakers they are always passing to and fro. I mus'n't forget the two old maiden ladies in well walk who have a Lap dog between them, that they are very anxious about. It is a corpulent Little Beast whom it is necessary to coax along with an ivory-tipp'd cane.

177 *Letter from John Keats to Fanny Keats*
21 April 1820
The British Library Board

As Keats grew more consumptive, both he and his doctors put the blame upon an overly nervous disposition which, in his case, was seen as an occupational hazard of the poetic life:

> The Doctor assures me that there is nothing the matter with me except nervous irritability and a general weakness of the whole system which has proceeded from my anxiety of mind of late years and the too great excitement of poetry.

Also in this letter is one of the first hints that Keats intended 'a Voyage' to restore his health, and the necessity of concentrating his mind upon more tangible things: 'They tell me I must study lines and tangents and squares and circles to put a little ballast into my mind.'

178 *Letter from John Keats to Fanny Keats*
14 August 1820
The British Library Board

In August Keats's nervous state was dramatically illustrated when a letter addressed to him was mistakenly opened (here referred to as 'an accident of an unpleasant nature'). 'Poor Keats was affected by this inconceivable circumstance beyond what can be imagined', wrote Maria Gisborne in her journal, 'he wept for several hours'. 'I am excessively nervous' he now writes to his sister, 'a person entering the room half choaks me'. For the first time the nature of his disease is hinted at, as is the journey to Italy:

> —'Tis not yet Consumption I believe, but it would be were I to remain in this climate all the Winter: so I am thinking of either voyaging or travelling to Italy. Yesterday I received an invitation from Mr Shelley, a Gentleman residing at Pisa, to spend the Winter with him: if I go I must be away in a Month or even less.

179 *Letter from John Keats to Fanny Keats*
23 August 1820
The British Library Board

Hearing of his sister's own ill-health, Keats is concerned that Fanny should not be overly affected by his illness, and, like him, lose her health due to morbid thoughts (a reason which he still believed to be the cause of his own illness):

> Do not suffer Your Mind to dwell upon unpleasant reflections—that sort of thing has been the destruction of my health—Nothing is so bad as want of health—it makes one envy Scavengers and Cinder-sifters. There are enough real distresses and evils in wait for every one to try the most vigorous health. Not that I would say yours are not real—but they are such as to tempt you to employ your imagination on them, rather than endeavour to dismiss them entirely. Do not diet your mind with grief, it destroys the constitution; but let your chief care be of your health, and with that you will meet with your share of Pleasure in the world—do not doubt it.

180 *Self-portrait of Joseph Severn (1793-1879)*
c 1820
Pencil, 25.4 x 17.8 cms
National Portrait Gallery, London

In offering to accompany Keats on the journey to Italy in September 1820, Joseph Severn earned himself a central place among the poet's circle of friends. Indeed, his dedicated nursing of Keats through the final illness earned him almost immediate public recognition; '[Keats] was accompanied to Rome' ended Shelley in his Preface to *Adonais*, 'and attended in his last illness by Mr. Severn, a young artist of the highest promise . . . His conduct is a golden augury of the success of his future career—may the unextinguished Spirit of his illustrious friend animate the creations of his pencil, and plead against Oblivion for his name!'

Severn, then a struggling young artist, first met Keats in 1816, when the latter was a medical student at Guy's Hospital. Their friendship grew, and a year later Keats gave him a copy of the 1817 *Poems* inscribed 'to Severn with all his Heart'. As an artist, Severn would accompany Keats to the British Museum and private exhibitions, and no doubt helped the poet towards his interest in fine art. He made two lifetime portraits, a charcoal sketch in 1816, and a miniature in 1819.

After Keats's death he remained in Italy, later, in 1861, becoming British Consul in Rome, where he was widely respected. For the rest of his life he was devoted to Keats's memory, a dedication that gradually developed into an affectionate, if misleading hagiography. His numerous posthumous portraits of the poet become increasingly idealised, in marked contrast to the first, animated sketch he made of Keats in 1816. His written reminiscences, edited by William Sharpe in 1892, are important but similarly unreliable.

Severn died in 1879, and was buried beside Keats. His tombstone gives great emphasis to those memorable five months when he nursed Keats through his final, tragic illness:

> To the Memory of Joseph Severn, Devoted friend and death-bed companion of John Keats whom he lived to see numbered among The Immortal Poets of England. An Artist eminent for his representations of Italian Life and Nature. British Consul at Rome from 1861 to 1872 and Officer of the Crown of Italy in recognition of his services to Freedom and Humanity . . .

DAVID COX (1783-1859)

181 *The Thames, off Gravesend*
Signed and dated 1820
Watercolour, 12 x 17.8 cms
By Courtesy of the Board of Trustees of the Victoria & Albert Museum

'On Sunday Morning', John Taylor wrote to Fanny Keats on 19 September 1820, 'Mr Keats went on board the Maria Crowther, for Naples, and about Noon reached Gravesend.—He did not go ashore, but entered at once on the kind of Life which he will have to lead for about a Month to come'. Taylor, with Woodhouse and William Haslam ('our oak friend' as Severn called him) had accompanied him in the boat there from Kent Docks, and now they left him. At Gravesend the *Maria Crowther* picked up Miss Cottrell, a young consumptive who with Keats, Severn, a Mrs Pidgeon, and the ship's captain, shared the cramped cabin through the voyage. Severn noticed her as 'a sad martyr to her illness—which is to a jot the same as Keats'. Severn himself went ashore. He wrote to Haslam:

> Keats took his breakfast well—I had proposed to go ashore to Gravesend—he thought this a good opportunity to have some things from the Chymists—which I got him—with 1/2 hundred Apples and 2 Dozen Biscuits—&c &c—the Captain was trying to buy a Goat for him—but was not successful—we all returned in a real full boat—to dinner—Keats was full of his waggery—looked well—ate well—and was well

JOHN BAVERSTOCK KNIGHT
182   Lulworth
Watercolour, 19.1 x 24.1 cms
*By Courtesy of the Board of Trustees
of the Victoria & Albert Museum*

Severn remembered that Keats last set foot in
England when the *Maria Crowther* anchored off 'the
Dorsetshire coast'. Traditionally, but with little evidence, this was thought to be Lulworth Cove, and
the area has entered into the generally hazy, almost
mythological terms of Keats's final months.

UNION MAGAZINE
183   Facsimile manuscript of 'Bright Star' Sonnet
February 1846
Private Collection

In February 1846, before the publication of Milnes's
Literary Remains, Severn sent the 'Bright star' sonnet
to the *Union Magazine*. He claimed that it was the
last poem Keats wrote, and that it was written in his
presence on the *Maria Crowther* when it was anchored off the Dorsetshire coast. He wrote to the editor:

> The shores, with the beautiful grottoes which
> opened to fine verdure and cottages, were the
> means of transporting Keats once more into the
> regions of poetry;—he showed me these things
> exultingly, as though they had been his birthright.
> The change in him was wonderful, and continued
> even after our return to the ship, when he took a
> volume (which he had a few days before given me)
> of Shakespeare's Poems, and in it he wrote me the

subjoined Sonnet, which at the time I thought the
most enchanting of all his efforts.

Several factors make it unlikely that the event took
place as Severn described it. The first signs of the sonnet are in a letter to Tom Keats from Scotland on 26
June 1818, when Keats talks of refining 'one's sensual
vision into a sort of north star which can never cease
to be open lidded and steadfast over the wonders of
the great Power.' In April 1819 Keats and Fanny
Brawne copied the sonnet into books – she into
Dante, and he (in a slightly revised version) in the
Shakespeare volume to which Severn refers. It is this
version (written opposite 'A Lover's Complaint') that
was printed in facsimile opposite Severn's letter.
Further, Severn's inscription in this volume reveals
that the book was not given to him until January the
following year, when they were in Italy. It seems likely
that Keats got out the volume on board, and read the
poem, and that Severn mistakenly thought he had
composed it then. In this sense, though, his merely
reading the poem was in fact his farewell to England,
Fanny Brawne and poetry.

JOHN ROBERT COZENS (1752-1797)
184   The Bay of Naples, from the Capo di Monte
Watercolour over graphite, 43.2 x 58 cms
Trustees of the British Museum

Illustrated in colour on p. 152

WILLIAM COLLINS (1788-1847)
185   Street in Naples
Watercolour, 19.9 x 15 cms
*By Courtesy of the Board of Trustees
of the Victoria & Albert Museum*

Naples was Keats's first experience of Italy, where he was finally released from 'the loathsome misery of Quarantine'. Though immediately struck by the richness of the city, he was also newly frustrated by his illness, which imprisoned him almost as effectively as quarantine had done: 'there is enough in this new Port of Naples to fill a quire of Paper' he wrote to Mrs Brawne on 24 October 1820, 'but it looks like a dream—every man who can row his boat and walk and talk seems a different being from myself . . . O what an account I could give you of the Bay of Naples if I could once more feel myself a Citizen of this world'. Eight days later his companion, Joseph Severn, reported him as 'breathing in a large room— with Vesuvius in our view—Keats has become calm— and thinks favourably of this place'.

186   Letter from Joseph Severn to Mrs Brawne
11 January 1821
The British Library Board

Severn gives an account to Fanny Brawne's mother of his and Keats's life at Rome, just over a month before Keats's death. Keats had written his last letter (to Charles Brown) on 30 November. Severn describes the pain of separation that Keats seems to have felt more than anything, but sees cause for hope in Keats's new feeling of resignation:

> Now he has changed to calmness and quietude, as singular as productive as good, for his mind was killing him. He has now given up all thoughts, hopes, or even wish for recovery. Dr Clark even thinks so. Nature again revives in him—I mean where art was used before.
>
> For three weeks I have never left him—I have sat up all night—I have read to him nearly all day, and even in the night—I light the fire—make the breakfast, and sometimes am obliged to cook— make his bed, and even sweep the room.

Severn goes on to describe the nightmare of their having to move rooms, the Italian law being 'that every individual thing, even to the paper on the walls in each room the patient has been in, shall without reserve be destroyed by fire'. He praises the attentions of Dr. Clarke, who 'still attends him with his usual kindness, and shows his good heart in everything he does . . . But for their kindness I am afraid we should go on very gloomily.' He concludes with his own longing for familiar surroundings, and feeling that the trip to Italy was pointless:

> my mind is carried to your happy Wentworth Place—for the hopeless advantages of this comfortless Italy. He has many, many times talked over 'the few happy days at your house, the only time when his mind was at ease.' I hope still to see you with him again. Farewell my dear madam. One more thing I must say—poor Keats cannot see any letters, at least he will not—they affect him so much and increase his danger. The last two I repented giving, he made me put them into his box—unread . . .

Keats on his deathbed, 1821, by Joseph Severn. The artist has written below: '28 Janry 3 o'clock mng. Drawn to keep me awake—a deadly sweat was on him all this night'. *(The London Borough of Camden from the Collections at Keats House, Hampstead)*

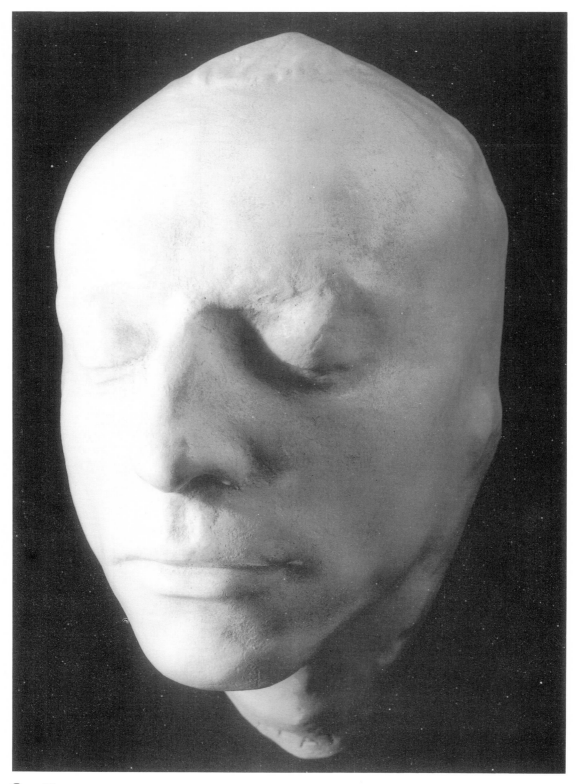

Cat. 188

WILLIAM BRIGHT MORRIS (1834-1900)

*187 Keats's Grave and the Pyramid of Cestius,
Testaccio Cemetery, Rome*
1870
Pastel, 17 x 25 cms
Private Collection

Keats was buried in the Protestant Cemetery in Rome
on 26 February 1821, close to Shelley's three year-old
son William. Shelley wrote of the cemetery in the
preface to *Adonais*: 'John Keats . . . was buried in the
romantic and lonely cemetery of the protestants in
that city, under the pyramid which is the tomb of
Cestius, and the massy walls and towers, now moul-
dering and desolate, which formed the circuit of
ancient Rome. The cemetery is an open space among
the ruins covered in winter with violets and daisies. It
might make one in love with death, to think that one
should be buried in so sweet a place.' Three years
later, Shelley's ashes were interred there, and later the

body of Severn, who often visited the place when in
Rome. He recalled to Haslam: 'Poor Keats has now
his wish—his humble wish: he is at peace in the quiet
grave. I walked there a few days ago, and found the
daisies had grown all over it. It is one of the most
lovely retired spots in Rome . . . with no sound in the
air but the tinkling of a few simple sheep and goats'.

GHERADI

188 Death Mask of Keats
*The London Borough of Camden from the
Collections at Keats House, Hampstead*

The original death mask of Keats was made, probably
by Gheradi, on 24 February 1821.

Cat. 189 Posthumous medallion of Keats by Girometti

9. AFTERLIFE

'Young Keats', wrote Shelley to Byron on 17 April 1821, 'whose 'Hyperion' showed so much promise, died lately at Rome from the consequences of breaking a blood-vessel, in the paroxysms of despair at the contemptuous attack of his book in the *Quarterly Review*'. 'I am sorry to hear what you say of Keats', Byron replied on the 26th, 'is it *actually* true? I did not think criticism had been so killing . . . Poor fellow! though with such inordinate self-love he would probably have not been very happy'. Shelley's sympathy and indignation was born out of his idea of the poet (not necessarily dependent on Keats himself) as a sensitive, beautiful spirit destroyed by the world, an idea he immortalised in *Adonais*. Byron, who famously described Keats in *Don Juan* as being 'snuffed out by an article', was sympathetic, but sceptical of Shelley's opinion, and always saw Keats as the youthful rhymester of 'self-love'. Neither of Keats's great contemporaries was therefore in a position to write a dispassionate, accurate picture of him.

But to present such a picture to the public was the desire of all Keats's immediate friends: 'My motive for writing Keats's life is that he may not continue to be represented as he was not', Charles Brown wrote to Dilke in January 1830, 'possibly I ought to add another motive,—that of revenge against Gifford and Lockhart,—aye, and Jeffrey'. But though everyone, including George Keats, felt that a biography should appear, there was never any agreement as to who was best qualified to write it. What is more, there was considerable difference of opinion over what the true portrait really was. So it was not until 1848, with the publication of Richard Monckton Milnes's *Life Letters and Literary Remains*, that a full-scale memoir appeared.

The same fate overtook the appearance of Keats's unpublished poems. In America, George Keats was claiming ownership of the estate, while in England Taylor was reluctant to produce anything more: 'I would like to print a complete Edition of Keats's Poems, with several of his letters', he wrote to John Clare in 1835, 'but the world cares nothing for him—I fear that even 250 copies would not sell.' There being no international copyright, a collected edition was published by Galignani in Paris in 1829, and versions of this appeared in America throughout the thirties and forties, but it was only in 1840, nineteen years after Keats's death, that the first English edition was published.

From then until the end of the century, Keats's reputation grew rapidly, particularly after the publication of Milnes's biography. Sumptuous editions, often illustrated, were appearing, and the Protestant Cemetery in Rome became a place of pilgrimage. He was an idolized figure among the new generation of poets (such as Tennyson), and the Pre-Raphaelite artists, who used his poems, particularly 'The Eve of St. Agnes' and 'Isabella', as subjects for their major oils. One of the most recent tributes to the poet who now stands, with Wordsworth, Coleridge, Byron, Shelley and Blake, as one of the six great 'romantics', is Tony Harrison's *A Kumquat for John Keats*, published in 1981.

Posthumous portrait of Keats, listening to a nightingale on Hampstead Heath, by Joseph Severn, 1845 *(London Borough of Camden from the Collections at Keats House, Hampstead)*

GUISEPPI GIROMETTI (1779-1851)

189   Plaque of John Keats
Plaster copy
*The London Borough of Camden from the
Collections at Keats House, Hampstead*

Girometti, the Italian sculptor, was a friend of
Canova, to whom Joseph Severn, when he came to
Rome with Keats, bore a letter of introduction from
Sir Thomas Lawrence. A carver of gems, cameos and
medallions, he was known personally to Severn,
Brown, Dr. Clark, and Woodhouse, who with Severn
commissioned this medallion. Completed a year or
two after Keats's death it was based on sketches by
Severn, the deathmask, and possibly Woodhouse's
own suggestions. It was placed beside the grave in
February 1876, and was generally thought to be an
unusually good likeness. John Hamilton Reynolds,
for instance thought it the best of all, and Charles
Brown commented: 'The bas relief he gave me of our
Keats delights me—never was anything like it; it
seems quite a piece of magic'.

ALFRED CLINT AFTER AMELIA CURREN
AND EDWARD ELLEKER WILLIAMS

190   Percy Bysshe Shelley (1792-1822)
Oil on canvas, 59.7 x 49.5 cms
National Portrait Gallery, London

When Keats's sonnet 'On First Looking into
Chapman's Homer' was published in *The Examiner*
on 1 December 1816, it was as part of an article on the
three "Young Poets", Keats, Shelley and Reynolds.
While Keats's relationship with Shelley was cordial, he
was also concerned not be in his shadow. The situation seems to have been that where the older (and
published) Shelley was anxious to give advice and
protection, Keats was equally anxious to fend off
what he saw as a threat to his poetic independence
and integrity; and he knew, well before the reviews of
Endymion appeared, that his image as Hunt's and
Shelley's *protégé* could be detrimental – 'I refused to
visit Shelley,' he wrote to Benjamin Bailey on 8
October 1817, 'that I might have my own unfettered
scope - and after all I shall have the Reputation of
Hunt's elevé—His corrections and amputations will
by the knowing ones be trased in the Poem—This is
to be sure the vexation of a day'. The first meeting
between Keats and Shelley, recorded in Haydon's

Journal, was earlier that year (20 January) at a dinner
at the home of Horace Smith, with Leigh Hunt and
Haydon as fellow guests. As was normal, there was a
heated argument on Christianity between Haydon
(a Christian) and Shelley and Hunt (atheists). Keats
gave his low opinion of this kind of occasion in the
same letter to Bailey:

> I went to Hunt's and Haydon's who live now as
> neighbours. Shelley was there—I know nothing
> about any thing in this part of the world—every
> Body seems at Loggerheads. There's Hunt infatu-
> ated—there's Haydon's Picture in statu quo.
> There's Hunt walks up and down his painting
> room criticising every head most unmercifully—
> There's Horace Smith tired of Hunt. The web of
> our Life is of a mingled Yarn.

By the time he was writing *Endymion*, he had
evidently succeeded in finding a measure of independence – he wrote to his brothers on 23 January 1818:
'the fact is he & Shelley are hurt and perhaps justly,
at my not having showed them the affair officiously
& from several hints I have had they appear much
disposed to dissect & anatomize, any trip or slip I
may have made.—But whose afraid Ay! Tom! demme
if I am.'

Shelley looked forward to receiving *Endymion* in
Italy: 'I hope that it will be included in my parcel,' he
wrote to Charles Ollier on 16 August 1818, 'He has a
fine imagination and ought to become something
excellent; but he is at present entangled in the cold

vanity of systems'. He obtained a copy at Leghorn in 1819, and gave his response to Charles Ollier on 6 September:

> . . . much praise is due to me for having read [*Endymion*], the Authors intention appearing to be that no person should possibly get to the end of it. Yet it is full of some of the highest & the finest gleams of poetry; indeed every thing seems to be viewed by the mind of a poet which is described in it.

Shelley repeated this criticism to Keats himself, in his letter to the younger poet inviting him to Italy (27 July 1820):

> I have lately read your Endymion again & ever with a new sense of the treasures of poetry it contains, though treasures poured forth with indistinct profusion. This, people in general will not endure, & that is the cause of the comparatively few copies which have been sold. I feel persuaded that you are capable of the greatest things, so you but will . . .
>
> In poetry *I* have sought to avoid system & mannerism; I wish those who excel me in genius, would pursue the same plan.

Keats's responded on 16 August 1820 that he was gratified that Shelley had found good in his 'poor Poem;—which I would willingly take the trouble to unwrite', and made his own comments upon Shelley's drama *The Cenci*:

> There is only one part I am the judge of; the Poetry, and dramatic effect, which by many spirits now a days is considered the mammon. A modern work it is said must have a purpose, which may be the God—an *artist* must serve mammon—he must have 'self-concentration' selfishness perhaps. You I am sure will forgive me for sincerely remarking that you might curb your magnanimity and be more of an artist, and load every rift of your subject with ore. The thought of such discipline must fall like cold chains upon you, who perhaps never sat with your wings furl'd for six Months together. And is this not extraordinary talk for the writer of Endymion? whose mind was like a pack of scattered cards. I am pick'd up and sorted to a pip. My Imagination is a Monastery and I am its monk.

In the Preface to *Adonais*, Shelley wrote: 'I consider the fragment of Hyperion, as second to nothing that was ever produced by a writer of the same years.' It was with *Adonais* that Shelley could really develop his idea of the fragile, wronged, Phaedrus-like young poet, something to which Keats would have been understandably reluctant to subscribe.

191 *Letter from Percy Bysshe Shelley to Marianne Hunt*
[29 October 1820]
The British Library Board

It was in *Hyperion* that Shelley first saw signs of future greatness. 'Keats's new volume has arrived to us,' he wrote to Marianne Hunt from Pisa on 29 October 1820, '& the fragment called Hyperion promises for him that he is destined to become one of the first writers of the age.—His other things are imperfect enough, & what is worse written in a bad sort of style which is becoming fashionable among those who fancy they are imitating Hunt & Wordsworth.'

192 *Letter from Percy Bysshe Shelley to Claire Clairmont*
[16 June 1821]
The British Library Board

'Let me see if I have any news for you,' Shelley writes to Claire Clairmont, and tells her of his immediate motive in writing *Adonais*:

> I have received a most melancholy account of the last illness of poor Keats, which I will neither tell you nor send you; for it would make you too low-spirited.—My elegy on him is finished: I have dipped my pen in consuming fire to chastise his destroyers; otherwise the tone of the poem is solemn and exalted. I send it to the press here, & you will soon have a copy.

PERCY BYSSHE SHELLEY
193 *'Adonais'*
Pisa: with the types of Didot, 1821
Private Collection

ADONAIS

———

AN ELEGY ON THE DEATH OF JOHN KEATS,
AUTHOR OF ENDYMION, HYPERION ETC.

BY

PERCY. B. SHELLEY

Ἀστὴρ πρὶν μὲν ἔλαμπες ἐνὶ ζωοῖσιν ἑῷος.
Νῦν δὲ θανὼν, λάμπεις ἕσπερος ἐν φθιμένοις.
PLATO.

PISA

WITH THE TYPES OF DIDOT
MDCCCXXI.

Adonais was written, at great speed, in June 1821.
Shelley arranged that a small edition be printed in
Pisa, thereby enabling him to correct it before sending it to Charles Ollier for publication in England.
'The poem is beautifully printed', he wrote to Ollier
in July, '& what is of more consequence, correctly;
indeed it was to obtain this last point that I sent it to
the press at Pisa.' In an earlier letter he had asked
Ollier to 'observe the great beauty' of the Didot type-
face. Created in France by Firmin Didot (1764-1836),
it has been called the first 'modern' face, characterised
by its vertical shading and hairline serifs.

194 *Letter from Joseph Severn to Charles Brown*
  1 January 1822
  The British Library Board

Severn is writing to Brown after Keats's death, referring to Shelley's *Adonais*, and the matter of Keats's
gravestone. The inscription, requested by Keats to
read simply: 'Here lies one whose name was writ in
water', was embellished by Brown so as to concur
with Shelley that Keats's death was hastened by 'enemies': 'This Grave contains all that was Mortal, of a
YOUNG ENGLISH POET Who, on his Death Bed, in the
Bitterness of his Heart at the Malicious Power of his
Enemies, Desired these Words to be engraven on his
Tomb Stone.' Brown later changed his mind, and
wrote to Severn in November 1836 of his desire 'that
not one word shall be there except those contained in
his dying request . . . Swayed by a very natural feeling
at the time, I advised more, but am now convinced of
the error, the sort of profanation of adding even a

note of admiration to his own words.' The design
Severn refers to was of a Greek lyre (copied from
one in the British Museum) with one string broken:

> I have received a copy of the Monody on Keats. I
> find many beauties in it, but is it not a pity so
> much beauty should be scattered about, without
> the balancing of lights and shades, or the opposi-
> tions of colours? In this poem there is such a want
> of repose,—you are continually longing to know
> what he will be at. It gave me great pleasure as a
> tribute to poor Keats's memory . . . The grave-
> stone is advanced, but not up yet. I cannot well
> recollect the Greek Lyre, so that they wait for the
> Drawings from London. I liked the inscription
> much, and it shall be done exactly.

Interestingly, Severn's criticisms of *Adonais* echo
Keats's own words in his last letter to Brown that 'the
knowledge of contrast, feeling for light and shade' are
'necessary for a poem', and his advice to Shelley that
he should 'curb your magnanimity and be more of an
artist'.

Severn later admitted that he owed many of his
future friendships to Shelley's praise of him in the
preface to *Adonais*, including that of William Ewart
Gladstone.

GEORGE HENRY HARLOW
195 *Lord Byron (1788-1824)*
  c. 1815
  Pencil and watercolour, H 22.5 cms (oval)
  Private Collection

'You speak of Lord Byron and me,' Keats wrote to
George and Georgiana on 20 September 1819, 'There
is this great difference between us. He describes what
he sees—I describe what I imagine—Mine is the
hardest task. You see the immense difference'. Not
only did he feel little kinship with Byron's style of
verse, Keats was also conscious of the elder poet's
fame. Haydon recalls an incident on 7 April 1817 in
which his rivalry was made explicit:

> Keats said to me today as we were walking along
> "Byron, Scott, Southey, & Shelley think they are
> to lead the age, but [*the rest of the sentence, consist-
> ing probably of eight or ten words, has been erased.*]"
> This was said with all the consciousness of Genius;
> his face reddened.

For his part, Byron was unsympathetic, and some-times savage in his attitude towards Keats and his poetry. Keats's attack on the Augustans in 'Sleep and Poetry' was not likely to commend itself to a fervent admirer of Pope, and Byron was averse to the 'Cock-ney' school typified by Hunt, '*that second-hand* school of poetry', as he described it to Shelley. Unlike Shelley, however, he did not see Keats as a martyr to poetry destroyed by reviewers. On 31 July 1821, he wrote to John Murray:

> Are you aware that Shelley has written an elegy on Keats—and accuses the Quarterly of killing him?—
>
>> Who killed John Keats?
>> I, says the Quarterly
>> So savage & Tartarly
>> 'Twas one of my feats—
>
>> Who shot the arrow?
>> The poet-priest Milman
>> (So ready to kill man)
>> Or Southey or Barrow.—
>
> You know very well that I did not approve of Keats's poetry or principles of poetry—or of his abuse of Pope—but as he is dead—omit *all* that is said *about him* in any *M.S.S.* of mine—or publica-tion.—His Hyperion is a fine monument & will keep his name—I do not envy the man—who

wrote the article—your review people have no more right to kill than any other foot pads.— However—he who would die of an article in a review—would probably have died of something else equally trivial—the same thing nearly hap-pened to Kirke White—who afterwards died of consumption.

Leigh Hunt recalled Byron asking the meaning of the phrase from the *Ode to a Nightingale*, 'a beakerfull of the warm South': 'the sort of poetry in which he excelled, was not accustomed to these poetical con-centrations. At the moment also, he was willing to find fault, and did not discern an excellence different from his own.' In his least generous moments, Byron would refer to Keats as 'that dirty little blackguard' and to his work as 'Johnny Keats's *p—ss a bed* poetry' and 'the *Onanism* of Poetry', but his most generous account was contained in a note to "Observations upon an Article in Blackwood's Magazine,", dated 12 November 1821:

> My indignation at Mr. Keats's deprecation of Pope has hardly permitted me to do justice to his own genius, which, malgré all the fantastic fopperies of his style, was undoubtedly of great promise. His fragment of 'Hyperion' seems actually inspired by the Titans, and is as sublime as Aeschylus. He is a loss to our literature; and the more so, as he him-self, before his death, is said to have been persuad-ed that he had not taken the right line, and was re-forming his style upon the more classical mod-els of language.

196 Letter from Lord Byron to John Murray
7 August 1821
The British Library Board

In these three letters to Murray, Byron questions Shelley's opinion that the reviews of *Endymion* has-tened Keats's death:

> I have just been turning over the homicide review of J. Keats.—It is harsh certainly and contemptu-ous but not more so than what I recollect of the Edinburgh R[eview] of "the Hours of Idleness" in 1808. The Reviewer allows him "a degree of talent which deserves to be put in the right way" "rays of fancy" "gleams of Genius" and "powers of lan-

guage". —It is harder on L. Hunt than upon *Keats* & professes fairly to review only *one* book of his poem.—Altogether—though very provoking it was hardly so bitter as to kill—unless there was a morbid feeling previously in his system.— —

197 *Letter from Lord Byron to John Murray*
18 November 1820
The British Library Board

P.S.—Of the praises of that little dirty blackguard KEATES in the Edinburgh—I shall observe as Johnson did when Sheridan the actor got a *pension.* "What has *he* got a pension? then it is time that I should give up *mine.*"—Nobody could be prouder of the praises of the Edinburgh than I was—or more alive to their censure—as I showed in E[nglish] B[ards] and S[cotch] R[eviewe]rs—at present *all the men* they have ever praised are degraded by that insane article.—Why don't they review & praise "Solomon's Guide to Health" it is better sense —and as much poetry as Johnny Keates.

198 *Letter from Lord Byron to John Murray*
26 April 1821
The British Library Board

Is it true—what Shelley writes me that poor John Keats died at Rome of the Quarterly Review? I am very sorry for it—though I think he took the wrong line as a poet—and was spoilt by Cockneyfying and Suburbing—and versifying Tooke's Pantheon and Lempriere's Dictionary.— —I know by experience that a savage review is Hemlock to a sucking author—and the one on me—(which produced the English Bards &c.) knocked me down—but I got up again.—Instead of bursting a blood-vessel—I drank three bottles of Claret—and began an answer—finding that there was nothing in the Article for which I could lawfully knock Jeffrey on the head in an honourable way.—However I would not be the person who wrote the homicidal article—for all the honour & glory in the World,—though I by no means approve of that School of Scribbling—which it treats upon.— —

GEORGE GORDON, LORD BYRON
199 *Don Juan Cantos 1,2 & 5*
Manuscript transcribed by Mary Shelley and corrected by Byron.
John Murray

Leigh Hunt recalled an incident with Byron in Italy: 'When I told him, that Mr. Keats admired his "Don Juan," he expressed both surprise and pleasure, and afterwards mentioned him with respect in a canto of it.' Byron may well have been surprised, for elsewhere Keats shows evidence of his dislike of the poem, so different from his own. In a letter to George and Georgiana (18 September 1819) he refers to it as 'Lord Byron's last flash poem', and Joseph Severn remembered them reading the poem to each other on the *Maria Crowther.* 'Keats resented the mocking cynicism of the shipwreck canto, and was so wrought upon that at last he flung the volume aside in contemptuous anger'. Byron's poetry, he declared, was based on a paltry originality, that of being new by making solemn things gay and gay things solemn. It is interesting that Richard Woodhouse should find, in the downbeat ending to 'The Eve of St. Agnes' an example of such Byronic cynicism; on 19 September 1819 he wrote to Taylor:

> [Keats] has altered the last 3 lines to leave on the reader a sense of pettish disgust, by bringing Old Angela in (only) dead stiff & ugly.—He says he likes that the poem should leave off with this Change of Sentiment—it was what he aimed at, & was glad to find from my objections to it that he had succeeded.—I apprehend he had a fancy for trying his hand at any attempt to play with his reader, & fling him off at last—I shod have thought, he affected the "Don Juan" style of mingling up sentiment & sneering: but that he had before asked Hessey if he co^d procure him a sight of that work, as he had not met with it . . .

Don Juan refers to Keats, in stanza 60 of Canto XI:

> John Keats, who was killed off by one critique,
> Just as he really promised something great,
> If not intelligible,—without Greek
>   Contrived to talk about the Gods of late,
> Much as they might have been supposed to speak.
>   Poor fellow! His was an untoward fate:—
> 'Tis strange the mind, that very fiery particle,
> Should let itself be snuffed out by an Article.

THE

POETICAL WORKS

OF

COLERIDGE, SHELLEY, AND KEATS.

COMPLETE IN ONE VOLUME.

PARIS

PUBLISHED BY A. AND W. GALIGNANI

Nº 18, RUE VIVIENNE

1829

200 *The Poetical Works of Coleridge, Shelley,
     and Keats*
     Paris: A. & W. Galignani, 1829
     Private Collection

201 *The Poetical Works of Coleridge, Shelley,
     and Keats*
     Paris: Galignani, n.d.
     Reissue of 1829 edition
     Professor Michael Jaye

The Galignani edition of Keats's poetry, the first collected edition, appeared in Paris in 1829. It was one
of a series of recent English poets that A. and W.
Galignani piratically published in the late twenties
that, in its cheapness, exploited the lack of international copyright. Drawing upon as much as it could
find, it includes, in addition to the three original volumes, 'The Human Seasons' and 'To Ailsa Rock'
(published in Leigh Hunt's *Literary Pocket-Book*,
1819), 'On a Picture of Leander' (published in 1829 in
the *Gem*), and 'In drear-nighted December' (which
appeared in the *London Literary Gazette* in September

1829. The preceding memoir relies upon the recollections of Leigh Hunt (the only writer who had published to date anything on Keats's life) in *Lord Byron
and his Contemporaries*; and the frontispiece portrait is
a weak version of the early sketch by Severn (which
also appeared in the Hunt volume).

202 *The Poetical Works of Coleridge, Shelley,
     and Keats*
     Philadelphia: DeSilver, Thomas, and Co, 1835
     Professor Michael Jaye

203 *The Poetical Works of Coleridge, Shelley,
     and Keats*
     Philadelphia: DeSilver, Thomas, and Co, 1836
     Professor Michael Jaye

204 *The Poetical Works of Howitt, Milman,
     and Keats*
     Philadelphia: Thomas, Cowperthwait and Co.,
     1840
     Professor Michael Jaye

205 *The Poetical Works of John Keats*
     New York: Wiley and Putnam, 1846.
     Professor Michael Jaye

The unauthorised Galignani edition was fully exploited by American publishers. The 1831 edition of poems
by J. Howe of Philadelphia follows the Galignani text
page for page, made only the smallest alterations to
the memoir and reproduced the frontispiece portrait.
From then until the 1850s this was the basis for a
wealth of editions, all with only very slight variants.
The prologue to the New York edition of 1846 claims
that 'the many editions already published of Keats's
works have sufficiently attested his popularity. His
reputation has been continually advancing since the
period of his lamented death.' His popularity in
America was certainly increasing, but these pirate
copies, with their second-hand texts and strategic
grouping of several authors in a single volume (in
one case Keats appears with Mary Howitt and H.H.
Millman), are principally evidence of the ingenious,
money-saving methods of American publishers.

206 *The Poetical Works of John Keats*
London: William Smith, 1841
Professor Michael Jaye

The first collected edition in England of Keats's poems appeared, 'By permission of the Proprietor' (that is, John Taylor), in 1840. It was a cheap paper-covered edition, part of 'Smith's Standard Library'. A more attractive second edition was brought out by Taylor and William Smith the following year, with an engraving of the drawing by Hilton as frontispiece.

207 *Letter from John Taylor to John Clare*
26 March 1821
The British Library Board

Informing Clare of Keats's death, Taylor expresses his desire for a memoir. It was his intention to write this himself, and *The Morning Chronicle* of 4 June 1821 contained the advertisement: 'Speedily will be published, with a portrait, *Memoirs and Remains of John Keats*. Printed for Taylor & Hessey, Fleet Street.' But there was opposition, from among others, Charles Brown ('I will not consent to be a party in a mere bookseller's job' he said), and the promised volume never appeared.

> The Life of poor Keats is ended at last; he died at the Age of 25. He used to say he should effect nothing on which he would rest his Fame till he was 30, and all his Hopes are over at 25. But he has left enough though he did not think so - and if his Biographer cannot do him justice, the Advocate is in Fault, and not the Cause. Poor fellow! Perhaps your feeling will produce some lines to his memory. One of the very few Poets of this Day is gone.

Clare wrote an epitaph, a sonnet published in *The Village Minstrel* (1821) – 'To the Memory of John Keats'.

> The world, its hopes, and fears, have pass'd away;
>   No more its trifling thou shalt feel or see;
> Thy hopes are ripening in a brighter day,
>   While these left buds thy monument shall be.
> When Rancour's aims have past in naught away,
>   Enlarging specks discern'd in more than thee,
> And beauties 'minishing which few display—
>   When these are past, true child of Poesy,
> Thou shalt survive. Ah, while a being dwells,
>   With soul, in nature's joys, to warm like thine,
> With eye to view her fascinating spells,
>   And dream entranced o'er each form divine,
> Thy worth, Enthusiast, shall be cherish'd here,
> Thy name with him shall linger, and be dear.

96   THE GOSSIP.

ON READING LAMIA, AND OTHER POEMS, BY JOHN KEATS.

Young, warm aspirant! thy mellifluous song
  Is as thine own " full-throated" nightingale,
Breathing her moon-light melody among
  Close-tufted trees, and sleeping larks, whose tale
Is hush'd until the orient sky be stained
  With barred chrysolite and jasper deep,
  And sweeter amethyst of purpling dye,
    All softly rainbow-grained —
Blended like trickling tears, when spirits weep
  In unison for earthly misery.

Lamia, and Isabel, oh! what a fate
  Were yours! so opposite, yet both so sad! —
Gladly we turn from Apollonius' hate,
  To gentle Madeline, in vestments clad
Of " rustling" silks, beneath the prism-like moon;—
  From choruses of woodland melody
    We turn, to where thy " light-wing'd Dryad" sings
      Her warm love-flushed tune,
  What time the gentle Fays assiduously,
    To load the chaliced flowers, ambrosia brings;

Soft, dewy drops! making an odorous bath,
  Where her sweet limbs Titania might enlave,
While lilies 'broidering the hedge-row path,
  Shook by attendant elves, fresh music gave! —
But now, alas! their mirth is turn'd to woe!
  For thou, who wert the muse's gifted child
    Hath passed away e'en like a favourite flower,
      Too sweet to thrive below;
  And now thy inspiration deep and mild,
    No more will soothe us in our summer bower!
                          G. V. D.

UNKNOWN AUTHOR
208 *The Gossip*
    London: J. Benson, 1821
    Professor Michael Jaye

The number of 19 May 1821 contains an elegy on Keats's death, by 'G.V.D.', entitled 'On Reading Lamia, and Other Poems, by John Keats'. Though minor, the elegy, in its classical strains, and images of weeping nature, anticipates *Adonais*.

WILLIAM HONE
209 *The Table Book*
    London: Hunt and Clarke, 1827, 1828
    Professor Michael Jaye

Hone describes his *Table Book* has 'a series of shifting scenes—a kind of literary kaleidoscope, combining popular forms with singular appearances—by which youth and age of all ranks may be amused.' There are three references to Keats, all of an overly-romantic nature. The first remembers 'a charming little grove in Well Walk, with a bench at the end; whereon I last saw poor Keats, the poet of the "Pot of Basil," sitting and sobbing his dying breath into a handkerchief.' The second reports on Keats's epitaph, and the third is a poem by 'Gaston', dated 13 September 1827, and

Hampstead, however, is the " place of groves;"—how long it may remain so is a secret in the bosom of speculators and builders. Its first grove, townward, is the noble private avenue from the Hampstead-road to Belsize-house, in the valley between Primrose hill and the hill whereon the church stands, with Mr. Memory-Corner Thompson's remarkable house and lodge at the corner of the pleasant highway to the little village of West-end. In the neighbourhood of Hampstead church, and between that edifice and the heath, there are several old groves. Winding southwardly from the heath, there is a charming little grove in Well Walk, with a bench at the end; whereon I last saw poor Keats, the poet of the " Pot of Basil," sitting and sobbing his dying breath into a handkerchief,— gleaning parting looks towards the quiet landscape he had delighted in—musing, as in his Ode to a Nightingale.

My heart aches, and a drowsy numbness pains
  My sense, as though of hemlock I had drunk,
Or emptied some dull opiate to the drains
  One minute past, and Lethe-wards had sunk:
'Tis not through envy of thy happy lot,
  But being too happy in thine happiness,—
    That thou, light-winged Dryad of the trees,
      In some melodious plot
  Of beechen green, and shadows numberless,
    Singest of summer in full-throated ease.
O, for a draught of vintage! that hath been
  Cool'd a long age in the deep-delved earth,
Tasting of Flora and the country green,
  Dance, and Provençal song, and sunburnt mirth!

entitled: 'Extemporaneous Lines, suggested by some Thoughts and Recollections of John Keats, the Poet'.

These, and the edition of *The Gossip* above, show that despite the lack of an immediate memoir or collected edition, Keats did not disappear from the public consciousness immediately after his death.

LEIGH HUNT
210 *Lord Byron and Some of his Contemporaries*
    London: Henry Colburn, 1828
    The Wordsworth Trust

Hunt's memoir of Keats was the first to appear. It is a slight reminiscence, consisting of occasional anecdotes, and quoting some of the poetry with brief comments. Throughout, there is the conviction that Keats was a man of genius, who would, in time, achieve the recognition he deserved. Its effect, however, was to incite fresh contempt from the Tory reviewers (Lockhart, for instance, was outraged that Keats should have been considered a worthy contem-

MR. KEATS.

WITH A CRITICISM ON HIS WRITINGS.

Mr. KEATS, when he died, had just completed his four-and-twentieth year. He was under the middle height; and his lower limbs were small in comparison with the upper, but neat and well-turned. His shoulders were very broad for his size: he had a face, in which energy and sensibility were remarkably mixed up, an eager power checked and made patient by ill-health. Every feature was at once strongly cut, and delicately alive. If there was any faulty expression, it was in the mouth, which was not without something of a character of pugnacity. The face was rather long than otherwise; the upper lip projected a little over the under; the chin was bold, the cheeks sunken; the eyes mellow and glowing; large, dark and sensitive. At the recital of a noble action, or a beautiful thought, they would suffuse with tears, and his mouth trembled. In this, there was ill health as well as imagination, for he did not like these betrayals of emotion; and he had great personal as well as moral courage. His hair, of a brown colour, was fine, and hung in natural ringlets. The head was a puzzle for the phrenologists, being remarkably small in the skull; a singularity which he had in common with Lord Byron and Mr. Shelley, none of

porary of Byron), and to dismay Keats's friends. Brown thought it 'worse than disappointing', commenting: 'it seems as if Hunt was so impressed by his illness that he had utterly forgotten him in health.' But until Monckton Milnes's biography appeared twenty years later, it was the main source of information about the poet.

CAROLINE SMITH

211   Richard Monckton Milnes (1809-1885)
Pencil and watercolour, 21.5 x 17.5 cms
Spedding Collection

Milnes was born in 1809, and was one of the 'Apostles' (with, among others, Tennyson, Arthur Hallam and Richard Chevenix Trench) at Trinity College Cambridge, who arranged in 1829 for the publication of *Adonais*. He debated at Oxford on the superiority of Shelley as a poet to Byron. After a period of travel in 1831-5 he became a prominent social figure, a minor liberal politician, a minor poet, and a generous supporter of authors. He was also known for his large library of erotica. In 1863 he became the first Baron Houghton, and died in Vichy in 1885.

In the 1840s Milnes's poetry was popular and highly thought-of, and at one stage he was talked of as a successor to Wordsworth as Poet Laureate. Landor is said to have maintained 'that Milnes was the greatest poet then living and writing in England', though Milnes himself recommended Tennyson for the Laureateship. His poetry has now been forgotten, and he is remembered for his patronage of other authors, both of his own time and (as in the case of Keats) of the recent past.

212   Letter from Charles Brown to Richard Monckton Milnes
17 October 1835
Trinity College, Cambridge

Charles Brown writes to Monckton Milnes, indignant at George Keats's efforts to block his publication of any of Keats's unpublished poems and biography:

Next February fourteen years will have passed since the death of our Keats; yet I am afraid an attempt to publish his relics will be put an end to in a violent manner. I have been duly warned that George Keats, his brother, has placed his Power of Attny in the hands of a certain party in London to withhold any one from publishing Keats's poems. It comes to this,—a point on which I am ignorant,—are his poems, published and posthumous, any body's property, when fourteen years shall have elapsed after his disease?

Fourteen years was then the period of copyright protection, and the 'certain party' was Charles Wentworth Dilke.

213   *Letter from John Hamilton Reynolds*
    to Richard Monckton Milnes
    26 June 1848
    Trinity College, Cambridge

As this letter shows, Reynolds too was willing (though not anxious) to put his own memories of the poet into publishable form. He writes to Milnes:

> If you find the work is too great a mortgage upon your time (I know it *cannot* be upon your wishes) rather than our rare Poet should go on *unbiographied* I would try an indifferent, though earnest memoir of him – with only such means as are open to me. Pray understand me – that the desire of my heart is that his memory & his Genius should be done justice to – & that *you* (with your ample means) should <u>*do*</u> it.

214   *Letter from Joseph Severn to Richard*
    Monckton Milnes
    Undated [c. 1847-8]
    Trinity College, Cambridge

Severn agrees with Milnes's wish that he should paint the latter's portrait, '& while you are sitting', he continues, 'I could tell you some [of] the many interesting things *not* in Browns life of Keats, and also explain my serious objections to its being published in any way.—As I was in doubt & did not like that my individual opinion should influence you I have consulted Dilke, who more than confirms it—I have lots of beautiful things about Keats which may inspire you to begin—'

RICHARD MONCKTON MILNES
215 *Life, Letters, and Literary Remains,*
    of John Keats
    London: Edward Moxon 1848
    Private Collection

LIFE,

LETTERS, AND LITERARY REMAINS,

OF

JOHN KEATS.

EDITED BY

RICHARD MONCKTON MILNES.

IN TWO VOLUMES.

VOL. I.

LONDON:
EDWARD MOXON, DOVER STREET.
1848.

Milnes was first encouraged to write his life of Keats by Charles Brown. The two men had first met at Walter Savage Landor's home in Italy in 1833. By 1841 Brown had decided to entrust the publication of Keats life and literary remains to him. 'Mr. Milnes is a poet himself,' he wrote to Severn on 21 March, 'an admirer of Keats and, in my mind, better able to sit in judgement on a selection for publication than any other man I know.' Brown gave him his own memoir and literary remains, expecting him to publish it intact with notes and comments. But in 1845, after Brown's death, Milnes was setting to work on his own biography. In the next three years he consulted nearly all the poet's friends, with the exception of Leigh Hunt, who 'could only encourage me by his interest and sympathy.' By a combination of tact, genuine enthusiasm and considerable private means, he managed to work with all their various quarrels, and, they were united in their satisfaction with what he wrote, and pleased with the reflected glory it threw upon them. Only Hunt, who was hurt by some of the contents of Keats's letters, was unhappy with it, objecting so strenuously that a new edition was out of the question. Strangely, Milnes himself had a low opinion of it: 'It is the biography of a mere boy . . . and therefore the literary interest is but small. . . . I cannot expect any reputation for the book.'

THE PRE-RAPHAELITES

> It is in Keats that one observes the beginning of the artistic renaissance of England . . . in the calmness of his vision, his self-control, his unerring sense of beauty, and his recognition of a separate realm for the imagination, Keats was the pure and serene artist, the forerunner of the Pre-Raphaelite School.
>
> Oscar Wilde, the *New York Herald*, 1882

When the Pre-Raphaelite Brotherhood was founded in 1848 (the year of Milnes's biography), its members, forward looking and iconoclastic, drew up a list of 'Immortals', 'the few far-seeing ones [who] revealed vast visions of beauty to mankind'. At their head was Christ (with four stars), who was followed by the author of *Job* and Shakespeare (both with three stars). Keats was one of the two-star immortals, who also included Dante, Homer, Chaucer and Goethe. This put him above Wordsworth, Byron, Milton and Raphael. Keats's poems of romantic medievalism, their concentrated, dreamlike sensuousness and intense colouring (as well as the traditional image of him as a solitary, misunderstood spirit), were an inspiration to the group of artists who came to see art as an antidote to the ugliness of life, secure in its own, absolute beauty and creating 'a separate realm for the imagination.'

OSCAR WILDE (1854-1900)
216 *Letter to W.M. Rossetti, enclosing monograph of the Protestant Cemetery, Rome*
14 July 1877
The British Library Board

'Knowing your love and admiration for John Keats,' writes the twenty-three year-old Wilde to William Michael Rossetti, 'I take the liberty of sending you a short monograph of mine on his grave at Rome . . . in hope that you might take up the question of having a suitable memorial erected to him. I am only a boy, and could not of course originate anything of the kind; but you with your great literary influence and eloquent pen might, I think, easily gain the honour of raising a statue of the divine poet.'

Visiting Keats's tomb, 'the holiest place in Rome', Wilde had, to the distress of his Catholic companions, prostrated himself on the grass. His monograph, published in the *Irish Monthly* in July 1877 sees Keats as a 'divine boy', 'a Priest of Beauty slain before his time', whose 'mean grave . . . and these wild flowers are but poor memorials to one so great as Keats'. His opinion of the medallion portrait was that it made Keats's face 'ugly, and rather hatchet-shaped, with thick sensual lips, and is utterly unlike the poet himself, who was very beautiful to look on.' He repeated this opinion in a letter to Lord Houghton, who replied that he thought the likeness a good one, and that Keats, far from being, Adonais-like, an unhappy warrior, 'was anything but unhappy, and he was recognised with unusual rapidity'.

Rossetti took some time to reply to this letter, and then said that there was no hurry for a statue, since in the fullness of time all great poets would have all the statues they deserved.

WILLIAM MICHAEL ROSSETTI (1829-1919)
217 *Life of John Keats*
London: Walter Scott, 1887
Professor Michael Jaye

When Rossetti's life appeared ten years after Wilde's letter to him, Wilde said in a review on 27 September that it was 'a great failure'. Rossetti's method of divorcing the central biography from chapters on the poems, his discussion of Keats's appearance and character, and his literary criticism was not quite successful, but more, Rossetti seemed to lack sympathy for his subject. His conclusion was that Keats 'was doomed to be the poet of youthfulness', unable to stand beside 'his great contemporary Shelley':

> it seems to me true that not many of Keats's poems are highly admirable; that most of them, amid all their beauty, have an adolescent and frequently a morbid tone, marking want of manful thew and sinew and of mental balance; that he is not seldom obscure, chiefly through indifference to the thought itself and its necessary means of development; that he is emotional without substance, and beautiful without control; and that personalism of a wilful and fitful kind pervades the mass of his handiwork.

DANTE GABRIEL ROSSETTI (1828-82)
218 Sonnet: 'John Keats'
Autograph manuscript
The British Library Board

Unlike his brother, Dante Gabriel Rossetti was a true Keats enthusiast. According to Lady Burne-Jones, he persuaded William Morris 'to give up architecture and take to painting, saying that if any man had poetry in him he should paint it, that the course of poetry had almost been run, but painting was still an unknown art in England, and that the next Keats ought to be a painter'. In this sonnet (published in *Ballads and Sonnets*, 1881) he compares the 'weltering London ways' with the beauty of Keats's imagination:

The weltering London ways where children weep
  And girls whom none call maidens laugh,—strange
                         road
  Miring his outward steps, who inly trode
The bright Castalian brink and Latmos' steep:—
Even such his life's cross-paths; till deathly deep
  He toiled through sands of Lethe; and long pain,
  Weary with labour spurned and love found vain,
In dead Rome's sheltering shadow wrapped his sleep.

O pang-dowered Poet, whose reverberant lips
And heart-strung lyre awoke the moon's eclipse,—
  Thou whom the daisies glory in growing o'er,—
Their fragrance clings around thy name, not writ
But rumour'd in water, while the fame of it
  Along Time's flood goes echoing evermore.

WILLIAM HOLMAN HUNT (1827-1910)
219 The Flight of Madeline and Porphyro
RA 1848
Oil on canvas, 77.5 x 113 cms
Guildhall Art Gallery, City of London

Illustrated in colour on p. 22

When Holman Hunt began this painting (of the climax to 'The Eve of St. Agnes') in 1846, he believed it was the first to be based upon the work of that 'still little-known poet'. Here Hunt has chosen as his subject the close of the poem where the lovers Porphyro and Madeline, safe in the power of their love, abandon the world of drunken revelry:

  They glide, like phantoms, into the wide hall;
  Like phantoms, to the iron porch, they glide;

Where lay the Porter, in uneasy sprawl,
With a huge empty flaggon by his side:
The wakeful bloodhound rose, and shook his hide,
But his sagacious eye an inmate owns:
By one, and one, the bolts full easy slide:—
The chains lie silent on the footworn stones;—
The key turns, and the door upon its hinges groans.

WILLIAM HOLMAN HUNT
220 The Flight of Madeline and Porphyro
Pencil, 7.4 x 9.7 cms
The Visitors of the Ashmolean Museum, Oxford

A pencil study for the above painting.

WILLIAM HOLMAN HUNT
221 Isabella and the Pot of Basil
1867
Oil on canvas
Laing Art Gallery, Newcastle upon Tyne

Illustrated in colour on p. 19

Keats based his poem 'Isabella; or, The Pot of Basil' (written in 1818) on a story in Boccaccio's Decameron. Isabella, rebelling against her brothers' wish that she marry a nobleman, is in love with Lorenzo. The brothers lure Lorenzo, a member of their own household, into a forest, where they murder him. Lorenzo then appears to Isabella as a ghost and tells her where he is buried. Isabella finds the body, severs the head and stores it in a pot with a plant of basil over it. The brothers steal the pot of basil, discover the festering head, and conscious-stricken go into banishment. Isabella dies of grieving for her 'basil-pot'.

Keats's friends thought 'Isabella' the finest thing he had yet done, and indeed it was his best-known poem for years after his death. 'Reynolds has returned from a six weeks enjoyment in Devonshire', Keats wrote to his brother and sister-in-law, 'he is well and persuades me to publish my pot of Basil as an answer to the attacks made on me in Blackwood's Magazine and the Quarterly Review'. But although he included it in the 1820 volume of poems, Keats was self-critical; 'Isabella,' he wrote to Richard Woodhouse in 1819, 'is what I should call were I a reviewer 'A weak-sided Poem' with an amusing sober-sadness about it.'

ARTHUR HUGHES (1832-1915)
222 *The Eve of St. Agnes*
1856
Oil on board; 58 x 29; 64 x 56; 58 x 29 cms
Tate Gallery, London

Hughes has designed his composition in the style of a medieval altarpiece: three separate episodes are shown on three panels. The first, left-hand panel shows Porphyro being shown into the castle by Madeline's nurse, and the centre panel shows him in Madeline's chamber. The right-hand panel, depicting their flight past the drunken porter, is clearly inspired by the earlier rendering of this scene by Holman Hunt (above). Hughes varies his lighting-effects according to the scene, the centre of the whole composition being the winter moon shining through the latticed window.

ARTHUR HUGHES
223 *La Belle Dame sans Merci*
c.1862
Pencil study
Tullie House, City Museum & Art Gallery, Carlisle

A study for the painting *La Belle Dame sans Merci* (1862-3), now in the National Gallery of Victoria in Melbourne. Where the painting has the knight on the ground with the lady on horseback, this sketch has both figures riding on the one horse, with the knight embracing the lady. Another study, in the British Museum, shows both figures on foot.

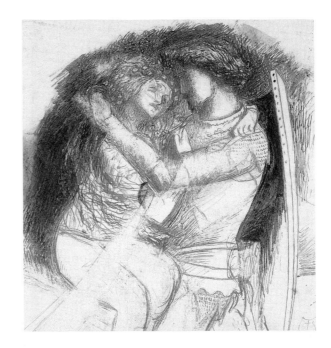

Sɪʀ Jᴏʜɴ Eᴠᴇʀᴇᴛᴛ Mɪʟʟᴀɪs (1829-1896)

224 Four pencil studies for 'Lorenzo and Isabella
Birmingham City Museum & Art Galleries

   a) The head of Isabella, and the brother
      34.8 x 24 cms
   b) The heads of the Serving Man, and the
      middle-aged woman seated at right
      23.1 x 17.3 cms
   c) The Old Woman seated at the right
      33.7 x 24.8 cms
   d) The Youth seated at the right
      23.1 x 17.4 cms

The studies are for Millais' oil, *Isabella* (1849), the first painting in which the artist followed the principles of the Pre-Raphaelite Brotherhood. William Holman Hunt wrote in *The Contemporary Review*: 'The first that we agreeed to do . . . was a series of designs for "Isabella". These were to be executed entirely on our new principles, and subsequently etched for publication. Millais chose as his subject the household of Lorenzo's brothers at meals.' The models were chiefly the artist's friends; Lorenzo, for instance, was modelled by William Michael Rossetti, and the man drinking from a wine glass on the far right was Dante Gabriel Rossetti.

Sɪʀ Jᴏʜɴ Eᴠᴇʀᴇᴛᴛ Mɪʟʟᴀɪs

225 The Eve of St. Agnes: Interior at Knole, near
Sevenoaks
Watercolour, 20.8 x 27.4 cms
By Courtesy of the Board of Trustees
of the Victoria & Albert Museum

Full on this casement shone the wintry moon,
And threw warm gules on Madeline's fair breast,
As down she knelt for heaven's grace and boon;
Rose-bloom fell on her hands, together prest,
And on her silver cross soft amethyst,
And on her hair a glory, like a saint:
She seem'd a splendid angel, newly drest,
Save wings, for heaven:—Porphyro grew faint:
She knelt, so pure a thing, so free from mortal taint.

Anon his heart revives: her vespers done,
Of all its wreathéd pearls her hair she frees;
Unclasps her warméd jewels one by one;
Loosens her fragrant bodice; by degrees
Her rich attire creeps rustling to her knees:
Half-hidden, like a mermaid in sea-weed,
Pensive awhile she dreams awake, and sees,
In fancy, fair St. Agnes in her bed,
But dares not look behind, or all the charm is fled.

Wɪʟʟɪᴀᴍ Eᴅᴡᴀʀᴅ Fʀᴏsᴛ (1810-1877)

226 Diana and Endymion
   Oil painting on paper laid on canvas
   Moss Galleries, London

Originally a portrait painter, in the 1840s Frost was best-known as a painter of mythical episodes, usually containing the tasteful eroticism of the kind seen here. He usually turned to Milton, Spenser and the ancients for his subjects. Keats appears to be his literary source on this occasion.

SIR EDWARD JOHN POYNTER (1836-1919)

227 *The Vision of Endymion*
1902
Oil on canvas, 50.8 x 38.1 cms
Manchester City Art Gallery

F. JOUBERT AFTER SIR EDWARD JOHN POYNTER

228 *Engraved version of the above watercolour*
London: E. Moxon, Son and Co., 1873
Professor Michael Jaye

Poynter has chosen the moment in Book One of *Endymion*, where Diana appears before the sleeping shepherd. Note how in engraving his original watercolour, Joubert has felt free to make changes.

And lo! from the opening clouds, I saw emerge
The loveliest moon, that ever silvered o'er

A shell for Neptune's goblet. She did soar
So passionately bright, my dazzled soul
Commingling with her ardent spheres did roll
Through clear and cloudy, even when she went
At last into a dark and vapoury tent—
Whereat, methought, the lidless-eyèd train
Of planets all were in the blue again.
　　　　　　　(*Endymion*, I 591-599)

WILLIAM REYNOLDS-STEPHENS (1862-1943)

229 *Happy in Beauty, Life and Love and Everything*
1896
Copper & bronze, inset with mother-of-pearl and precious stones, on an original oak stand with wood inlays, metal fittings and ornament, 172 cms high
Private Collection

This relief, with its inscription from Keats's *Lamia* was first exhibited at the Royal Academy in 1896, and, with its stand, in the same galleries in 1898. It was subsequently shown at the Fine Art Society's exhibition 'Sculpture for the Home' (1902) with the title of *Youth*, and the catalogue for that exhibition contains the following note:

The mirror in the background typifies (by the sunrise scene) the unclouded brightness of youth's outloook into life . . . [on the stand are] emblems of spring, the narcissus, and a bird singing to his mate.

Where Reynolds-Stephens comments upon the naive, and to some extent narcissistic optimism of youth, Keats depicts a young man ensnared by a love of the immortal which his mortal frame cannot support:

The cruel lady, without any show
Of sorrow for her tender favourite's woe,
But rather, if her eyes could brighter be,
With brighter eyes and slow amenity,
Put her new lips to his, and gave afresh
The life she had so tangled in her mesh:
And as he from one trance was wakening
Into another, she began to sing,
Happy in beauty, life, and love, and every thing,
A song of love, too sweet for earthly lyres,
While, like held breath, the stars drew in their
                    panting fires.
                ('Lamia', Bk I, 290-300)

230 *The Poems of John Keats*
     The Kelmscott Press, 1894
     The British Library Board

Keats's appearance in the Kelmscott Press, founded by William Morris and Emery Walker in 1891, shows how generally admired his poetry had become by the end of the century. The books were not always suitable for reading; the intention was that they should be artefacts in themselves. The beauty of Keats's work was now thought suitable material for fine printing.

THOMAS HARDY

231 *Rome. At the Pyramid of Cestius near the Graves of Shelley and Keats*
     1887
     Manuscript with violets
     The British Library Board

Thomas Hardy visited Rome with his wife in 1887, and went to the Protestant Cemetery. In this poem he meditates upon the identity of Cestius, now forgotten, who, though seeking to memorialise himself, in death performed and still preforms the more wonder-

ful task of 'beckoning pilgrim feet' to the graves of 'Those matchless singers', Shelley and Keats. Like Wilde before him, he noticed violets growing on the grave, and like Wilde he picked and preserved some of them.

       Who, then, was Cestius,
         And what is he to me?—
Amid thick thoughts and memories multitudinous
         One thought alone brings he.

       I can recall no word
         Of anything he did;
For me he is a man who died and was interred
         To leave a pyramid

       Whose purpose was exprest
         Not with its first design,
Nor till, far down in Time, beside it found their rest
         Two countrymen of mine.

       Cestius in life, maybe,
         Slew, breathed out threatening;
I know not. This I know: in death all silently
         He does a finer thing,

In beckoning pilgrim feet
With marble finger high
To where, by shadowy wall and history-haunted
                                   street,
Those matchless singers lie . . .

Say, then, he lived and died
That stones which bear his name
Should mark, through Time, where two immortal
                                Shades abide;
It is an ample fame.

The editor has his opinions on Keats's early death:

> When he was eighteen he fell in with a rollicking set of young fellows, all of literary ambitions and aspirations. The days of deep drinking had not passed, and it was no disgrace to be seen under the influence of a bottle of wine or a stiff glass of punch. This kind of life had a peculiar fascination for Keats, and he gave himself up to it without limit. There is little doubt that his manner of life for the next three or four years had much to do with bringing on the trouble which shortened his career.

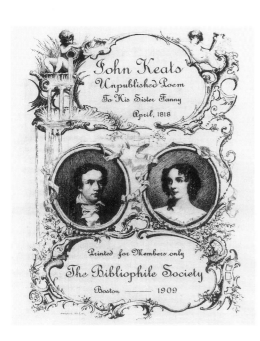

[JOHN KEATS]
232 *Unpublished Poem to His Sister Fanny*
April, 1818
Boston: Printed for Members Only the Bibliophile Society, 1909
Professor Michael Jaye

This volume, expensively printed on vellum for the Bibliophile Society, set in black-letter text and limited to 489 copies, testifies to Keats's ultimate popularity and respectability in America. In claiming the discovery of an unpublished poem it is, however, at fault; the lines are actually by John Hamilton Reynolds, and were published in the *Examiner* in June 1818 (signed J.H.R.), and then in *The Garden of Florence.*

WILL LOW
233 *Illustrative Designs for the Odes & Sonnets of John Keats*
London: John Bumpus, 1888
The British Library Board

ROBERT GIBBINGS (1889-1958)
234 *Engravings for Lamia, Isabella,*
The Eve of St. Agnes & other poems
Golden Cockerell Press: 1928
The British Library Board

JOHN BUCKLAND WRIGHT (1897-1954)
235 *Illustrations for the Collected Sonnets*
of John Keats
The Halcyon Press, 1930
The British Library Board

DAVID GENTLEMAN
236 *Illustrations for the Poems of John Keats*
New York: The Heritage Press, 1966
The British Library Board

TONY HARRISON (1937-)
237 *'Them & [uz]' from 'The School of Eloquence'*
Rex Collings: 1978
Private Collection

'The School of Eloquence' is a sonnet sequence where the poet has the inarticulate speak; in 'Them and Uz' the schoolmaster demands that Keats be read with R.P. (Received Pronounciation). He claims Keats for the exclusive few, whereas the poet, through his subversive wit, reclaims him for the many.

In reviewing these poems, Harold Pinter wrote:

avaracious appetite for language. Brilliant, passionate, outrageous, abrasive, but also, as in his family sonnets, immeasurably tender'.

TONY HARRISON
238 *A Kumquat for John Keats*
Bloodaxe Books: 1981
The British Library Board

'A Kumquat for John Keats' is an affectionate and witty love poem that throughout pays tribute to Keats for his tough ambiguities, for his understanding of the indivisible relation of melancholy and joy.

TONY HARRISON
239 *A Kumquat for John Keats*
Original Manuscript
Private Collection

This notebook gives privileged access to a modern poet at work. One hundred and twenty-four lines involves some eighty pages pages of workings, characterised by changes of pen, colour of ink, and the occasional personal collage. The earliest jottings are dated 1979.

JOHN KEATS
240 *Endymion*
London: Taylor and Hessey, 1818
Private Collection

This is Wordsworth's own copy of *Endymion*. Wordsworth has signed the flyleaf: 'Wm Wordsworth / Rydal Mount / May 25'. Keats had read to Wordsworth part of the poem (the 'Ode to Pan') when Wordsworth visited London in December 1817. Wordsworth's well-known response was recorded by Haydon (some thirty years after the event):

I said he has just finished an exquisite ode to Pan—and as he had not a copy I begged Keats to repeat it—which he did in his usual half chant, (most touching) walking up & down the room—when he had done I felt really, as if I had heard a young Apollo—Wordsworth drily said
"a Very pretty piece of Paganism"—
This was unfeeling, & unworthy of his high Genius to a young Worshipper like Keats—& Keats felt it *deeply*—so that if Keats has said any thing severe about our Friend; it was because he was wounded—and though he dined with Wordsworth after at my table—he never forgave him.

Nothing in Keats's letters, however, supports Haydon's last remark, that Keats 'never forgave' Wordsworth.

Lenders to the Exhibition

Thomas Agnew & Sons Ltd., London
Reg Alton
Ashmolean Museum, Oxford
Birmingham City Art Gallery
The British Library, London
The British Museum, London
Brotherton Library, Leeds University
Courtauld Institute Galleries, London
Fitzwilliam Museum, Cambridge
Guildhall Art Gallery, Corporation of London
Guildhall Library, Corporation of London
Professor Michael Jaye
Laing Art Gallery, Newcastle upon Tyne
Lincolnshire County Council: Usher Gallery, Lincoln
London Borough of Camden from the Collections at Keats House, Hampstead
Manchester City Art Gallery
Moss Galleries, London
John Murray, Publishers
National Gallery, London
National Portrait Gallery, London
Royal Horticultural Society
Science Museum, London
John Spedding
Tate Gallery, London
Theatre Museum, London
Masters and Fellows of Trinity College, Cambridge
Tullie House, City Museum & Art Gallery, Carlisle
Victoria & Albert Museum, London
Wellcome Institute Library, London
Whitworth Art Gallery, University of Manchester
The Worshipful Society of Apothecaries of London

Among the generous owners who have lent to the exhibition several wish to remain anonymous.

Select Bibliography

Allott, Miriam, *The Poems of John Keats*, Longman, 1970

Bush, Douglas, *Selected Poems and Letters*, Boston, 1959

Forman, Maurice Buxton, *The Letters of John Keats*, Oxford, 1931

Garrod, H.W., *The Poetical Works of John Keats*, second edition, Oxford, 1958

Rollins, Hyder Edward, 2 vols., *The Letters of John Keats*, Cambridge, 1958

Stillinger, Jack, *The Poems of John Keats*, Harvard, 1978

Adami, Marie, *Fanny Keats*, London, 1937

Altick, Richard D., *The Cowden Clarkes*, Oxford, 1948

Bate, Walter Jackson, *John Keats*, Massachusetts and London, 1964

Blackstone, Bernard, *The Consecrated Urn*, London, 1959

Blunden, Edmund, *Keats's Publisher*, Oxford, 1940

Blunden, Edmund, *Leigh Hunt's "Examiner" Examined*, Archon Books, 1967

Bodurtha, Dorothy Hyde & Pope, Willard Bissell (Eds.), *The Life of John Keats by Charles Armitage Brown*, Oxford, 1937

Bush, Douglas, *John Keats*, London, 1966

Chilcott, Tim, *A Publisher and His Circle*, London and Boston, 1972

Cowden Clarke, Charles and Mary, *Recollections of Writers*, Centaur Press, 1969

Eliot, T.S., *The Use of Poetry and the Use of Criticism*, Faber & Faber, 1933

Finney, Claude L., *The Evolution of Keats's Poetry*, New York, 1963

Gittings, Robert, *John Keats*, London, 1968

Gittings, Robert, *John Keats. The Living Year*, London, 1954

Gittings, Robert, *The Odes of Keats and their Earliest Known Manuscripts*, London, 1970

Goellnicht, Donald C., *The Poet Physician. Keats and Medical Science*, Pittsburgh,1984

Hewlett, Dorothy J., *A Life of John Keats,*London, 1937

Holmes, Richard, *Shelley, The Pursuit*, London, 1974

Jack, Ian, *Keats and the Mirror of Art*, Oxford, 1967

Jones, Frederick L. (Ed.), 2 vols., *The Letters of Percy Bysshe Shelley*, Oxford, 1964

Jones, Leonidas M. (Ed.), *The Letters of John Hamilton Reynolds,*Nebraska, 1973

Jones, Leonidas M., *Selected Prose of John Hamilton Reynolds*, Harvard, 1966

Jones, Leonidas M., *The Life of John Hamilton Reynolds*, Hanover and London, 1984

MacGillivray, J.R., *Keats, A Bibliography and Reference Guide*, Toronto, 1949

Matthews, G.M., *Keats, The Critical Heritage*, London, 1971

Muir, Kenneth, Ed., *John Keats: A Reassessment*, Liverpool, 1959

Owings Jr., Frank N., *The Keats Library*, London, 1978

Parson, Donald, *Portraits of Keats*, New York, 1954

Perkins, David, *The Quest for Permanence: The Symbolism of Wordsworth, Shelley and Keats*, Harvard, 1959

Pope, Willard Bissell (Ed.), 5 vols., *The Diary of Benjamin Robert Haydon*, Harvard, 1960

Redpath, Theodore, *The Young Romantics and Critical Opinion 1807-1824*, London, 1973

Ricks, Christopher, *Keats and Embarrassment*, Oxford, 1974

Rollins, Hyder Edward, *More Letters and Poems of the Keats Circle*, Harvard, 1955

Rollins, Hyder Edward, 2 vols., *The Keats Circle*, Harvard, 1948

Schwartz, Lewis M., Keats *Reviewed by his Contemporaries*, New Jersey, 1973

South, John Flint, *Memorials*, Centaur Press, 1970

Sperry, Stuart M., *Keats the Poet*, Princeton, 1974

Spurgeon, Caroline F.E., *Keats's Shakespeare*, Oxford, 1929

Taylor, Basil, *Joshua Cristall*, London, 1975

Walker, Carol Kyros, *Walking North with Keats*, New Haven and London, 1992

Ward, Aileen, *John Keats. The Making of a Poet*, London, 1963

Wise, T.J., *Catalogue of the Ashley Library*, London, 1924

INDEX

Note: figures in italic refer to illustrations